Chapter 1

# Window Shopping

## *creating appealing gardens*

HARRODS, SELFRIDGES, Smith and Caughey. The world's big department stores have two things in common: a serious shortage of toilets and amazing window displays. Christmas is the best time to go window gazing when these big stores pull out the stops to impress. Partitions and drapes, mannequins and movement: each carefully contrived scene seeks to draw you in, and where your eyes go, your heart and (the store hopes) your wallet will follow. Often several windows will play on the same theme or each window may be distinct with its own mood and 'story' to tell. For men's aftershave it's angular mannequins posing within sharp metallic spaces while at women's lingerie, the window bursts with sexy plum curtains and curves.

### Display tactics:
*creating captivating compositions in the garden*
What if each flower bed in your garden was t separ a sce

In each pocket of planting you have the chance to create a composition — a picture which, just like a shop window display, will tell a story, evoke a particular mood and look dynamic year round. Some beds might develop the same theme, working together to give a unified feel. Others might become stand-alone compositions sculpted from living plants.

As we look afresh at our own garden beds here are some of the tricks to be learnt from a shop-window approach.

### Overall impression:
*creating instant appeal*
Shop displays have the 'wow' factor — the first overall impression that either attracts or repels us. Our garden beds should similarly be instantly appealing. You don't have to have a degree in botany to know whether you are impressed straight away

Vivian Papich is a master of composition and each corner of her garden is a carefully thought-out piece of theatre. Here she orchestrates textures and colour — even spray painting an old tree stump to reflect the flowers of *Agapanthus* 'Streamline'.

with a particular group of plants. Our first impressions are determined by many factors discussed in this book. Colour is an important first drawcard along with dramatic shapes and textures. The general tidiness and health of your plants also have a lot to do with that instant appeal. Chapter 10 is devoted to using colour. Using shapes and textures is touched on in most chapters.

## A style or theme:
*creating unity and a sense of purpose*

Style is what sets the mood of a shop display or a garden and is important to the 'big picture' that gives everything on display a sense of unity and purpose. For example, if everything in a shop window is purple, instantly the window has impact, whether things are grouped nicely or not. Expensive shops ooze class, not just because of the products they are selling but also because every product in the window seems to be related to its neighbour. Subtle lighting, coordinated materials, expensive, real wood stands — everything is sending the same message: 'We are the top end of the market.'

This sense of unity and purpose is instantly attractive. Style can be as simple as a mood like 'hot, fast and exciting' or 'soothing, restful and soft' for a shop display. In our gardens it might be more specific but the style underscores everything that is included in any display; it takes a ragtag bunch of players and makes them into a winning team. More of this is looked at in Chapters 2 and 5.

## Main point of interest:
*providing initial focus*

Eyes are creatures of habit. After that initial glance, if we like what we see, our eyes look for something specific to look at. Like Formula One cars, they like to race around at first but then like to pull in for a pit stop, to alight at one particular point for a few seconds. We view paintings in the same way: as well as good overall shapes and colour there is usually some main feature that draws our attention, particularly before we start to notice other peripheral details. In a shop display

---

Singing the same song: plants linked by a clear theme like these subtropical bromeliads and dark *Aeonium arboreum* 'Schwarzkopf' provide a dramatic sense of escape in the garden.

it may be a slogan or perhaps a group of figures. In our garden beds there might be a particular 'feature' plant or plants that stand out from the crowd. What you might use is discussed in Chapters 3, 6 and 12. Make sure there is a stand-out star feature or massing of plants to provide that primary point of focus.

## Details:
### adding extras

After a refuel at the 'pit stop' our eyes set off again, zooming about, but this time they go in search of interesting details. Without the details we quickly tire of any image. In music a melody is just a nice tune to whistle to, but add in all the other notes and it becomes a symphony that we can enjoy again and again; within which we are constantly discovering something fresh and new. Details add depth to the sensory experience. In the shop window they might include particular products placed about, the backdrop or the type of fabric worn by a figure. In our gardens it will be a particular flower or fruit that we notice on closer inspection; perhaps the light illuminating a leaf or the papery texture of the bark of a tree.

Details are important but a feast can be as unpleasant as a famine – so go easy as we don't want our borders to become the equivalent of a junk shop when we intended them to be a treasure trove. At the other extreme are those in search of restful simplicity who struggle with the idea of any small details at all, finding them 'bitty' or distracting to the overall picture. The trouble is that an overly simplistic approach looks sleek and in scale when it is wrapped round a large building like a public library but in a domestic setting it can be so simplistic as to be dull. Even in the simplest of schemes there is room for a few surprises and 'added extras'. The details of the garden are touched on throughout this book; adding extras is looked at in Chapter 14.

Our eyes zoom about looking for small details. If they're lucky they get to land somewhere like this: *Vriesea splendens* stealing the show from golden oreganum and black mondo grass (*Ophiopogon*).

## Depth:
### creating movement and perspective

The best window displays draw us in quite literally with a sense of three dimensions for realism. The spaces and shadows and the apparent changing of perspective as we view one object against another from different angles makes for a lively and intriguing set up. (Compare this to the 2D attraction of a poster.) In our garden borders, even when space is at a premium, if we can build up a sense of depth and perspective by layering our plants against each other, we can create a sense of movement and depth. Although doing this consumes space, it can make the whole garden feel bigger.

One of the most obvious ways to add depth to your planting is to make your beds deeper, which we look at below. Other tricks to give an illusion of depth include playing with leaf shapes and colours (see Chapters 10 and 11).

## Flower bed shapes:
### playground or prison?

The first building block of our planting is the space where we want to put our plants. Some spaces are so small or awkwardly shaped that planting in a creative way will always be a challenge. Before we even look at plants and planting it is best to see if we are making the most of the space available. Garden

Slide the lawn to one side — you don't need beds on every side of the lawn. This tidy hedge stands alone as a restful feature and the wall would be perfect for kids with a football. You can then make a decent-sized bed in another part of the garden.

---

beds are like the canvas on which we are about to paint, so getting them right is an essential first step.

Take a fresh look at your garden. Call them flower beds, gardens, shrubbery or borders, you will see that most of the plants in your garden are confined to well-defined, finite spaces. Maybe you have an amorphous island bed in the lawn or a small geometric pocket against a wall cut from a patio or deck. Most of us have at least one place where a flower bed is notoriously long and thin. Traditionally punctuated with standard roses or pencil conifers 'the long strip' is a thorn in the side of good design and planting. Such beds are the most difficult to plant well, especially in any naturalistic fashion, yet at the same time in today's smaller gardens they seem to be the only spaces left between neighbouring driveways or those anorexic, wind-blown gaps down the side of our houses.

In Chapter 15 we will look more closely at the challenge of narrow beds. For now, though, take note of the number and shape of different flower beds in your garden, and consider at the outset how you might alter them to make them more plant-friendly. Each space should be like a playground and not a prison: a place where your plants look like they are enjoying themselves.

## Soil preparation

The success of a good planting can stand or fall on how well you prepare the soil initially, and then how well the plants you choose are suited to the site. You may be blessed with a rich and deep volcanic soil or you may be cursed with a sticky clay — either way get to know your soil and improve it as much as you can before you start. A pH test will indicate which plants may grow best in your garden: those favouring acidic or alkaline soils. Test kits are available from garden centres. Most often your soil will just need a boost with applications of compost and general-purpose fertiliser.

## Big really is best

When we bought a new bed for our bedroom, with kids on the way, everyone told us to buy king size or at least as big as possible. 'It seems huge now but when you have children you'll see!' was the sort of thing people said with knowing looks. Garden beds are the same. Plants grow up and they need space to spread out. There is a misconception that larger flower beds mean more work. I find the opposite to be true. With more room between my plants it is easier to get into a border to weed, and I don't find I have to be cutting everything back as much as each plant has a bit more elbow room. Structural shrubs often take up most of the space anyway so if we mulch well under these at least, the higher-maintenance areas of perennials, annuals and bulbs become quite manageable. So where it is practical, make your beds on the generous side — you'll wonder where all that space goes when you plant.

### Creating depth and interest

It is not just the matter of size which is important but of depth. You could have a border the size of a Pacific atoll but if it is shaped like a piece of spaghetti — stretched down the side of the lawn for 200 metres — there is precious little opportunity to have much fun visually. With your plants lined up one next to the other, things can easily start to look as exciting as a queue at the supermarket

Deep borders give your plants room to breathe and allow you to plant boldly. Here variegated aralias float above *Geranium macrorrhizum* and grassy *Phalaris arundinacea* 'Picta' at Sezincote, an English garden with an Indian theme.

rather than a tempting shop window. Deep borders enable you to layer plants, allowing each to be set off against those behind and in front. A layered border is as rich and decadent as a tiered gateaux — there is that sense of three-dimensional spark. Apart from maintenance worries the other more valid reservations you might have about making your existing borders deeper is the sacrifice of living space. The back yard used to be thought of as somewhere to hang the washing and send the kids out to play, but now it's all about 'outdoor living'. We all want a space for a chair and tables, maybe a barbecue and even a pool. It's not much use creating great planting if we aren't out there enjoying it. If you have children they will still want somewhere to kick a ball around. So how do we fit all that in and still have beautiful planting?

## Achieving a balance between living space and garden

The answer is a bit of give and take. We often design our gardens with the lawn or paved area in the middle and the garden beds dribbled round the perimeter in anorexic strips which follow the boundary rather like measly piping round a fat cake. By sliding the lawn to one side you might have to sacrifice a flower border (no great loss) but you gain space on the opposite side to enlarge the planting there and do something more exciting. The side of the garden where you have a tidy hedge or an attractive fence or wall might be a good

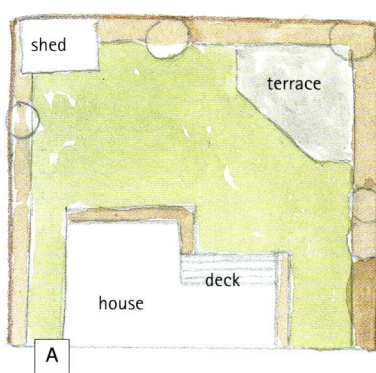

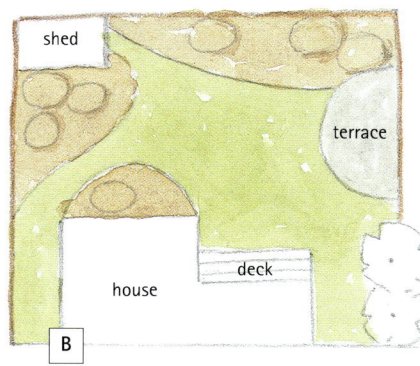

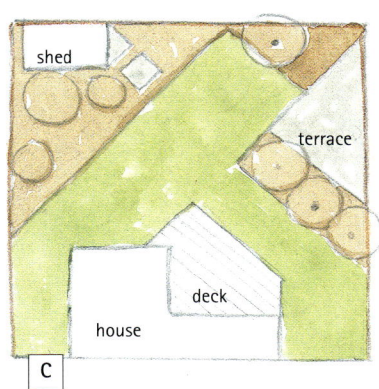

A  A traditional garden: long thin borders dribbled round the edges.

B  By removing some borders altogether and enlarging others, there are less edges to trim and deeper borders allowing for more creative planting.

C  An alternative diagonal approach creates interesting angles and triangular borders that lend themselves to creative plant grouping.

place to sacrifice having much planting at all. Instead let the terrace or lawn make a wall-to-wall carpet so you can enjoy some uncluttered simplicity and build up a generous planting in another area — perhaps where that ugly shed or brightly painted neighbour's house need hiding.

Another trick designers use to make flower bed shapes deeper and more interesting is to rotate any lawn area, paved areas or deck shapes to 45 degrees, thereby removing all those long, straight edges (see diagram on page 13). Instead, you are left with several deep triangular spaces, notably in the corners, which are always opportunities for creating some depth. These three-dimensional spaces break up the squareness of a garden and create heaps of interest even before you put the plants in. If you have a smaller garden, however, don't rush to just slice the corners off the lawn — the obvious thing to do. Obvious as corners are for planting, in small gardens filling every corner with plants can actually hem you in and create an amorphous 'blob' of living space in the middle with any element of surprise lost. An alternative is to create a large border jutting out into the central space to divide it a little. A corner can be a useful area to have as a seating area instead, which will draw you right out into the garden to make full use of the space available. Though in very small gardens deep borders might be totally impractical, make the creation of at least one or two meaty borders a priority in your design if you can.

## FOOD FOR THOUGHT

☆ Imagine a picture frame around each area of planting in your garden — would it hold together as a shop window display?

☆ How many distinct garden beds do I presently have in my garden?

☆ Which beds are large and spacious? Which are small and fiddly?

☆ Are there some beds I can remove all together, some I could enlarge and others I could just simplify in shape?

## REMOVING BEDS

People who most often equate garden beds with lots of work usually have masses of pint-sized beds in all manner of tortuous shapes. Small beds are high maintenance because often they have lots of edges to trim and even when they don't adjoin lawns, garden edges are like magnets to weeds. Seeds blow across paving and settle in the hollow along the edge and, being often the sunniest and most cultivated part of the garden, what self-respecting weed seed wouldn't grow? In getting the balance right between living spaces and borders consider which smaller beds you could remove. Here are three classic high-maintenance scenarios.

### Drive edge
*Problem:* You step out of the car and get entangled in the rose bushes. You spend a fortune on annuals to edge the drive each year.

*Solution:* Just grass it over. If the lawn is flush with the drive you will minimise the need to edge it. Put those annuals in pots by the front door and put your feet up.

### Island bed
*Problem:* A specimen tree or shrub in a lawn can look fine, but island beds look invariably silly unless you have several acres and can attempt something sweeping and grand à la Beth Chatto. Just as a small pond is a puddle so a small island bed can have all the charm of a freshly dug grave. Large island beds divide a garden up and provide screening; small island beds look like measles all over your front lawn.

*Solution:* Grass them over; whoever does the lawn mowing will be eternally grateful.

### The bit between the dustbin and the back door
*Problem:* In laying functional paths and drives it is easy to be left with awkward-shaped pockets of bare ground where we optimistically imagined an oasis of green. Against a house the eaves will prevent any rain falling near the walls of the house; and foundations under the soil can mean any beds here can be about as hospitable as a long stint in Alcatraz. Out in the open, small, odd gaps between paving are another nuisance to look after. Many are either driven over or trampled over and are often just too small to ask any plant to make its presence felt in any meaningful way.

*Solution:* Pave them over with matching materials. Simplicity is best in areas that get a lot of use.

Chapter 2

# Enjoying Plant Shapes

THE GARDEN IN twilight is a bloodless sight, drained of colour and smelling of leaves and damp earth. It's not the gangs of mosquitoes, quickly catching onto a whiff of flesh, nor the death of snails crunching as I tread down the path that takes my attention, but the drama of shapes caught in the failing light.

The comforting sight of a hebe hanging out on the corner becomes a reassuring dollop of smoothness telling me where the path turns, but lurking behind are some edgier characters: the dagger leaves of phormiums poised and poking skyward. An oily mat of something flat (is it thrift?) oozes out over the path, and is broken in places by rude shafts of verbascum that polevault out of nowhere. So cheerful by day, these now loom with gothic menace — dark candelabras with every last flame snuffed out. Seed heads and silhouettes, reassuring mounds and menacing spires — it's no wonder the snails are out in force enjoying the show.

Even in twilight this border would be a feast of varied outlines with a mound of *Crassula ovata*, architectural agaves and aloes, and a grassy *Dasylirion*. The flames of *Toona sinensis* behind add a spire-like lift.

The more angles you see your garden from, the more you will unravel how it works. So taking a trip into the garden in twilight is a great design experience. Twilight strips the garden of its stronger colours. All the subtle nuances of leaf and petal are blurred in shadows and we can appreciate the general flow of forms – the ups and downs of it all. Ups and downs are very important in gardening. Think beyond leaves, shoots and flowers and imagine your borders doing the 'Full Monty' – stripped down to all but the basic shapes. Does it all still hold up as an attractive composition? Without a good basic arrangement of shapes everything else you do in the garden will be built on shaky foundations. Plant shapes – often called plant 'form' – are what give the garden its bones. We may not always consciously notice them but we certainly appreciate their presence.

When you look at your planting at twilight, unimaginative planting will look as interesting as a bowl of cold porridge and good planting will look as dynamic as the roof-scape of an old city or a stretch of coastline.

A good variety of shapes makes for excitement and drama but, as with all design ingredients, balance is everything. Too enthusiastic a mixture of different shapes can make things look restless and lumpy like a child's toy box tipped out. (Remember those clunky conifer beds planted in the seventies?) The plants with strong form will add the guts to your garden. Like croutons in a bowl of runny soup they hold the plan together, form a meaningful framework and carry the less substantial players in the scheme. In turn the softer plants have their part to play, helping to link together the more structural elements with a mellow softness. Good planting is all about teamwork.

## Some things different, some things the same:
### unity and diversity

In design there is always a tension between unity and contrast. Remember those kitchens that were once fashionable, where the blinds, cushion covers and crockery, even the kettle, had to match – usually in red and white? We've moved on from such contrived surroundings. We still want the main kitchen elements – the dishwasher, the oven and the refrigerator – to match but we also want some spontaneity and surprises to provide a personal touch and to break the predictability. In the garden it's the same.

This principle of variety and contrast over an underlying feeling of unity is one of the most important principles not just

---

A Jekyll and Hyde character: thalictrum begins life as a neat mound then explodes into a cloud of mauve smoke. Ethereal shapes like this bring height and lightness to stodgy planting.

16  Enjoying Plant Shapes

in gardening but in all schools of design, and it is a hard balance to get right. If everything were the same — plant shapes, sizes and colours and the like, we would end up with a homogeneous nothing. On the other hand, if we become obsessed with contrasting foliage, colours, leaves and styles the effect will be one of chaos. Our garden plants work together best when there is at least one thread linking them together. Often it will be your underlying theme or feel that has influenced the choice of plants. The other major connecting thread is that of repetition where key plants are massed and threaded through a planting scheme or where a particular colour or landscaping material is repeated. These help the border to tell the same story. Over these underlying themes you will add variety and spice — seasonal effects and contrasting flowers, plant shapes and leaf shapes and textures. While the unifying elements tell the story and bring meaning to the garden, the excitement of contrasts and diversity add sparkle and drama.

## The recipe for a shapely border:

### combining plant shapes

By understanding the basic shapes of plants, we will easily spot where our existing planting is weak and needs a 'pick me up' so that we get interesting changes, not just in height but in form too. Combining plant shapes is like making bread. There are some basic ingredients that you use in quantity nearly every time you bake, like mats of groundcover, spiky plants and the rounded mounds of structural shrubs that form the body and structure of the border. Then there are the optional extras like spires and weeping plants. Like spices and raisins added to bread dough, you throw these in in moderation to bring life and variety to the basic mix.

Below is a list of some of the main ingredients in the garden recipe. You won't want to use all of them all of the time but each has a part to play in the drama and each brings its own particular character to the garden. While spikes and spires are energetic, weepers and carpeters are more sombre. While blobs are smug and self-contained, sideswept plants reach out to interact with their neighbours.

Obviously some plants will not fit neatly into any one category — a thalictrum for example, like many perennials, is a wonderfully elastic Jekyll and Hyde character that begins as a neat mound of leaves in winter and skyrockets upwards in spring. Here perhaps the most exciting part of the life cycle is the one to consider when planning a suitable home for such a plant. Other plants just sit on the fence with indistinct outlines. These are no less valuable, but to have a sharp and focused sense of shape you will need at least some well-defined contrasts between the shape of one plant and the next.

The shape of flowers, though not as important as that of the plant as a whole, is another aspect of planning to think about. Large flowers like the goblets of magnolias or the trumpets of lilies are very dominant in season and other smaller flowers are massed in striking spikes or plumes. Although a border can't always be planned around flower shapes, where possible try to contrast large blooms with small, horizontal shapes with verticals. In this way you will enhance the games being played by the more permanent shapes in your grand plan.

### Fat blobs

Blobs are a comforting, replete presence in our borders and in life. Where, after all, would a good steak be without a comforting dollop of mashed potato to nestle up to? Simple mounds create instant bulk in your borders, giving a comforting sense of solidity and mass. Lavender, santolina or a hebe with typical middle-aged spread might settle themselves down with their rear end sprawled out over a rather narrow path.

If you can, resist the temptation to trim these characters back, or worse still slice the sides off their rounded forms. Though they take up rather a lot of valuable space they add an appealing solidity and weight to the garden. Think of them like islands in an ocean. Smaller plants nestle round them like small boats anchored offshore, enjoying the protection and shelter provided. The result is a relationship between large and small forms that looks naturally balanced.

### Rounded shrubs

Shrubs are the main group of plants that take on a distinct rounded outline — more so if we trim them. If the leaves are small like in a berberis, you get a satisfying

smooth look that is crisp and distinct. But if the leaves are large as in a cotinus or hydrangea, the result will be more textural but less definite in outline. It is the plants with crisper outlines that have more impact in the border than those with fuzzy edges, which melt into the crowd. This means that 'smooth' plants, the likes of santolina, heathers, hebes and box, have to be placed with special care as they become major 'stars' within the whole plan.

Those chameleon-like plants which morph as the seasons change will keep you on your toes. Lavenders start out as a loose but well-rounded bump but things quickly grow and swell and then a Mohican of flower erupts, giving a loose and diffused outline. Only when you trim the flowers off a month later will you have those wonderfully precise spheres again, giving a sense of focus amid the more blurry chaos of high summer.

Plants are eternal rebels, constantly smashing down our little design rules and blobby plants don't need to be smug little balls; they can billow and tower — in the shape of spun candyfloss. Many of New Zealand's beautiful divaricating plants, for example, take on billowing forms rather than forming simple mounds. The amazing *Coprosma virescens* rises like a

Divaricating plants bring a fuzzy, wire-netting quality to rounded forms and are almost unique to New Zealand's flora. Here a dwarf kowhai (*Sophora prostrata*) adds some solidity to a leafy tapestry including grassy *Acorus gramineus* 'Ogon' and carnivorous pitcher plants.

---

plume of tawny steam from a geyser, and in smaller spaces the well-behaved *Muehlenbeckia astonii* makes a writhing ball of wire-netting twigs. With a bit of clipping it is easy to enhance the billow in many of these shrubs and exaggerate their organic forms.

The Japanese are experts at turning

an unadventurous hummock of azalea or even an unpromising pine into a swagger of cloud-like beauty. Such shapes still have the friendliness of a rounded outline but rather more spirit than a simple ball.

### Mounded perennials

It's easy to think of perennials as rather formless — just flowers on stalks — but many provide distinctive mounds of leaf that can be structurally important even when there isn't a flower in sight. *Coreopsis verticillata* 'Zagreb' is a wiry customer and only explodes gold for one month a year but I grow it as much for the froth of fine leaves, which make a pleasingly dark hummock among the looser planting of gazanias and red blood grass (*Imperata* species). Similarly non-running Michaelmas daisies like *Aster lateriflorus* 'Horizontalis' contribute solid roundness even in winter when, drained of life, the deep-brown hummocks add interesting texture to the bareness all around.

### Don't overdo spheres

Rounded forms add weight and punctuation to your planting but if overused they can give the impression that your garden has broken out in boils so go easy on the attractiveness of spheres. People who are unsure of how to prune shrubs notoriously live by the motto 'if in doubt, beat it into submission with shears'. With every shrub duly shorn and manicured, this simplistic mentality results in gardens that look more like a bag of marshmallows than something animated. The beauty of humps is often contextual; it is only when they sit alongside contrasting forms like the edginess of spiky leaves, the looseness of perennials or a tight spire that they really come alive.

> ## PLANT PICKS: BLOBS
>
> ★ **Smaller plants:** argyranthemum, *Artemisia* 'Powis Castle', aster (compact types), azalea*, *Callistemon viminalis* 'Little John', coleonema, conifers (many), *Convolvulus cneorum*, *Coreopsis verticillata* 'Zagreb', *Crassula ovata*\*, erica*, *Erysimum* 'Bowles Mauve', *Euphorbia griffithii*, *Geranium psilostemon*, hebe, *Metrosideros carmineus*, santolina, skimmia*, solidago (dwarf types) (see also topiary list page 38 and hedging list page 138)
>
> ★ **Spherical flowers:** acacia, allium, dahlia hybrids, echinops, hydrangea*, monarda, paeonia, rhododendron* (some), rosa hybrids (some), tagetes (marigold), zinnia
>
> ★ **Trees and large shrubs:** abelia, *Brachyglottis greyi*, camellia*, coprosma, hebe, hibiscus, hydrangea*, lantana, leonotis, olearia, *Pinus mugo*, pittosporum, protea, rhododendron*, royina, spiraea
>
> *\* suitable for shady conditions*

### Upswept

I love plants with that surprised look, rather like Marilyn Monroe when she walked over a ventilation grille in the classic movie *The Seven Year Itch*. Branches and leaves that sweep upwards and outwards have a wonderfully uplifting effect on us. They can lead our eyes up and out of a tight corner, increasing the feeling of spaciousness in a small garden and their upward mobility rings an optimistic note in a design.

The inverted cone shape looks charming when seen in the folds of a fern or an explosion of native toetoe flowers or a grassy miscanthus. However, it looks stiff and unfriendly in something like a 'Kanzan' cherry where branches make a rather contrived and rigid shuttlecock shape, which doesn't seem to suit the tissue-paper texture of the flowers. Other trees carry off the feeling of upward mobility much better, such as cercidiphyllum, Judas tree (*Cercis siliquastrum*) or a maple like *Acer palmatum* 'Senkaki' on which, especially

in winter, every twig glows orange and reaches for the heavens.

Like warm thermals sweeping ever upwards, plants with a sense of verticality lift our spirits and even without a breath of wind their very shape suggests movement. A buddleia will explode like a fireworks display — fat arrowheads of bloom shooting out in all directions. Grasses are invaluable for ascendant inclinations and not just the bamboos. A fountain of miscanthus, native toetoe,

> ### PLANT PICKS: UPSWEPT
>
> ★ **Smaller plants:** amaranthus, *Asplenium aethiopicum**, astilbe*, *Blechnum gibbum**, *Campanula lactiflora*, epidendrum, *Leptocarpus similis* (oioi), *Matteuccia struthiopteris** (ostrich fern), miscanthus, perovskia, polystichum*, restio, sansevieria (mother-in-law's tongue), sarcococca*, watsonia (see also many spiky plants list page 29)
>
> ★ **Trees and large shrubs:** *Astartea fasicularis*, *Azara microphylla* (vanilla tree), *Bambusa gracilis** (fairy bamboo), beilschmiedia* (taraire), *Berberis* 'Helmond's Pillar', buddleia, cestrum, *Cordyline nigra**, *Cortaderia richardii* (toetoe), *Cupressus arizonica/torulosa*, *Disanthus cercidifolius*, *Elegia capensis*, *Fagus sylvatica* 'Dawyck Purple', *Juniperus chinensis* 'Kaizuka' (Hollywood juniper), *Kunzea ericoides* (kanuka), *Lagerstroemia fauerii*, leucadendron, *Ligustrum japonicum* 'Rotundifolium', *Liriodendron tulipifera* 'Fastigatum', *Malus* 'John Downie', *Olearia solandri*, *Pseudopanax lessonii* 'Sabre'*, pyrus, *Rhopalostylis sapida** (nikau palm), *Spartium junceum* (Spanish broom), *Toona sinensis*, *Viburnum bodnantense**
>
> *\* suitable for shady conditions*

chionochloa or one of the evergreen restios from South Africa will all add grace to any planting.

In a garden you can make the upswept feel a major theme by using only upwardly orientated plant forms such as spikes and spires. Phormium could be placed in front of Hollywood juniper (*Juniperus chinensis* 'Kaizuka'), with planting of kniphofia and astilbe flower spikes in front. The danger with this approach is that your garden can have a rather 'startled' air — the unsettling look of a possum caught in car headlights. Upswept plants make a more balanced composition if contrasted with downswept forms and those with a horizontal plane such as farfugiums and hostas with plate-like leaves.

### Tearful weepers

Not every weeping tree looks like it has just been to a funeral, but we do tend to associate trailing plants with sorrow and modesty. A weeping cherry planted with

a rigid pencil of 'Swane's Golden' cypress was the hallmark cliche of the seventies for a dash of drama, but today we want our contrasts to be a little more subtle. Weeping plants need especially careful placement if all the downward growth is to be displayed to best advantage. The weeping pussy willow has rather given trailing plants a bad reputation — this pudding basin dollop of leaf grafted onto a peg-like leg really does have the hound-dog blues. In its wake has come all manner of cascading clones: head-hanging cherries and gloomy elms.

Often the trouble with these examples is that they are not natural weepers but are grafted onto woefully inadequate stems. By the second year new shoots have hidden the trunk — all the growth hits the floor and any elegance is lost. You are left with a static blob rather than anything more animated. As we have seen there is nothing wrong with a blob in the right place but don't think that a weeping Japanese maple will give you the waterfall look. It makes a fantastic hummock but there is precious little sense of downward movement.

In contrast the best weeping plants are far from gloomy. They don't hang limply — they plunge. The billowing cascade of a great willow or Kashmir cypress (*Cupressus cashmeriana*) is as engaging as a mountain stream with rivulets of growth splashing out in many individual torrents. These plants bring a sense of dynamic movement to the shapes in your border.

### Trailing plants

Along with the larger weeping trees and shrubs there are the smaller trailers that are useful at the front of plantings, draped over awkward slopes or retaining walls. Different species each have different personalities. Some of the groundcover grevilleas like 'Bronze Rambler' are excellent for covering a dry,

---

*Opposite*

*Like a dollop of mashed potato next to a steak, a comforting mound soothes the soul, but be careful not to overdo it. Here native plants are clipped Japanese-style in dramatic cloud shapes that take the humble blob to new heights, adding a definite sculptural feel.*

## PLANT PICKS: WEEPERS AND TRAILERS

★ **Smaller plants:** *Campanula poscharskyana*\*, columnea, *Convolvulus sabatius*, graptopetalum, *Hakonechloa macra* 'Aureola'\*, *Helichrysum argyrophyllum*, *Grevillea* 'Bronze Rambler'/'Fanfare', *Platycerium bifurcatum* (elkhorn fern)\*, *Sedum morganianum*, *Silene maritima*

★ **Trees and large shrubs:** *Agonis flexuosa*, *Betula pendula* 'Youngii', *Callistemon viminalis*, *Cercidiphyllum japonicum*, *Coprosma propinqua/prostrata/kirkii*, *Cordyline* 'Red Fountain', dracophyllum\*, *Leptospermum scoparium* 'White Cascade', *Malus* 'White Cascade', palms like butia and *Rhopalostylis sapida* 'Chathams'\* (Chatham Island nikau), *Pseudopanax ferox*\*, *Rhopalostylis baueri*\* (Norfolk Island nikau), *Salix babylonica*, 'Shinus molle', *Sophora japonica* 'Pendula', *Ulmus glabra* 'Pendula' (weeping elm)

*\* suitable for shady conditions*

sunny bank and with a drop of suitable stature to leap off, vigorous trailers like prostrate rosemary or *Coprosma* 'Prostrata' can bungi jump to their heart's content. The secret of getting the best from these majestic trailers is to give them room to perform. Don't plant them on top of a knee-high wall, for like Samson's hair you will find yourself forever neutering them by having to cut off their magnificent dangling locks. Save trailers like these instead for head-height walls where they can do the death plunge in style. Be aware also that such rampant growers billow out sideways a good deal as they cascade, so along a narrow pathway you will need slimline plants like *Helichrysum argyrophyllum*, which will dribble more sedately instead of doing a Huka Falls leap.

Some plungers lend more of a sense of movement than others. While some are wispy and hesitant, curling up at the tips as they lower themselves downwards, others do the death plunge with no hesitation. The tender succulent *Sedum morganianum* is at the peak of droopiness (if I can mix my metaphors). The growths are ghostly and rope-like and the overall effect is of an intricately braided hairpiece. And while some plants fall in attractive strands, other trailers like pinks (dianthus) and *Convolvulus sabatius* are really just blanketers; they ooze over the edges of our gardens in great swags and are perfect for softening hard edges — like honey drizzled over a cake.

Doing the death leap in style: like a giant wig, a variegated toetoe (*Cortaderia selloana* 'Gold Band') learns how to hang its head from the old master next door — a weeping willow. While these two take the plunge, a *Crinum moorei* in the foreground adds a touch of upward mobility.

## Spires

Istanbul has its minarets and Cambridge has its church steeples. Where would the skylines of the world be without the needle-sharp punctuation added by narrow vertical forms? There is something immediately arresting about a spire firing itself skyward with all the sureness of a rocket launch. In gardens spires are always conspicuous, whether lining paths with rhythmic precision, rallying themselves at gateways to announce an entrance or threading their way through more slovenly plants like bugles calling us to wake up. Spires lead our eyes upwards, and the dramatic contrast they present to the more horizontal planes of the garden is a key dynamic to exploit in any planting. They also anchor down looser planting as firmly as javelins pushed into a picnic rug and this gives a garden bed, particularly island beds, a sense of permanence.

However, spires carry a 'handle with care' warning. In boring borders it's all too easy to throw in a pencil juniper for a quick fix, only to find that it dominates the scene and distracts from everything else you are trying to do. Spires need to be used carefully because they are so visually arresting. They work well with similarly pronounced forms such as tight blobs and spiky plants as well as forming a groomed element amid looser forms. The particularly smooth spires made by some conifers and by topiary was made for formal gardens where it can draw the eye along a path or vista to a focal point. A single spire will always look lonely and incongruous on its own but grouped they look comfortable, especially if you vary the heights a little or let nature and the vagaries of your soil do it for you. Sophisticated designers might cough into their cappuccinos, but a good approach to varying heights and grouping such major shapes in a garden is to see it as a 'Daddy Bear, Mummy Bear, Baby Bear' scenario. Perhaps with a scowling 'Teenager Bear' lurking characteristically three steps behind, not wanting to be seen with the rest of the group (see diagram).

### Climbers as spires

Spires are uncompromisingly architectural, so if you want a softer effect with vertical thrust, a good solution is to use columns of climbers trained on tripods and poles. Using climbers for upward mobility brings colour and bolder leaf shapes into the spire equation and adds height when space is tight. On a fence or wall a climber can get into the neighbours' or under your eaves but on a pole it can bask in the sun without getting into trouble. Informal branches make excellent supports for lighter climbers like annual sweet peas, tropaeolum (nasturtium) and eccremocarpus, but for native tecomanthe or evergreen ivies use a strong pole set in concrete. Clematis, trained up wigwams of branches, are especially effective in a cottage-style planting for colour after the roses have finished. Climbers like these can be mixed to give columns of interest for much of the year — gelsemium in winter, jasmines in summer and a blast of rich purple from grapevines like *Vitis vinifera* 'Purpurea' to finish.

### Flower spires

Alongside the usual spires of conifers and topiary you can introduce more subtle ascendant forms with spikes of flower such as needle-sharp *Veronicastrum*

---

## PLANT PICKS: SPIRES

★ **Smaller plants:** *Agastache foeniculum, Bulbine latifolia, Calamagrostis* x *acutiflora* 'Karl Foerster', *Campanula latifolia*, cardiocrinum\*, *Cimicifuga simplex* 'Atropurpurea'\*, delphinium, digitalis\* (foxgloves), eremurus, echium, *Epilobium angustifolium* var. *album*, knophofia, lupinus, lythrum, perovskia, persicaria, puya, *Salvia confertiflora, S.* 'Indigo spires', *S. nemorosa* 'Ostfriesland', *S. superba* varieties, sisyrinchium, veronica, *Veronicastrum virginicum, Verbascum chiaxii*

★ **Trees and large shrubs:** agave (flowers), aloe, *Cassia didymobotrya*, cereus (cactus), *Cupressus sempervirens* 'Totem', *Juniperus communis* 'Hibernica', *Juniperus scopulorum* 'Skyrocket', *Salix humboldtii* (Humboldt willow), *Taxus baccata* 'Fastigiata' (Irish yew), *Thuja orientalis* 'Pyramidalis' (see also climbers on poles list page 128)

\* *suitable for shady conditions*

*virginicum* or the contemporary rusty needles of *Digitalis ferruginea* – a stunning perennial foxglove. The classical architecture of acanthus, eremurus and delphiniums are invaluable for impact but are here today and gone tomorrow. Treat them as important added extras rather than as essential structural elements in your plan because the effect is fleeting. In the contemporary garden you might go for succulent beschorneria, aloes and yuccas where the stunning architecture of the blooms plays just as important a role as the leaves in the right season. Or go for the classic Mediterranean scene stealer, *Echium pininana* with its mauve-blue towers punching a clean spring sky.

Sleek flower shapes like this break up into the space above less graceful plants and produce a sense of rhythm and animation that works especially well alongside flowers with a horizontal plane like achilleas, crocosmias and solidago. Often the seed heads that remain, like those of verbascum, continue the good work and stretch out the interest. Every garden, whether it is funky and minimal or traditional and cottage style, needs a spire or two. Even where you don't want the distraction of 'flowers' and instead prefer form and foliage you might be surprised how a towering spike of *Eucomis pole evansii*, or *Eryngium pandanifolium*, the wave of a grass such as *Deschampsia* or the small clublike heads of purple plantain will cut through the static space and bring a strong sense of architecture and life to your planting.

In summary:
- Keep spires in proportion to the rest of your planting.
- Group them.
- Use flowers and seed heads as much, if not more, than you do conifers and topiary.
- Consider climbers on poles for looser vertical form.

## Mats

Rolled out at our feet, mats are the first plants we come to at the threshold of the garden. Cushion plants, groundcovers or rockery plants: whatever you call them they are the lower-growing shrubs and perennials that form a vital ingredient in the recipe. Some people assume every groundcover is easy-care but the term simply describes a flat growth habit. Groundcovers come in a kaleidoscope of personalities: some will blanket the ground and reduce weed growth; some, like forget-me-not, will tiptoe quite literally through your tulips and nicely cover over all your mistakes. But the finer ones like thyme and chamomile seem to attract weeds with the veracity that a cowpat attracts flies. Groundcovers neatly divide into the shade-tolerant types and the sun lovers, but whatever their preferences they all provide that last layer of foliage and flower as our eyes drop downwards from tree to shrub to ground. Like a cup that sits comfortably in its saucer, or a steak served in a rich sauce, so many of our larger garden plants look a bit 'unfinished' until they are skirted in a drizzle of low-lying leaf. It's the finishing touch that helps them sit comfortably in the border. It is no accident that groundcovers are called 'cushion' plants. As well as the low-maintenance myth,

another misconception is that mat-like plants are to be only confined to the edge of the border. Though they are perfect for softening a path edge, that ground-hugging outline comes into its own in many other ways. Here are a few ideas.

### Placemats

Around a pot or a piece of sculpture placed in the border, where larger plants would swamp and conceal, a low groundcover can create the perfect setting. Choose foliage colours to match and link with the feature you are showing off – rather like a colour-coordinated placemat would set off the object under which it is placed. In a Mediterranean corner at Ayrlies Garden I pepped up a bank of echiums (dazzling in spring but very pedestrian for the rest of the year) with agaves set in terracotta pots. The pots were effective but still looked like they had been shoved in (which they had). To make them look more integral to the scheme, and to draw extra attention to each pot, they were raised up on bricks, which were hidden with wide pools of the succulent *Echeveria elegans*. This created alcoves of icy grey texture as a setting for each pot. Glaucous mats like *Pimelea prostrata* or *Acaena caesiiglauca* would similarly look the part dribbled beneath lead or steel containers while the bronzy colour of libertias sits well around copper objects.

---

**Opposite**
Prevented from climbing through a neighbour's fence or getting into your attic from an outside wall, climbers on posts or pea sticks bring colour and texture to the spire-like equation. For a more contemporary twist you could use tecomanthe or trachelospermum (star jasmine).

Vita Sackville-West tried dwarf narcissus and even hollyhocks in these beds at Sissinghurst in England. Successive gardeners sensibly brought things down to size with this thyme lawn — pretty in season but hopeless for walking on and an awful lot of work to keep free of weeds.

itself if it is shaped and styled carefully. At Sissinghurst garden in England there are two slab-shaped borders planted entirely with thyme. Giving a lawn-like effect for much of the year, in summer they come alive — marbled with swirls of pink and white like some map of the moon threaded with busy bees.

As a gardener there, one of the most intricate jobs I did was to weed this tapestry every so often. With bottoms in the air, four of us would beaver away, armed with screwdrivers and knives. It was tedious work but always fun for the crowd of onlookers it would draw. It certainly taught me how much hard work groundcovers can be.

Generally, the smaller and finer your groundcover the more work is involved in keeping it weed free. Large expanses of flat planting work best where they won't get easily trampled on and where they don't meet the strong vertical of a fence or wall, which always makes for an ugly angle. On undulating land a lawn of mondo grass or Spanish shawl (*Heterocentron elegans*) makes a wonderfully restrained foreground to other planting beyond and might provide a simple setting for a sculpture, a rock or a special feature plant displayed alone like a nikau palm or a swanky bromeliad like *Alcanteria imperialis*. On a smaller scale a trough or large pot is a great place to create a mini lawn, threaded with small succulents to make a living 'table top' feature on a sunny terrace.

### Spotlights

The four best foliage colours to lighten a border are grey, cream, yellow or lime. Groundcovers used in these hues are especially useful in lighting up dark corners, especially under the skirts of larger shrubs, which are apt to go bare at the base. I love marjoram, either the limy gold form, *Origanum vulgare* 'Aureum', or the newer variegated variety 'Country Cream'. Majoram tends to burn in full sun but sheltered under larger plants it forms soft, illuminated duvets. Use light colours to brighten the gloom but take special care with plant choice as many plants with coloured leaves lose their intensity or turn green in shade or when they dislike the conditions.

### Groundcover lawns

Used exclusively en masse, groundcovers can be shaped and trimmed to form a two-dimensional expanse of low texture that can become quite architectural in

## Pizza topping

This is a trick used by many designers to cover a flat, boring area where you don't want to create a jungle or lose a view into another part of the garden. A reliable groundcover is planted over the area to make a lawn (this is your pizza base). Then onto this you sprinkle your salami or olives.

Enliven lawns of a purple acaena or *Muehlenbeckia axillaris* with taller-growing clumps of anything from carex to arthropodium or bromeliads. When your flower beds are crammed with plants it provides a good change of pace to come to a corner where just two simple elements are juxtaposed in a slightly theatrical way.

The plants you pepper about need to be strong enough to cope with the intense competition of the groundcover, which needs to be flat enough so that it doesn't billow up and swamp the 'topping'. Flat natives like acaena, pratia, raoulia and pimelia are great combined with a sprinkle of dwarf divaricates like *Coprosma* 'Mangitangi'. For a tropical look, cycads, cordylines, aloes or taros dotted in a bed of Spanish shawl or the blue succulent *Senecio serpens* can create a very tasty combination.

## Rivers

It's easy with groundcovers to use them as edging plants which follow the line of a flower bed or path edge in a predictable way. But by planting such plants perpendicular to the natural flow, threading them at right angles towards the depths of the border you can effectively break up long, drawn-out plantings and create the illusion of depth. Rivers of texture like this can also cause the eye to pause and be led towards surprises hidden in the depth of your planting — a pool of silvery pulmonarias grouped under a shrub, for example.

Shade lovers are ideal for this, used to form textural carpets in the wasted space under large shrubs. Take ajuga, for instance: like many shade-tolerant evergreens it provides a leafy carpet when deciduous shrubs above are bare and dull and brightens the spring border with rich blue spikes just before the canopy above closes in. This is the sort of perfect partnership that the best gardens are made of — a layered effect where, as one tier takes the curtain call, the next act is waiting in the wings to carry on the show. By layering your planting two or three plants take up the space of one so your picture becomes richer. Most gardens are full of golden opportunities to weave carpeters under deciduous shrubs and trees. In shade, weeds are often less of a problem and here some woodland groundcovers actually live up to the hype and keep the baddies out.

A river of flat *Coprosma* 'Hawera' seeps out ready to engulf a verbascum rosette and beyond the bronzy *Carex testacea*. Mats are like pizza bases and often look better interspersed with other shapes.

### PLANT PICKS: MATS (GROUNDCOVERS)

★ **Smaller plants:** acaena, armeria (thrift), aubrieta, bergenia, *Brachyscome iberidifolia*, *Cerastium tomentosum*, convallaria*, *Cornus canadensis**, doronicum*, drosanthemum (ice plant), epimedium*, gazania, *Geranium* 'Pink Spice', *Gunnera prorepens**, *Hebe pinguifolia* 'Pagei', *Iberis sempervirens* (Candytuft), isotoma, *Juniperus squamata* 'Blue Star', lamium*, lampranthus (ice plant), leptinella*, *Lithodora diffusa*, *Origanum vulgare* 'Country Cream', osteospermum, *Pachysandra terminalis**, *Pimelea prostrata*, *Salix repens*, *Senecio serpens*, stachys, thymus, *Veronica pedoncularis**

★ **Tougher groundcovers:** *Acorus gramineus* 'Variegatus'*, ajuga*, *Blechnum penna-marina**, *Campanula glomerata*, *Ceratostigma plumbaginoides**, *Coprosma* 'Hawera', *C. acerosa*, *Crassula multicava**, *Euphorbia amygdaloides* var. *robbiae**, *E. cyparissias*, *Geranium macrorrhizum**, *G. oxonianum*, geum*, hedera* (ivy), *Hypericum calycinum**, *Juniperus communis* 'Prostrata', *Luzula sylatica**, *Lysimachia nummularia**, *Persicaria affinis*, *Phlomis russeliana*, *Pratia angulata*, symphytum*, *Trachstemon orientalis**, *Vinca minor**, viola*

*\* suitable for shady conditions*

## Spikes

This chapter is about plant form, not foliage, but with spiky plants the whole form of the plant is shaped by the leaves and it is hard to separate the two. At twilight the spears of an aloe, a yucca or a drift of iris make arresting exclamation marks in garden beds, contrasting beautifully with softer shapes. We most often associate spiky plants with desert-themed gardens, full of angular agaves, doryanthes and beschorneria; it is certainly easy to find plants to add some architecture in such gardens but with lots of spiky plants put together it's so easy to overdo it. The result can be as relaxing as a battle scene from The Lord of the Rings with daggers pitched against swords,

javelins flailing skywards against spears. Too many spiky plants in any scheme can create an unsettled and restless atmosphere. We don't necessarily want every garden bed to be soothing but it's a wasted opportunity when spiky plants are not shown off against a contrasting background. Obviously, if the rocky desert look is what you are after you won't want the tropical swagger of hibiscus nor the frothing softness of a philadelphus as counterpoints, but softer plants that have a bit of the arid look about them will come in useful. Whipchord hebes, skeletal artemesias, sea buckthorn, tamarisk and the wire-netting fuzz of New Zealand divaricates like *Coprosma crassifolia* will all look at home in an arid scheme while still providing a softer complement to the spikes.

Spikes can give either downward or upward movement. These *Aloe thraskii* combine spiky architecture with a weeping sense of movement. The mats of gazania (left) are the perfect accompaniment.

## PLANT PICKS: SPIKES

★ **Smaller plants:** aciphylla, agave, aloe, *Aristea ecklonii**, asphodelus, astelia*, beschorneria, bletilla*, bulbine, bulbinella, crocosmia, crocus*, dianella*, *Dierama pulcherrimum* (angel's fishing rod), dietes, iris (bearded, ensata, *laevigata, sibirica*), kniphofia (red hot poker), libertia*, *Orthrosanthus multiflorus*, phormium (flax), schizostylis, tillandsia, tulbaghia, watsonia, *Zephyranthes candida*

★ **Succulents:** see desert garden plants list page 53

★ **Trees and large shrubs:** abies (fir), araucaria, cordyline, picea, *Yucca elephantipes*

*\* suitable for shady conditions*

At the other extreme cottage gardens, being so rich in soft perennials, can lack the sense of architecture and crisp form which spikes can bring. But there are many spiky plants that still have a cottage look about them. The eminent Edwardian plantswoman Gertrude Jekyll loved her yuccas as strong structure at the end of borders and plants like dietes, sisyrinchium, hemerocallis and iris all contribute a sharpness of form with a feel that is still sympathetic.

## Horizontal forms

Whether it's the folds in the hills of a landscape, the rhythmic ripple of the sea or just the layers in a rich cake, forms and shapes layered horizontally sit easily and comfortably with our eyes. It was perhaps the gardens of the East that first celebrated the beauty of trees sculpted by wind and heavy snowfalls to make distinct tiers. Today many of the classic sideswept plants we enjoy come from Chinese and Japanese gardening tradition, from elegant, flat-topped cherries to delicate maples that glow in spring and autumn. The idea of clipping bushes and training bonsai into cloud-like shapes also originates from the Orient and can add a wonderfully relaxed mood to any garden, taking an amorphous blob and turning it into something of elegance. The Japanese often use pines and clipped azaleas to form tiered sculptures but New Zealand natives like small-leaved coprosmas and totara respond equally well to cloud pruning for the richly layered look.

## Espalier

In more formal designs we can steal techniques of pruning from European traditions too, to introduce a strong sense of horizontal form along paths or boundaries. Fruit trees with lateral branches bent down and trained in parallel lines are called espaliers. Traditionally the technique was used to produce a heavy fruit crop against warm

garden walls but today we can train all manner of shrubs along horizontal wires in the open or on walls. Shrubs like pyracantha and even kowhai can produce living sculptures that echo the lines of a formal garden.

## Pleaching

Pleaching is a similar technique to espalier, in which a standardised avenue of trees like limes or hornbeam are trained so that their branches grow horizontally along wires and meld together. The finished effect can produce a theatrical sense of trees holding hands with beautiful patterns of parallel branches. If a pleached avenue is left to grow bushy before being clipped you can create a sort of hedge on stilts. This might be useful for hiding the neighbours or dividing the garden up without killing the sense of space altogether. Any tree that responds well to clipping can be used for this from callistemons (bottlebrush) to *Leptospermum nitidum* 'Copper Sheen'.

## Creating layers

Individual plants with a well-developed sense of horizontal form make elegant features in the garden with tiered branch structures layered one on the other. The flowering dogwoods — *Cornus contoversa* and *Cornus alternifolia* cultivars in particular — are deservedly the most well-known trees for sideswept good looks. Decked with creamy bracts in spring they deserve the comparisons with wedding cake. Though not as elegant as cornus, many conifers such as *Juniperus* x *pfitzeriana* are wonderfully explosive in the way they reach ever outwards. The fact that they sometimes take up a lot of room may have caused their fall from favour but with annual clipping it is easy to keep them in bounds. Using shears is fatal with conifers as it tends to obliterate their character and make them into formless blobs. Use loppers instead and just cut back firmly the strongest growths each year for a more naturalistic and animated effect.

With some plants, notably achilleas, crocosmias, lacecap hydrangeas and some umbellifers like dill, the sideways shimmer comes not from form or foliage effects but from the architectural flowers. The charm is fleeting but no less valuable, especially when contrasted with upright flower spikes.

## Ribbon planting

A layered feeling in the garden can be introduced not just by individual plants but in the way you mass shrubs and perennials in tiers and ribbons through your flower beds. Ribbon planting — the laying out of perennials and annuals in narrow, overlapping strips rather than clumps — was first advocated by Gertrude Jekyll. This arrangement allows several curtains of colour and texture to be overlaid in a small space. As one plant finishes flowering the idea is that another layer springs up behind or in front to continue the effect. It takes a degree of work to keep plants from swamping each other but the result is that plants that individually have little shape provide an effective sense of horizontal form when planted en masse. Throw in the odd rude interruption of a blobby shrub or a few spires to add some surprises.

---

The leaf arrangement on a Japanese maple (*Acer palmatum*) creates a relaxing layered feel that is echoed in the waterlily and even the arum flowers (*Zantedeschia*). Providing a dynamic vertical contrast at the pond edge is the grass *Hakonechloa macra* 'Aureola'.

### PLANT PICKS: HORIZONTAL FORMS

★ **Flower form:** achillea, *Aster lateriflorus* 'Horizontalis', crocosmia, *Echinacea purpurea* 'Magnus', helenium, hydrangea* (lacecap types), sedum, solidago, viburnum*, xeronema

★ **Trees and large shrubs:** *Acer palmatum**, *Albizia julibrissin* (silk tree), *Azara microphylla*, *Clerodendrum trichotomum**, *Coprosma* 'Beatsons Brown', *Cornus controversa** and *Cornus alternifolia**, *Helichrysum petiolare*, idesia, *Juniperus* x *pfitzeriana*, *J. virginiana* 'Grey Owl', *J. sabina* var. *tamariscifolia*, lagerstroemia, lepidothamnus, leptospermum, loropetalum, pinus, *Prunus* 'Mount Fuji', schizophragma*, stewartia*, *Viburnum plicatum* 'Mariesii'*

* suitable for shady conditions

Horizontal flowers of *Achillea millefolium* 'Red Beacon' weave through *Crocosmia* 'Lucifer' — a sculptural perennial for high summer.

## Loose weavers

The loose weavers are those plants with no well-defined form of their own. Many bulbs and annuals fit into this category; they are simply flowers held above a threadlike stem with little body to speak of. Structurally these plants add little to the border in terms of form until they flower, but they bring colour and seasonal surprise and as such are no less important in the overall recipe. Floppy perennials are often ignored in planting schemes because they lack strong form. But even without their flower contribution, their very looseness is in itself an asset. Such plants blur the edges of other planting; they flop easily into ugly corners and froth around those awkward underskirts where older shrubs are starting to go bare at the base. Like a serving of cream poured over a bowl of crumble, such plants often don't taste strongly themselves but as they drizzle themselves

### PLANT PICKS: LOOSE WEAVERS

★ **Smaller plants:** ageratum*, ajuga*, *Alchemilla mollis*\*, aquilegia*, asters, centaurea (cornflower), centranthus (false valerian), chrysanthemum, dianthus, dicentra*, epimedium*, erigeron, *Eryngium giganteum*, *Euphorbia polychroma*, felicia, gaura, gazania, geranium — most including *sylvaticum*\*/*oxonianum*/'Anne Folkard', geum*, osteospermum, primula*, saxifraga*, sisyrinchium, viola*

★ **Annuals:** alyssum, antirrhinum, *Calendula officinalis*, digitalis*, erysimum (wallflower), eschscholtzia, gypsophila, impatiens*, *Helichrysum bracteatum*, limnanthes, lobelia*, malva, mimulus*, nemesia, nicotiana*, papaver, petunia, *Salvia splendens*, tagetes, tropaeolum*, verbena

★ See also many deciduous bulbs list page 132

*suitable for shady conditions*

If you're not careful, loose weavers like these white ornithogalum bulbs and annual statice can make things as formless as minestrone soup. Here the strong path edge and balloon of clipped box steadies the sense of chaos.

into the corners they make everything taste better. Plants like hardy geraniums, alchemilla and asters are wonderful for adding body and fullness to your garden. In planning a border, if different plants were guests at a party, perennials would be the hosts of the event — not always wanting the limelight but moving around, helping everyone else to mix and have a good time.

## FOOD FOR THOUGHT

Look at different corners of your garden at the major planting. See how each plant fits into a shape category.

☆ Are certain plant shapes repeated or do you have a bit of everything?

☆ Do you have good vertical and horizontal elements as well as blobs?

☆ Are your spires grouped or alone?

☆ Is everything unbalanced with too many spires and nothing spiky or are there just too many forms in a chaotic mixture?

☆ At the other extreme, is everything rather shapeless — a porridge of formless froth?

Chapter 3

# Impact Plants

*architecture and topiary*

A TOILET ROLL on wheels. It's not a kind description but it sums up the tourist motor home or camper van rather well — a white box struggling up Arthur's Pass enjoying the open road and not noticing the queue of traffic banked up behind. The motor home has been forgotten by stylists and designers. Like the humble shed, it is just too small and slow to warrant any attention. Instead the architects are busy building bridges and banks — the big impressive projects that win awards for corporations — clad in concrete with steel girders, glass and sails hanging off the sides. Nature is different — she crafts even the humblest creation in amazing 3D detail. From a towering redwood to a humble seed pod, sublime architecture is woven into every thread of life — we just need to look.

## Architectural plants

Ask any architectural plant where it stands in the pecking order of plant shapes and textures and it would tell you that it is head and shoulders above the competition. Call them what you will — feature plants, accent plants or architectural statements — certain ingredients in your planting will always stand out from the crowd and you need them in some form or other. They are the cream that will help your garden hit the big time and they know it. Structural plants hold their heads up and shine. There are many reasons these plants think so highly of themselves but it often boils down to that most basic of boasts — size. Architectural plants have it big; if it's not big leaves then it's height and if it's not height then it's busty flowers, with big pods and fat stems, and preferably a combination of the whole lot.

But it doesn't end there, for true architecture isn't just about quantity, it is also about quality, construction and design. If you're into sci-fi movies like me it's not the biggest spacecraft that stick in the mind but those with the best shape. Most plod along, more like flying cutlery drawers than elegant pieces of

Don't call them stuck up — they are just confident: architectural plants like these swanky flowering aloes know they are big and beautiful and aren't afraid to strut their stuff. Such clean lines and slick shapes especially suit bold contemporary architecture.

## PLANT PICKS: ARCHITECTURAL GRASSES AND SEDGES

★ *Calamagrostis x acutiflora* 'Karl Foerster', *Chionochloa conspicua/flavicans, Cortaderia richardii/splendens, Cyperus papyrus, Deschampsia cespitosa, D.* 'Smart Grass', *Eragrostis trichodes, Hakonechloa macra* 'Aureola'*, *Helictotrichon sempervirens, Luzula sylvatica*, Miscanthus sinensis* 'Morninglight'/'Gracillimus'/'Variegatus'/ 'Zebrinus', *Molinia caerulea, Stipa gigantea*

*\* suitable for shady conditions*

## PLANT PICKS: ARCHITECTURAL WOODY PLANTS

★ **Shrubs:** aralia, carmichaelia, cornus*, divaricating shrubs (see page 116), *Ficus lyrata/dammeropsis/roxburghii, Hydrangea quercifolia*, Justicia carnea, Ligustrum japonicum* 'Rotundifolium', macropiper*, *Marattia salicina** (King fern), pseudopanax*, *Rosmarinus officinalis,* schefflera*, *Solanum laciniatum* (poroporo), viburnum*, wigandia, *Yucca filamentosa*

★ **Climbers:** *Beaumontia grandiflora* (herald's trumpet), campsis, *Clematis armandii,* humulus, lapageria*, monstera*, passiflora, philodendron*, schizophragma, *Tecomanthe speciosa*, Vitis coignetiae,* wisteria

★ **Trees:** abies, *Acer palmatum*,* agathis*, agonis, alberta, Aloe bainsii, *Araucaria columnaris* etc., brachychiton, *Cecropia peltata*, Cedrus atlantica* 'Glauca' (many other conifers), *Chorisia speciosa,* cordyline*, dracaena, *Ensete ventricosum* (banana), erythrina, *Eucalyptus pauciflora, Magnolia grandiflora, Meryta sinclairii*, Podocarpus macrophyllus** (Buddist pine), *Radermachera sinica,* tree ferns*

*\* suitable for shady conditions*

intergalactic architecture, but Star Trek's *Enterprise* will always stand out from the crowd — a sort of frisbee with toilet rolls attached. Luckily, nature too is a master designer with similarly outlandish tastes. Plants may be constrained by gravity but you wouldn't think so to look at some.

### Larger-than-life foliage

The thread common to all architectural plants is that they strut their stuff with confidence and style. They can have many different kinds of foliage but again that foliage is larger than life — scalloped, ribbed, voluminous or, if nothing else, at least arranged in an eye-catching way.

Take the humble carrot. It belongs to a family of brilliantly sculptured masterpieces, from the lacy doilies of sweet Cicely (*Myrrhis odorata*) to the cathedral-sized magnificence of fennels and angelica. Not all are big, but all are perfectly formed — they are the spacecraft of the garden and from humble beginnings in spring they boldly go where few plants have been before. From unpromising mounds of leaf, great shafts emerge. Ribbed like the pillars of a church, they push upwards at great speed and produce on top a hooded sheath like a dollop of melted candlewax. As this leathery lid peels back, from within a thousand tiny flowers cartwheel outwards, held on a framework of umbrella spokes.

It's a ridiculous set up in a way — a monster plant with puny little flowers, like midges gathered on the back of a dinosaur. Beneficial insects soon crowd in to feed and bask, and as the flowers fade they form purses of seed which, if left standing and not tidied away, will remain to entertain through winter — dressed in frost or snow before collapsing in a mass of burnt-out wreckage before next year's seedlings set forth.

The whole carrot family is gutsy, dynamic and fun. Every part of the plant is interesting but people don't use them. Why? Perhaps it's because they perform for a relatively short time and seed about. But that fleeting moment is all part of the specialness.

### Dynamic structure and form

We often associate architectural plants with good foliage but nice leaves alone don't make for good design. Several dynamic plants don't have any good leaves to speak of at all. *Verbena bonariensis*, for example, dresses to

---

Opposite below

With flowers balanced on skeletal rods *Verbena bonariensis* is an ethereal construction that deserves a position at the front of a bed so you can peer through its translucent form. It flowers for months then spoils the fun by seeding about rather too energetically.

**Above**
The subtropical style lends itself to architectural excess. This glamorous line-up begins with purple *Cordyline* 'Red Fountain', alocasias, bright coleus and a glowing *Cordyline australis* 'Albertii' to finish.

> ## PLANT PICKS: ARCHITECTURAL SOFT PLANTS
>
> ★ **Bulbs:** especially: amorphophallus*, arisaema*, cardiocrinum*, crinum*, dracunculus, eucomis, haemanthus*, lilium*, scadoxus*
>
> ★ **Succulents:** (see plant list page 53)
>
> ★ **Annuals:** *Amaranthus*, *Ammi visnaga* (bishop flower), anethum (dill), cleome, cosmos, helianthus (sunflower), limonium (statice), moluccella (bells of Ireland), *Nicotiana sylvestris**, nigella, *Onopordum arabicum*, *Persicaria orientale*, *Salvia sclarea*
>
> ★ **Soft evergreen plants:** *Acanthus spinosus**, agapanthus, alpinia, *Artemisia arbrotanum*, *Astelia chathamica**, celmisia, *Elegia capensis*, *Euphorbia characias*, *Geranium maderense**, *Helleborus argutifolius**, *Iris pallida* subsp. Pallida, *Pachysandra terminalis**, melianthus, *Myosotidium hortensia**, phormium, restio, strelitzia, *Xeronema callistemon*, zantedeschia*
>
> ★ **Deciduous plants:** *Achillea* 'Moonshine', *Aconitum carmichaelii* 'Arendsii'*, *Allium sphaerocephalon/aflatunense*, *Amsonia tabernaemontana*, *Angelica archangelica**, *Angelica gigas**, aquilegia*, *Astrantia major* 'Claret' and 'Shaggy'*, canna, *Cimicifuga simplex* 'Atropurpurea'*, *Cynara cardunculus*, *Cyperus papyrus*, *C. alternifolius* 'Nanus'*, *Digitalis ferruginea/parviflora/lanata**, *Echinacea purpurea*, *Echinops ritro*, *Eupatorium purpureum*, *Filipendula rubra* 'Venusta', *Foeniculum vulgare* 'Purpureum', hedychium, *Helianthus salicifolius*, *Liatris spicata*, *Macleaya cordata*, meconopsis*, *Persicaria amplexicaulis*, *Phlomis russeliana*, polygonatum* (Solomon's seal), rheum*, *Salvia confertiflora/madrensis*, *Sedum spectabile*, *S. telephium* 'Matrona', strelitzia, *Telekia speciosa*, thalictrum, *Tiarella cordifolia**, *Verbena bonariensis*, *Veronicastrum virginicum*
>
> *suitable for shady conditions*

impress, wearing very little at all — no dinner-plate foliage or big flowers. Here, it's the strength of the wiry stems and the very translucent but powerful presence of the plant that makes it stand out. We wonder how it stands up at all.

Similarly euphorbias like *Euphorbia characias* and many grasses have relatively dull leaves but they are arranged in a dramatic way, in whirls and fountains, often on long, arching stems or combined with dramatic flowers. So structure and form are essential for drama; but size counts too — it magnifies the qualities that are there.

Another misconception about feature plants is that they are so outlandish and loud that they are only for modern gardens — funky bromeliads and bananas for a Pacific theme and spiny aloes for the desert look. Architecture, however, should be an essential part of every garden scheme. Dynamic structures act like anchor points of distinctiveness among the less 'Hollywood' members of your plant team.

In the cottage garden, style is not compromised by introducing the odd yucca or canna among the roses but the fleeting spires of thalictrum flowers, aconitum and nodding racemes of cimicifugas are more dramatic in their season, even without the colour that they bring. Cardoons (*Cynara cardunculus*) and annuals like bishop flower (*Ammi visnaga*) and giant tobacco plant (*Nicotiana sylvestris*) provide that delicious combination of softness and stature. In any garden they come into their own when plants of substance are thin on the ground and they undergird the lighter flutter of flowers.

## Positioning architectural plants

Feature plants are like living sculptures and as such need careful placing where the background will not detract from their forms. A plain wall or fence is the ideal setting but background plants with fine leaves and unobtrusive textures also make good companions, especially if they are in a contrasting colour. Alternatively, by placing architectural plants out in the open you can remove all distractions and allow them to be seen from many different angles. On the bend of a path, in an island bed or rising from a gap in paving or a stretch of gravel are all excellent places to showcase your most structural stars.

Lighting can play an important part in the planning too. No other plant elements in the garden will benefit more from some clever illumination than architectural plants. By choosing a place that catches morning or evening sun you can accentuate shapes and shadows, but after dark artificial lighting comes into its own, creating exaggerated silhouettes and casting magical shadows onto nearby walls.

# Topiary

Smart and crisp, topiary, like little else in the garden, can perk up flabby planting and add a powerful dash of style. Begun by the Romans, topiary — where plants are clipped and trained to form exaggerated forms — has a long and noble association with gardens. The regular clipping ensures a density of growth and a solidity of form that makes it half way between a sculpture and a planted element. Whether it is blobs, cones, spirals or spires topiary shapes always stand out from the crowd and draw the eye, so their size, shape and placing is especially important. As any plant hummock acts as an anchor so a topiary performs the same task but to a greater degree.

Topiary works best in three situations. A simple topiary plant can be used firstly to give a feeling of stability and permanence to areas of light and frothy planting. Where perennials and annuals predominate, its strong and smooth form provides a useful anchor point, holding the looseness together — the same effect a rather stern school principal would have on a class of unruly children.

Secondly, topiary also works a treat in structural borders where lush foliage predominates and a sleek and smooth contrast would be as welcome as a cool beer after devouring a bowl of nachos.

The third area of usefulness is in formal gardens where symmetry and rhythmic lines are needed. But don't get too rigid: in the tradition of Japanese gardens, shape your topiary into natural and abstract forms for a more organic and characterful finish. One of the most satisfying elements I've added to a garden were a cluster of lonicera balls huddled under a group of nikaus and a clump of taro. The fat paddles of the taro, the architecture of the palms and the comfortable smoothness of the topiary set up a vigorous tension while the overriding greenness held everything together.

---

The soothing effect of topiary is used to great effect by Julie Russell in this confident set-up, combining silver cardoon (*Cynara cardunculus*) and beschornerias that echo the vibrancy of camellia flowers in their gutsy flower spikes.

Impact Plants 37

**Left above**

Forget pompous formality and try some fun and self-expression with the shears. This dressing table with its silvery ivy mirror and thyme lawn carpet is part of a complete bedroom scene fashioned from plants.

**Left below**

Melting like church candles: topiary at Great Dixter that began as proud but uptight peacocks has metamorphosed into something altogether more abstract and characterful, thanks to some sensitive clipping.

### PLANT PICKS: TOPIARY

★ **Smaller plants:** *Buxus sempervirens*, *Coprosma* 'Cappucino'/'Cutie'/'Mangitangi', hedera, *Lonicera nitida*, *Muehlenbeckia complexa*, *Pittosporum* 'Little Squirt'

★ **Trees and large shrubs:** carpinus (hornbeam), *Coprosma* 'Beatsons Brown', *C.* 'Beatsons Gold', corokia, *Escallonia macrantha*, *Euonymus japonicus*, ilex, *Laurus nobilis*, osmanthus, pittosporum, *Podocarpus totara*, *Prunus lusitanica*, royina, *Taxus baccata* 'Fastigiata' (Irish yew), tecomaria, *Waterhousea floribunda* (weeping lily pilly)

At Christopher Lloyd's home, Great Dixter in England, two abstract topiaries greet you at the front door. Like dollops of mashed potato they lurch about drunkenly like the house itself. What's intriguing is that a photograph shows that they began life in the 1930s as pristine peacocks in wooden tubs. Since then they have rooted into the ground and been allowed to choose their own identities thanks to some sensitive clipping. Sometimes when we release the reins a little like this what emerges is something far more interesting than anything we might have imagined.

Another great use for topiary is in adding humour to the garden. I'm currently working on a life-size moa in my own patch. Like Mr Lloyd's peacock my *Coprosma* 'Beatsons Brown' began as something quite different but it's hard to tell a headstrong native that it is destined to a life as a boring ball when it longs to spread its flightless wings.

Suitable plants for topiary are ideally slow growing. They often have fine leaves, which will give a smooth look, but larger leaves can work too provided you don't wreck them too often with clipping.

## Standards

Craggy old roses lashed to old broom handles have given the idea of standardising plants a bad name. Standardising is when we train a tree or a shrub up onto a single stem. Apart from weeping specimens, which are often grafted onto an upright rootstock, with most standards you basically get the visual impact of a blob on a stick. It sounds a bit coarse, but the result can give an unusually airy, light feel to a border. Many people find the toffee apple look to be just too contrived but standards are useful tools when you want to step out a rhythm in a dramatic way or when you need a sense of height in a limited space.

The secret of good standards is in using unobtrusive stakes if they are needed at all, and in getting the spacing right. Spaced too widely in formal schemes one standard will not relate to the next. In a more casual scheme, providing you get the heights uniform, it can look quite charming when some heads are more swollen than others.

Spacing standards close together has become quite the thing to do in trendy little courtyards where perky pieces of potted bay or box eagerly line up along a wall or down some steps — as if they are queuing for the bus. Such intense repetition gives you a touch of Versailles chic in a space the size of a postage stamp, but it's a technique that quickly

---

We associate standards with formality, but here Ben McMaster has used standardised lavenders in a looser way — massing them with cypress (*Cupressus sempervirens*) for a distinct Mediterranean feel. As we will see later the principles of repetition and simplicity add to the drama.

### PLANT PICKS: FOR STANDARDISING

★ argyranthemum, buxus, camellia, *Coprosma karo* 'Red'/'Yvonne', escallonia, euryops, *Ficus hilleri*, fuchsia, *Genista* 'Yellow Imp', ilex (holly), *Juniperus chinensis*, *Juniperus chinensis* 'Kaizuka' (Hollywood juniper), *Laurus nobilis*, *Lavandula dentata*, *Lonicera nitida*, osmanthus, *Prunus lusitanica*, rhaphiolepsis, rosmarinus, *Sophora* 'Dragons Gold', vaccinium (cranberry)

### PLANT PICKS: FOR POLLARDING

★ callistemon, carica (fig), casaurina, catalpa, *Cotinus* 'Grace', erythrina, gleditsia, hymenosporum, lagerstroemia, poplar, salix, tilia (lime)

### PLANT PICKS: FOR PLEACHING

★ alnus (alder), carpinus (hornbeam), gleditsia, hymenosporum, lagerstroemia, malus (apples — crab apples), platanus (plane tree), prunus (plums, apricots, peaches), sorbus aria (whitebeam), tilia (lime), olea (olive)

A twist on conventional pollarding: bending a willow sapling over to make a stunning silhouetted shape shows that tortured trees have a place in the garden. The regrowth can easily be trimmed back to the main frame each year.

---

## FOOD FOR THOUGHT

✩ What are the most architectural plants in the garden? Are you using them to full advantage?

✩ Have you considered using deciduous architectural plants which will add dynamic changes through the seasons?

✩ Is there a tree you could limb up creatively or allow to form an attractive apron of branches?

✩ Are you taking advantage of topiary in the garden?

✩ Is your planting very loose and fluffy? It might need the addition of topiary or architectural plants.

✩ At the other extreme, is your planting crowded with bold foliage? There may be scope to introduce smooth topiary shapes.

---

becomes predictable and formulaic if you try it again and again round the garden. Save it for your most intimate and sophisticated entertaining areas where you want a heightened sense of theatre.

### Standard trees

As with all garden features overuse is a killer and the most common abuse of standards is when every tree in the garden is mutilated and limbed up to form a lollipop. If given time many trees like nyssas, weeping pears and pin oaks form magnificent aprons of growth with exciting 'caves' underneath. Often when we defrock such specimens all we do is reveal a crusty patch of dry, uncompromising bare earth that will support neither lawn nor garden. Us blokes are especially 'trigger happy' when it comes to the chainsaw or bowsaw. But vent your slash-and-burn instinct on the firewood pile instead and leave at least a few of your trees with some dignity.

### Pollarding

One legitimate way to chop and torture trees is to pollard them — growing a tree into a standard and then pruning it back hard each few years to a single stem so a fuzzy mass of loose top growth is produced. Indestructible plants like the willow and poplar are traditionally used but many species can be tried. Callistemons work well as do gleditsia, hymenosporum and lagerstroemia. The benefit of pollarding is that you get significantly larger leaves with the vigorous regrowth, as well as a nice loose shape and, in deciduous species, wonderfully explosive branch structure to enjoy all winter. A pollard is ideal where you need height and lightness without the tight formality (and regular clipping) of a piece of topiary.

Chapter 4

# Humps and Hollows

*planting for balance and dramatic topography*

What is it about the coast that we love? Headlands, bays, coves and plunging cliffs. If only we could arrange our plants in such an exciting way.

IT'S A SWELTERING hot day at Muriwai. The gannets seem quite unfazed by the heat but with a baby, a rucksack and a shameful amount of excess fat I'm panting when I get to the top. It's a surreal place — birds polka-dotting the ledges and stacks, and the stench of guano. The view's worth the climb though: plunging cliffs, the muffled boom of waves slapping into a cavern somewhere under my feet and then, further off, scrawled lines of surf piggybacking into the wide bay with nowhere else to go on a hot day.

## Coastline appeal:
*creating unpredictability and drama*

We are either turned on or off plants by first impressions. Colour is often the prime drawcard but after that it is the general grouping and arrangement of plant shapes that we notice first. You can fill your beds with the most interesting botanical collection but unless it has instant appeal to the average person, then design wise it's not worth a heap of beans.

My granddad, like many people of his

generation, liked his chrysanthemums at the back of his flower beds and his pinks along the front. His plants were always arranged like a stiff family wedding portrait with starchy tiers of faces. It makes sense in a way – the taller plants hide the fence and the smaller plants get lots of sun at the front. The trouble was that everything looked about as comfortable as a pack of choir boys at a carol service. You could almost feel the plants wanting to break out and let their hair down. Now, I try to arrange plants so that they echo the contours of a coastline rather than marching along in tiered rows. A coastline basically has the low stuff at the front and the cliffs at the back, but along the way there are plenty of surprises and drama. Valleys cut deep clefts down to the sea and the flat sands don't just make a strip along the front, they create arcing bays that cut deep inland between muscular headlands.

In your garden, as well as the general ins and outs, you can build the drama by allowing spire-like yuccas or verbascums to jut out at the front of the border like rock stacks poking out of the ocean. The hollows under large shrubs and trees become your caves, to be filled with bright treasures – perhaps woodland plants like silver lamium and pulmonaria or bromeliads and rhizomatous begonias for a tropical look. In long borders especially, the inclusion of headlands of substantial plants creates a sense of surprise as you walk along to see what is in the next 'bay'. It also masks the predictability of a boring boundary.

Getting away from the tired 'low at the front, big at the back' formula will break the mould of predictability by creating an ebb and flow as hypnotic as the tide.

### Anchor things down

At the coast, it is the massed landforms that make the backbone of the landscape. So too in our gardens the planting needs weighty elements to form the skeleton that holds the border together. Like the ballast in a ship, large, bulky shrubs or plants with a strong sense of architecture provide the sense of stability to hold together all the looser planting. These anchor plants need to have a sense of permanence and weight, forming the framework around which smaller, less permanent plantings ebb and flow. A small tree is the ultimate 'anchor point' but spires work well too. A good example is Irish yew, which is tight in form and would make a powerful anchor point.

Like ballast in a ship, the clipped *Coprosma* 'Beatsons Brown' in the centre of this 'hot' border at Ayrlies Garden provides permanence and stability to the busy planting all around.

## A balanced composition of shapes

As well as including a good backbone planting in our gardens, how we arrange those key plants is important. Most often we want a good general spread of varied shapes — a balanced composition. An effective way to get balance is to imagine each flower bed is a life-raft floating on the open sea. Then imagine the bulkier plant elements like awkwardly shaped packing cases or cargo loaded on top. Lighter spires and slender plants are like people. In this scenario, to prevent a total capsize we would rightly put the largest masses towards the centre grouped together. Smaller items would naturally be distributed round the edges and should someone need to stand near a corner we would be sure to place another person on the opposite corner to prevent the raft from tipping. This is what designers mean by creating a sense of balance, and in island beds in the garden, which aren't anchored down into the wider design by hard landscaping, a sense of balance is especially important.

Balance doesn't always occur within the same border. Either side of a doorway, for instance, you might want to achieve the same sense of fullness in your planting. The plants may not be a slavish reflection of each other but their density and proportions should relate. Similarly in a square space such as a lawn area, if you site a large tree or piece of sculpture toward one corner it will help visually if 'anchoring' plants are massed on the opposite corner to create a sense of stability (see diagram). Along a very formal border you will want a very even distribution of forms but as double borders approach a house entrance or a set of gates, planting might swell and rise to draw attention and add weight to where the main focus is to be drawn. Attractive plant shapes contrasted together are a great start but how we distribute those shapes within any given space is crucial for success. Let's look at some different ways of distributing our plants.

See the garden as a life-raft with trees and shrubs arranged so that they don't capsize the design. The garden above left is over-weighted in one corner. By planting in the opposite corner a sense of balance is achieved (above right).

The same principle works where garden features or architecture are crooked or irregular. Plants can help redress the balance, as shown in the diagrams to the right.

## Blocky planting

Men seem to love blocky planting where everything is arranged in well-defined slabs of one sort or another. Blocky planting is tidy and precise: plants are kept firmly in their place. Planting in distinct groups also makes designing a garden on paper quite straightforward and many designers opt for this approach. After all, formal grouping of plants gives them greater impact and gives a clean, unified look that is easy to maintain and has a restful simplicity about it.

The bold, blocky approach has a long tradition too. The formal gardens of the Renaissance were defined by very structured and formally grouped plant elements. In the 1930s it was Roberto Burle Marx who first began using plants in a modernist way. Rather like a child would colour in a picture with bold, simple slabs of a single colour so he planted South American parks and gardens with vast sheets of a single species, arranged to make abstract patterns, and designers have been copying him ever since.

Some people just love to see a bit of soil between their plants, despite the weeds it may attract. For them the blocky look is ideal, but with every plant at arm's length, a border treated like this can start to look like a troupe of Irish folk dancers with their arms held by their side and no interaction. In nature plants often mix and mingle in complex associations so why should we separate them cleanly in our gardens? Another disadvantage if this approach is used exclusively is that a garden where everything is set out in distinct blocks can become formulaic

Bold blocks of colour add clarity and confidence to a garden but you need plants that won't let you down.

and dull — as characterless and clinical as a doctor's waiting room. Moreover, because each species is massed, the choice of plants is limited to those that will perform for most of the year in their allotted space. In a more diffuse planting there is room to dibble in a few luxuries — plants like spring bulbs or lobelias that pop up and entertain for just a short period. These plants will not hold up as prime players in a planting scheme but in the shadow of more year-round performers they give us an exciting side show before diving for cover.

Filled with plants that neither flop nor billow, blocky gardens can seem rather too 'tame' and sterile. But thankfully designers like Wolfgang Oehme and James van Sweden in North America have shown how to combine the looseness and seasonality of tough perennials with the blocky way of planting. Gardens can thus appear logical and controlled yet still be loose and free.

### BLOCKY PLANTING

Advantages

- Easy to look after.
- Crisp and neat.
- Allows simplicity and boldness.

Disadvantages

- Plants don't interact.
- Can look sterile and boring.
- Short of detail and surprise.
- Needs careful plant choice.

## Dotty planting

Are you going dotty? Take a look outside the window. Just as blocky planting can become monotonous so over-busy, fragmented planting can start to resemble the bottom of a handbag with all manner of bits and pieces shoved in — all of them justified in being there no doubt, but with no overall sense of order and control. If, like me, you love to collect plants and you only have a small garden, then you are especially susceptible to catching the 'busyness' disease. They say variety is the spice of life, but whether it's plants, pots or garden accessories, bittyness in all its guises is the worst enemy of good design. It's ironic that the keener you are to garden the more you have to fight the urge to bung in just one more treasure. Bittyness starts when we decide (with some justification) that rather than spend a small fortune on three of the same weigela shrubs to make a decent splash, we buy instead one weigela, a purple cotinus and an upright juniper. The weigelas were going to form the anchor of your border and already you have removed their power to pull everything else together. Things are starting to get busy and that's before we have even looked at the smaller details like bulbs and annuals. Look at the shrubs in any one garden bed and ask yourself: 'Is there one of everything, or have I planted in groups and repeated my structural plants?'

In order to look comfortable the main structural planting in the border should be in groups of the same sort. If you achieve a simple structure then the peripheral plants can become a little busier without distracting from the overall cohesion. Another way bittyness spreads through a garden bed is when we find a plant we particularly like, say a red penstemon or some bright annuals, and we split them up to make more. So far so good, but the trouble is that instead of planting our offsets so they relate to the original parent plant, we dot them about up and down the bed so that they become scattered individuals with little impact and no relation to one another. They say a little goes a long way but in good design take your little and either bin it or bulk it. In the defence of busyness it does have its advantages. Busy borders are interesting with lots to see and with a wide variety of plants. If one sort is past its best or has not yet emerged there is usually something else having a fling.

### DOTTY PLANTING

Advantages
- Lots of variety.
- Plenty to see.
- Always something in season.
- Good interaction between plants.

Disadvantages
- Little sense of order, control or cohesion.
- Little overall impact.
- No relation between plants.
- No clarity and crispness.

Even with a coherent colour scheme this garden looks like it has a bad case of measles with dots of this and that and plants scattered rather than arranged in relaxed but meaningful groups. To create some chemistry, always gather your plants together.

A special form of dottiness that can look quite beautiful is meadow-style planting where a palette of plants is repeated in a diffuse matrix — we look at this intentional sort of intense repetition in Chapter 8.

Right above

Low, flat plantings increase the sense of spaciousness in this garden. They lap at the shores of a 'sea' of chamomile, making a beautifully restrained centrepiece.

Right below

In a billowing planting a simple iron arbour clothed in clematis makes an intriguing 'cave'. The pot containing a structural cordyline draws our eye in, creating a nice sense of depth.

### FOOD FOR THOUGHT

☆ Do the overall contours of your planting have coastal appeal? Even in formally shaped beds it often should. (Try looking at your planting at twilight or in low evening sun to get a better idea of its contours.)

☆ Do low plants flow out from the depths of your planting, back to front? Are there caves and outlying 'rocky stacks'?

☆ Are you too dotty or blocky in your approach? Do you have one of everything in your garden or have you repeated some key elements — especially trees or shrubs?

☆ Look at the plants that are repeated in the garden: are they repeated in a purposeful way to create headlands and hills to anchor down looser planting?

Chapter 5

# The Stylish Approach

*choosing a unifying theme*

I'M KNEE DEEP in heather and the wind is whipping it into waves. Beyond the smell of sheep poo and bracken, somewhere miles above me a skylark is going ballistic. The mingling of heather swathes with moor grass and gorse weaves patterns not unlike the surface of the moon. Amid this, huge cusps of granite poke their head up on the high ground like crooked old teeth. I'm up on the moors. England. Summer. But it's all only in my head. In reality I'm in New Zealand wondering how to take all that beauty and mood and recreate it with my barrowload of carex and a pocket handkerchief-sized plot to play with.

## Choose a guiding style or theme

Window displays, and in fact most works of art, have a distinct style or theme that sets them apart from the crowd. There is an overall look that every element within the composition reinforces. Similarly, when our planting has a guiding theme such as my desire to make a garden reminiscent of a wild moor, it not only creates mood and atmosphere in the garden but it also helps you plan and plant with purpose.

When you decide to create your vision, maybe a 'tropical paradise' or a cooling 'blue and white' garden, suddenly shopping for plants becomes more focused, more of a challenge, and more fun. Often we are overwhelmed with plant choice anyway, so in fine-tuning the end product we want to achieve, we turn buying plants into a treasure hunt rather than a case of a random 'bag a bargain'.

## Choose the look and plan with purpose

Like morning mist, 'style' is one of those hard to grasp design jargon words like 'balance' and 'proportion', but it basically encapsulates the look you want to achieve in any particular corner of the garden. It might be based geographically — maybe a Mediterranean look, the

It may be the props that are guiding the theme in this 'Alice in Wonderland' border but the plants, like woolly *Senecio cineraria* and red verbenas, are also adding just as much to the whimsical atmosphere.

moorland memory mentioned above, or if you really want to impress the neighbours, your 'Yak Lands of Mongolia' border. You may want more of a fantasy theme, say an 'Ice Border' full of jagged, angular yuccas and icy blue and white colours.

Whatever you choose, get a picture of something in your mind and then stick to it. Special places affect us so deeply that we instinctively want to somehow capture them and take them home. From my moor it might be a sprig of heather but more often it's a few photos or a memory rekindled when we see a magazine picture or a movie that recalls that special place.

These are all great sources of inspiration for those little details that will make all the difference to the finished product.

As well as memories, movies and magazines as inspiration, a theme can be a total fantasy dreamt in your wildest dreams. Often a colour theme is part of the idea — we will look at that in Chapter 10. A theme doesn't have to sound pompous and grand, it may be as simple as a general look you want to achieve or a mood you want to feel when you go into a particular part of the garden. You might say, 'I want this part of the garden to feel light and airy. I want tall, see-through plants that move in the wind and fine foliage — lots of grasses and not much colour.' It sounds a bit vague but in fact this is a great starting point in planting with purpose and having a foundation on which to base all your future planting decisions.

Whether we consciously think it or not, we usually know when a garden is planted with purpose; there is an innate sense of order and direction that really gives the garden an edge. Planting that is a hotchpotch of random ideas and tastes is as unsettling as being made to eat a plate of bacon, apple pie and curry mixed together. In other words, a stomach churner! Even a wilderness garden,

The purist may want to stick to a single united style for their property but for the adventurous there is often scope to integrate several themes into one garden.

This alcove is shady and intimate — perfect for a Japanese-inspired courtyard.

Formal style: low maintenance and a clean look to complement the house architecture at the front.

Swirling shapes and lush planting create a native/subtropical look in the back garden. The sculpture, set in a pebble koru, acts as a focal point from both the deck and the woodland walk.

A curving woodland walk hides the narrowness of this side of the garden.

seemingly chaotic and ecologically planted, has by its very nature a uniform style and look about it. The owners have deliberately excluded gharish exotics — they have stuck to their theme and all the plants are telling the same story. That's why sticking to a particular theme works; your plants look like they are there for a reason. They look 'at home' together like a comfortable family. The alternative is to have your plants looking like an assorted jumble of people waiting at a bus stop — no interaction or chemistry and everyone looking like they are going someplace else.

### Keep themes simple

As well as bringing a sense of focus, themes add harmony not only to your plants but to the garden as a whole. There is a case to be made for having only one theme and sticking to it. It keeps things simple and allows you to develop an idea more fully. In choosing too many themes in a small area things can get confusing and muddled. Imagine if a simple trip to the front door involved passing your 'Cottage Garden Corner', your 'Desert Alcove' and negotiating a stream at your 'Peruvian Cloudforest'; visitors would have jetlag before they got to the doorbell.

Simple themes are most successful but if you can't hold yourself back, you will want more than just one, and as most gardens have a natural front/back divide there is scope for at least two different treatments within your plot (see diagram). As well as front and back gardens, the strip down one side of the property might become a natural place to take advantage of a different microclimate to create perhaps a mossy woodland feel. A tiny alcove created by the walls of your house might provide yet another separate space in which to have fun with another theme. It might lend itself to a Japanese-style composition; for example, to be viewed from a particular window for a self-contained scene.

### Keep themes separate

Between major themes it seems best not to overlap them but to keep them distinct and separate from one another. The supreme theme garden for me is Biddulph Grange, a Victorian garden in north-west England where at every twist and turn ingenious tunnels and two-sided summerhouses lead you through a series of garden 'rooms'. From the Japanese garden a pergola tunnel emerges into an Egyptian court; a small pinetum wraps around, ending in a rocky rhododendron glade reminiscent of the Himalayas; entering a cave there you eventually

*We needn't produce a slavish copy when developing our theme. This Japanese-inspired space has distinct New Zealand touches, like the scleranthus to replace traditional moss.*

emerge from a Tudor cottage! The concept works because each area is hidden and doesn't interfere with the next.

We might not be quite so theatrical in our own gardens but we can have fun with mood and style on different sides of the house or in different garden 'rooms'. Look for natural divisions in your layout so different styles won't clash. It only takes one palm poking over a fence to spoil the effect of a soft perennial planting. Neutral shrubs or hedges can act as buffer zones between different areas.

Enclosed areas separated from other parts of the garden are good places to create gardens with a unique flavour. With its moss and maples a Japanese theme lends itself to shady corners.

## Themes and house styles

Creating a style is as much about the hard landscaping as the soft, so of course your walls and paths, furniture and pots should lead and reflect the style of the planting. House architecture is often so dominant a part of a garden that it tends to dictate the kind of style you will choose in the first place. Clean, modern houses suggest clean, modern gardens rather than rustic abandon, while an old villa would suit something looser. This idea is fine if you have a nice-looking house but if you have something rather less than a palace, despite what the garden books say, just turn a blind eye to it and let your imagination wander.

## Laying out your style: formal or informal?

If you are the sort who likes hospital corners when you tuck in the bed sheets and creases ironed into your underpants, then whatever style of garden you go for will end up formal in design. You will insist that your garden plants stand to attention and line up with military precision.

Formality is not so much a style in itself but rather a way of laying out all the other styles. A desert garden can be laid out formally or informally, though the latter seems to work best. Pacific rim and cottage gardens work equally well whether sophisticated or informal and very rustic.

There are no rules — it boils down to your own preference. Many gardeners, however, wheel out the old advice: 'don't mix formal and informal'. It's true that when designing your flower beds and path shapes, geometrical circles and arrow-straight lines do lose their integrity if you start to throw in snaky wiggles, but informal-style planting works beautifully within a very formal design — just look at famous gardens like Sissinghurst or Hidcote in England. There's something exciting about the tension between the control and order of straight-path edges contrasting with the exuberance and spontaneity of the plants within. Many of the world's great gardens use this formal/informal spark in their fabric; laying soft planting over geometric bones.

The formal look is a great thing in the garden, bringing that sense of order and reason to a design. We feel safe with formality, there are clear rules of symmetry and repetition that we can follow, but so often we avoid launching out into a more free-form expression of ourselves lest our curves become convoluted wiggles and our informality turns into chaos.

## When formal gets military

Formality gives a crisp, sharp look but don't use it mechanically, especially with your planting.

We all like to march around and feel in charge from time to time. Who doesn't enjoy the sadistic pleasure to be had from beating a bush into submission with the shears, for example. But if you are an orderly sort of person ask yourself whether, in your garden, you are acting more like a circus master or a military dictator. Both jobs require exacting leadership and strength but while the military dictator demands straight lines and total submission, at the circus your firm hand is there to produce: not submission but a dazzling show. Many formal gardens are spoilt by being almost too regimented — like the minimalist homes we see in glossy magazines they look great but not especially friendly, or realistic. Sure it makes sense to have places where there is regular repetition and taller plants toward the back, but there is room too for a lighter touch. Looser planting between and around the formal elements will actually accentuate the formality by the contrasting association so don't be afraid of letting go a little — the results might surprise you.

Often creating a sense of style can be as easy as introducing a few key plants that are iconic indicators for that particular style. Here, for a spark of inspiration, is a whistle-stop tour of some popular styles with some of the plants that typify 'the look'.

## Mediterranean style

Mediterranean, like any style, is a generalised conglomeration of features and ideas from a vast range of places as diverse as California, South Africa, Tuscany, Provence and even parts of New Zealand — anywhere you can grow an orange in fact. The important thing is that it feels hot, rustic and mildly productive. The Mediterranean climate is characterised by moderately hot, dry summers and mild, moist winters with often poor, freely draining soils. As a result the plants that grow well are often aromatic with a grey, protective coating on the leaves (lavender, for example) or are waxy and succulent like aloes or yuccas.

It's amazing how little it takes to imbue your garden with Mediterranean flavour; you only have to buy an olive jar and throw a citrus tree into a pot and visitors will instantly feel they are on the Côte d'Azur.

Much of the look borrows its emblems from agriculture, with plants that are both productive and beautiful at the same time. Figs, citrus, vines and billowing olives are all pretty essential. Olives can be overdone — they grow enormous and drop leaves for 12 months of the year but without them you can't impress friends by wheeling out your home-made snacks steeped in garlic and orange rind. Olives do take well to clipping: the variety 'Manzanillo' is said to be more compact but in tighter spaces similar-looking alternatives are available. Examples include native *Olearia virgata* or *Elaeagnus angustifolia*, which has sweetly scented flowers and shimmering leaves.

Scent is another important part of the recipe. Many dry-climate plants release aromatic oils as the sun works its magic

---

Even on a dull day stucco walls and drought-tolerant plants like these silvery *Convolvulus cneorum* and impressive *Euphorbia charachias* hybrids evoke the sunshine of the Mediterranean.

> ### PLANT PICKS: THE 'MED' LOOK
>
> ★ **Smaller plants:** acanthus, agave, aloe, argyranthemum (marguerite daisy), beschorneria, convolvuolus, doryanthes, eucomis, euphorbia, *Foeniculum vulgare* (fennel), furcraea, melianthus, osteospermum, pelargonium, most salvias especially *S. officinalis* (sage), yucca
>
> ★ **Trees:** acacia, cercis, citrus, cordyline, eriobotrya (loquat), olea (olive), palms (see page 54), pencil conifers, *Cupressus sempervirens* is a Tuscan essential
>
> ★ **Climbers:** bougainvillea, *Ficus carica* (fig), jasminum, passiflora, *Petrea volubilis*, plumbago, *Rosa banksiae*, solandra, wisteria, vitis
>
> ★ **Shrubs:** especially grey-leaved types, callistemon, ceanothus, cistus, datura, *Echium fastuosum*, gardenia, heliotropium, hibiscus, isoplexis, lavandula, nerium (oleander), pelargoniums, *Phlomis fruticosa*, plumeria (frangipani), rosmarinus, tamarisk, teucrium, tibouchina, zauschneria

so as well as lavender, orange blossom and cistus, use herbs like rosemary and sage. Also try small lawns or seats carpeted with chamomile or thyme; they will charm the pants of everyone, but will need some intensive care to keep the weeds out.

Mediterranean places are often steep and coastal so if you have a slope the obvious thing is to create terraces where you can show off some serious rustic stonework or dazzling white plaster walls. Use predominantly coastal plants, like marguerites, echiums and euphorbias and don't be afraid of using bright colours – they don't look so washed out in the bright light. Let rip with hot pink pelargoniums, oleanders and – hottest of all – the essential bougainvillea, which is the natural choice for the pergola. Even if your local weather isn't crash hot you need a pergola to create the illusion that you need somewhere to get out of the sun. Cover it with grapes and bask in the illusion. Garden style helps us escape everyday life; we can lounge in the back yard and imagine the Aegean Sea lapping just over the lavender hedge.

## Desert style

A desert planting is one of the hardest styles to fit comfortably into a garden setting. Its inherent austerity means you will inevitably see through to any walls or fences beyond so these need to look like attractive parts of the design because screening them in lush planting will counteract the parched effect you are aiming for. A simple stucco wall can be incredibly effective as a backdrop, especially if you use it to cast dramatic shadows with subtle garden lighting. Stone is also a good material to use, particularly if you can link it through to rocky outcrops to emphasise a rugged, inhospitable feel. Rocks seem to go hand in hand with the look even though many deserts have no rocks at all!

Desert planting is on the sparse side so leave gaps between your plants and cover with a shingle mulch that matches the colour of your feature rocks. (Water-rounded pebbles are hardly appropriate in a desert but more often than not you will get away with it.) Desert-type plants are very striking and need plenty of space to best show their architecture. The strong, often spiky shapes fit well with contemporary architecture and are best if left uncluttered. The harsh textures can seem a bit cold and uncompromising, however, so try and weave in a bit of softer planting as a contrast. Under upright cactus-like cereus even a low aloe like the beautiful *Aloe spinosissima* will create a duvet of leaf that will glow with orange candles in winter.

Being such inhospitable places, the desert look needs plants that look like they haven't had a decent meal in weeks. New Zealand divaricates make suitably meagre mounds of wire-netting twiggyness. Grey-leaved, drought-tolerant shrubs like calocephalus and fine artemisias like 'Silver Queen' will also look suitably dishevelled. A desert doesn't have to be made only of the archetypal prickly

---

### TIPS TO MAKE YOUR DESERT SMILE

○ Don't be tempted to mix too many brightly coloured succulents together – the result can be very busy.

○ Some succulents colour better if they are underfed.

○ In cold areas often it is wet feet and not the cold that kills in winter. Improve drainage and cut down on the fertiliser to toughen your plants.

Plants have the power to transport us. With distinct Mexican architecture like this your planting has to go with the flow and heighten the illusion of faraway places. Note how the fescue grasses help soften the harsh architecture.

cactus and succulents. Real desert ecosystems are complex communities of shrubs, bulbs, grasses and opportunist annuals that spring to life at the mere whiff of rain. All too often we throw in a few aloes and echerverias, landscape with rocks and gravel mulch, and leave it at that. Additions like gazanias, moraea corms, sedums and small euphorbias will bring some softness, seasonality and colour to an otherwise rather hard textural palette. Use bright colours or white, which in deserts attracts pollinating insects that come out at dusk. Orange colours work well with the predominant greys and browns of foliage and bright yellows will bring in the sun even on dull days.

Small grasses can be useful to cover the ground and can be chosen for a sun-baked appearance. Examples are many of the New Zealand carex and fescues, such as rich brown *Carex flagellifera*.

A desert style is one of the few styles that is limited to a certain microclimate. You need a fairly frost-free locality and a site with good drainage and all-year sunshine. The soil you can change by building it up and incorporating humus and grit, but the other factors are fixed. A good site is against the north side of the house in the rain shadow of the eaves where other plants would soon curl up their toes. High-rainfall areas can be suitable as long as you provide plenty of drainage. Some 'desert' lookalikes such as aloes actually go yellow if they don't get enough water.

## PLANT PICKS: THE DESERT LOOK

★ **Smaller plants:** anigozanthos, *Artemisia* 'Silver Queen', astelia, bulbine, crassula, drosanthemum (ice plant), echeveria, eucomis, gazania, lachenalia, lampranthus (ice plant), libertia, nerine, oxalis, *Pimelea prostrata*, sedum, sparaxis, *Wachendorfia paniculata*, fine grasses like briza, *Carex* 'Frosted Curls', festuca, *Molinia caerulea*

★ **Palms:** (see tropical palms list page 54)

★ **Bold succulents and cacti:** aeonium, *Aloe arborescens/bainsii/ferox/pluridens/ thraskii*, agave, *Beaucarnea recurvata* (ponytail palm), beschorneria, *Cereus jamacaru*, crassula, doryanthes, dracaena, furcraea, *Kalanchoe beharensis/grandis/thrysiflora*, *Opuntia monocantha* (prickly pear), *Yucca elephantipes*

★ **Parched-looking shrubs:** (see divaricating plants list page 116), *Calocephalus brownii*, cassinia, *Coprosma* 'Mangitangi', *C. virescens*, *C. brunnea*, *C. acerosa* 'Red Rocks', corokias, *Hebe tetragona*, *Genista aetnensis*, holocladium, *Muehlenbeckia astonii*, *Myrsine divaricata*, olearia, *Spartium junceum*, westringia, *Zauschneria californica* (Californian fuschia)

## Subtropical style

Your husband may not have the physique for it, but at least you can make him feel like he's Tarzan with a suitably lush jungle oasis. Many of us dream of a Pacific Island paradise — the swish of palm trees, dappled shade studded with the outlandish blooms of hibiscus, exotic orchids and the smell of gardenia. We want the greenery without the leeches and tigers. The subtropical look combines dramatic foliage with explosive flowers. Because many of the ingredients are shade lovers and can be massed in impenetrable jungle walls, it is a theme that especially suits today's smaller gardens with fences to hide and neighbouring buildings that cast shade for much of the day. The approach to jungle planting is often informal with plants richly layered from bromeliads and

Jungles don't always need to be garish. Gorilla-sized bromeliads (*Alcanteria imperialis* 'Silver Form') make a fitting centrepiece in this jungle glade. Even with all the strong textures, by avoiding artificial variegations and the distraction of flowers, the result is a surprisingly naturalistic and restrained scene.

### PLANT PICKS: THE SUBTROPICAL LOOK

★ **Smaller plants:** alpinia*, arisaema, arthropodium*, begonia*, bromeliad*, caladium*, canna, catalpa (coppiced), clivia*, colocasia*, crinum*, dahlia, ferns* (many), gunnera, haemanthus*, hedychium*, *Heterocentron elegans*, hypoestes (polka dot plant)*, impatiens*, iresine*, *Nicotiana sylvestris*, *Philodendron* 'Xanadu'*, phormium, pilea* (aluminium plant), rheum*, rodgersia*, scadoxus*, strelitzia, tradescantia*

★ **Climbers:** bougainvillea, campsis, hoya*, mandevilla, monstera*, philodendron*, stephanotis, tecomanthe, thunbergias

★ **Compact palms and lookalikes:** *Brahea edulis*, *Chamaerops humilis*, *Cordyline australis**, *Cycas revoluta**, *Phoenix roebelenii**, *Rhapis excelsa** (lady palm), *Musa velutina*, *Rhopalostylis* (nikau)*

★ **Trees and large shrubs:** *Cecropia peltata**, *Chorisia speciosa* (floss silk tree), *Cordyline nigra**, *Fatsia japonica**, *Ficus dammaropsis**, hibiscus, *Luculia grandifolia*, meryta* (puka), paulownia, plumera (frangipani), pseudopanax*, *Radermachera sinica* (Canton lace), *Schefflera actinophylla*/arboricola*/'Condor'**, *Schizolobium paraphyllum* (Brazilian fern tree), trevesia*, monstera*, *Musa ventricosa* (dwarf banana), tree ferns*, vireya rhododendron*

*\* suitable for shady conditions*

### TIPS FROM THE JUNGLE

○ Big leaves don't make small spaces feel even smaller — quite the opposite is true.

○ Good feeding and watering are essential to most subtropicals.

○ A jungle can be refined and even subtle if you avoid strong leaf colours and let shapes and textures provide the drama instead.

Spanish shawl (heterocentron) at ground level, elephant-leafed taros and vireya rhododendrons at chest height and palms and bananas swaying overhead. Unlike some other styles it is the plants and not other garden features that are the main event. Bright colours seem to best reflect the exuberance and flamboyance of this approach so don't hold back.

One of the great things about a 'Pasifika'-style garden is that it allows you to integrate many New Zealand natives into the scheme like bold puka (*Meryta sinclairii*), flaxes and cabbage trees, which are themselves subtropical. Hard features like pots and seats tend to play second fiddle to the drama of the plants.

Palms can quickly outgrow their welcome so choose smaller types or lookalike cycads that won't reach for the skies and rupture your borders in years to come. Bananas too can easily engulf a small plot so go for lush lookalikes such as *Canna edulis* and safe gingers (hedychium and alpinia). In colder climates where it takes more cunning to go subtropical it seems the challenge becomes irresistible and sometimes the most wonderful exotic escapes are forged in the flames of adversity. With all those architectural forms the lush look is a style that especially suits contemporary designs and low-maintenance gardens.

## Cottage style

In New Zealand as I write, cottage gardening has become mothballed along with thermos flasks and Val Doonican sweaters. Everybody wants pebbles and yuccas. In Europe the cottage garden has been hijacked by trendy eco-designers who have grafted it onto the sleek clean lines of modernism with Frankenstein-like results — shiny steel and glass boxes bursting at the seams with wildflower meadows. If you don't have an allium and a grass then your name is dirt. However, true cottage gardens have simple and unselfconscious roots — the small gardens of the working class who grew vegetables in rows and poked in flowers where they could.

Today, with chocolate box and calendar pictures filling our heads we imagine thatched cottages or in New Zealand the colonial villa with verandas draped in roses and more often than not a gargantuan wisteria. Where would the cottage garden be without a rose or two? I feel a bit sorry for roses — they look great with tropical plants but like the Spice Girls they have been tarred with a certain brush and no one lets them play beyond the cottage look. So get a rose and you're off to more than a good start. Cottage gardens often have impractical paths made of bricks or crazy paving — preferably a mixture of the two guaranteed to trip you up. Arches too are an essential — dripping with a mountain of jasmine, a wisteria or a rose or three, and of a size that is awkward to walk under. Bending and stooping is after all part and parcel of the cottage experience, for there is lots to see at all levels and most of it is flopping over the path trying to trip you up.

Traditionally vegetables were mixed in with the huge variety of flowers and herbs but nowadays we have relaunched that particular fad and called it a potager. If you don't have vegetables then you must have flowers at least. In the cottage garden flowers come first and foliage is

### PLANT PICKS: THE COTTAGE LOOK

★ **Smaller plants:** traditional perennials with soft outlines and bright colours: achillea, alchemilla, aquilegia*, argyranthemum, artemisia, asters, campanula*, cheiranthus, chrysanthemums, crocosmia, dahlias, delphinium, dianthus, euphorbia, geranium*, helenium, helianthemum, hemerocallis, lavandula, lavatera, leucanthemum, lupinus, lysimachia, osteospermum, penstemon, rudbeckia, sedum, solidago, tiarella*

★ **Plants that seed themselves about:** alcea (hollyhock), digitalis (foxloves), lunaria (honesty), myosotis (forget-me-not), papaver (poppy), reseda (mignonette), viola

★ **Climbers:** especially: clematis, climbing roses, humulus, lathyrus (sweet pea), lonicera, parthenocissus

★ **Bulbs:** (see bulbs list page 127) especially: anemones, crocus, lilies, narcissus (daffodils), tulipa, and for late summer amaryllis, colchicums, eucomis, nerines

★ **Trees and large shrubs:** roses have become something of a trade mark but need not be essential. Soft, rounded outlines and decidious-type trees and shrubs are most suitable: abelia, berberis, cotinus, deutzia, forsythia, fraxinus, hydrangea*, malus, philadelphus*, pyrus (pear), quercus, rhododendron*, ribes, sorbus, spiraea, syringa, viburnum*, with topiary in buxus (box) and taxus (yew)

*suitable for shady conditions*

With plants seeding and weaving, the cottage garden look is an exuberant celebration of softness and colour. Here, seeders like the foxgloves and blue Chinese forget-me-not (*Cynoglossum amabile*) will need judicious thinning, but at least when they have passed the foliage of hostas, stachys and bearded iris in the foreground will add more permanent structure.

more of an added extra. The plants are soft and billowy and everywhere. Today's gardens planted in the cottage style tend to include a bigger proportion of good foliage plants and shrubs, providing year-round interest.

To distill the essence of the cottage look into a few key words, I would describe it firstly as **romantic**, where everything is so full and free that a garden teeters on the edge of chaotic and wild but is held together by the line of a path or the firmness of a ball of wobbling topiary. There is also a sense of **simple rusticity** where a straight path is slightly kinked rather than perfect and a bench is of crude, wooden construction rather than highly stylised and ornate. The two characteristics of '**diversity**' and '**fullness**' abound with every plant group represented from climbers to shrubs, bulbs to trees but with perennials always at the fore. The whole is woven into an informal tapestry, with plants leaning onto one another and jostling for space. It is very much a melting pot of plants where sometimes the individual ingredients seem blurred but the whole has a unity and more often than not a gentle softness rather than using shock tactics. To the uninitiated, fearing heaps of maintenance, the mixture can seem overwhelming, but it need not be the case if you use newer compact and disease-resistant plants and cut down on the number of self-seeders.

## FOOD FOR THOUGHT

☆ What sort of theme(s) would I like for my garden?

☆ What sort of plants usually typify this theme/style (think of personal experiences, movies, magazines and the like)?

☆ At present what is the general theme of my garden? Are my plants all telling a similar story; giving a unified look?

☆ Where is there opportunity in my garden to create separate areas with planting of a different theme or mood?

☆ How do I make my hard features and landscaping tie in with the theme(s) I have chosen for my planting?

Chapter 6

# Drama

*creating excitement in the garden*

Even the most attention-grabbing plants have to play supporting roles beside this elaborate mosaic water feature in Kevin Kilsby's garden. A 'set piece' like this is ideal placed at the end of a vista or as a surprise breaking up a long border.

DO YOU REMEMBER Bob? You know, he was the one clinging on to the life-raft between the vicar and the lady in the blue dress when the ship broke open like a Christmas cracker. He fell off with the funnels just after Leonardo di Caprio scooped up Kate Winslet and set her afloat on a bit of bed-head.

Love, betrayal, special effects – even a dance number: *Titanic* was a great rollercoaster ride of a movie but no one remembers Bob or the hundreds of other extras – just Leonardo with his boyish smile and lily-white Kate with that pouty mouth. The extras are never as well remembered as the stars but they are just as important in making the story work.

The cast of plants we use in the garden work in a similar way. There are the show-offs that play the lead parts and the lesser mortals helping the story along. It's a team effort and if you get it right your cast of characters will turn in an Oscar-winning performance.

A bit like our shop window scenario, to be dramatic our planting has to tell a story. In *Titanic*, if there wasn't a coherent plot linking all the set pieces together,

This garden comprises an 'all star' cast but without quieter linking plants there is little obvious chemistry between such prima donna plants as *Carex hachijoensis* 'Evergold' (bottom), *Agave attenuata* and *Pisonia brunoniana* 'Variegata' (top).

then we would soon, quite literally, lose the plot. You can spot those garden borders that have lost their way; they are often full of interesting moments but there is no common thread to link them together. The result is the horticultural equivalent of a bag of liquorice allsorts — great plants but no story. The things that provide continuity in a border are, firstly, an all-embracing theme or style; within this there are colour themes (green leaves providing the most basic and essential sense of unity); finally, there is repetition, where certain materials and plants pop up again and again rather like the narrator spinning a good yarn.

## The problem with drama:
*feast or famine*

The process of building up a good border, for me, usually involves creating first the backdrop then a solid cast of stars as my feature planting. Lastly I have some fun finding a supporting cast to complement. There are two mistakes we often make as we audition plants with which to build a border. On the one hand we get star struck and try to build a meaningful story with only dramatic plants, which leads to a restless cat fight of prima donnas all vying for attention. Gardens where spikes and balls, paddles and purple leaves are all strutting their stuff can be a bit like an Arnold Schwarzenegger movie — all action but very little story to draw you in and engage you at a deeper level. What we need is a little moderation in how many stars we use in any given area.

At the other extreme we aim too low: we collect together a bunch of subtle plants and wonder why the result is sending us to sleep. It's easy to fall in love with those soft and subtle species. Cottage gardeners are especially susceptible to this oversight. In October their gardens look amazing but once foxglove, valerian, aquilegia and forget-me-not have done their dash, by December there is little left to see — just a formless soup of spent stems and leggy roses. What's needed are some accent plants to add form and foliage that will go the distance: bold cannas or cardoons (cynara) or shrubs like *Cotinus* 'Grace' are perfect candidates for the job to carry the other planting when it runs out of steam.

With drama it seems to be the case of feast or famine but the best gardens combine a little of both extremes. Some areas may be loud and brash while other parts are mellow and relaxed. By creating different levels of drama in different parts of your garden you will create a nicely textured sense of mood as you move from one space to another. Even within a single planting, there is room for both drama and subtlety so that the stars play alongside their supporting cast.

## The stars

In any great production the stars carry the show and play all the major parts. Whatever we call them: feature plants, accent plants or show-offs, these are Leonardo di Caprio plants — they have the confidence and charisma to hit the high notes and make you feel that you have got your money's worth.

The difference between the star and the supporting cast is seen in the quantum leap between a highly bred dahlia and a lowly hebe. While the hebe shuffles along in its slippers — small leaves, tiny flowers, a humble hummock as comfortable and familiar as a hot-water bottle — the dahlia erupts on the scene like a geyser. Before long it has overshadowed the neighbours and is flamenco dancing its way down the border in shocking flamingo pink. Love it or hate it, this brazen performance certainly produces a response — and that's what drama is all about.

A hibiscus bush is undoubtedly a prima donna too. Like the dahlia it invests all its talent in the floral fireworks but these, sad to say, don't last forever. In winter it's a different story for both plants; they exit with their tails between their legs — the dahlia snubbed rudely out by the first frost and the hibiscus becoming a bundle of bony old twigs for the cold season. Drama doesn't have to be a year-round effect: in the garden as on Broadway a production can have a limited season. Indeed, sometimes the short length of a performance makes it even more special like the lilies in high summer or chrysanthemums that are so redolent of darkening days and falling leaves. It's good to have stars like these, especially if they are staggered through the year so they don't all do a curtain call at the same time. There are those who bounce on in act one in spring and then the late arrivals at the finale. But as well as these fly-by-nights we also need feature plants which are more enduring — the Clint Eastwoods and Meryl Streeps who will stand the test of time. These plants usually rely not on flower power primarily to elicit a winning performance but instead use glamorous foliage and the dramatic shapes that we have already looked at to dazzle and delight.

## The supporting cast

A movie where every actor was trying to be the star would be a complete bore — an indigestible helping of show-offs all competing for attention. In recent years, however, form and texture has been so emphasised that the other subtle qualities that some plants contribute are forgotten. Take plumbago and agapanthus, for example: both are blue and flower in summer. While agapanthus flowers only briefly but dramatically at Christmas it has bold foliage that looks good all year — it is a star. Plumbago, however, is a large, formless blob of a bush with nondescript leaves. At first glance is it any wonder it is not used much? But

*The supporting roles offered by self-seeders like white* Lychnis chalcedonica, Centranthus ruber *and* Echium plantagineum *are just what this busty rose needs to look its best.*

### STAR TACTICS

Dramatic plants always use one or more of the following tactics:

- strong form,
- striking foliage,
- bright colours,
- strong architecture.

plumbago goes on flowering much longer than agapanthus at a time in high summer when flower colour is thin on the ground. It doesn't seed about either and its gentle humpbacks are a great backdrop for spiky plants like yuccas or the spires of *Cupressus sempervirens* 'Totem'. So in context, plumbago might do a better job overall than its more glamorous counterpart.

Mundane plants may not get the blood boiling but they work quietly behind the scenes, creating the appropriate setting in which the prima donnas can strut their stuff. They build an atmosphere and give a garden a feeling of completeness, either adding a sense of intricacy and detail or providing some meaty structure.

Background plants vary in the way that they work. Some are structural elements providing bulk and mass to a planting, such as blobby plants like hebe, choisya, nandina and coprosma. Others, like hardy geraniums and hemerocallis, provide flower power and lush swags of greenery to fill out the garden.

Still other supporting cast members include the weavers and seeders that are flexible enough to fill in the gaps and add a final dusting of detail like a rich custard making a dessert taste even better. Lastly a few, like perennial lobelias and some bulbs, add interest, be it ever so briefly, at an unusual time of the year.

As gardening grabs you, you realise that you can't take the plants seen on a garden centre shelf at face value. Many valuable plants look dreadful cooped up in a pot and many cannot be judged on that first impression. In a garden context, however, working as part of the team of plants, they may play an essential role at a certain time of the year. To rely on the obvious good lookers to build a satisfying garden would be like trying to get to the moon by recruiting the contestants from a Miss World contest to build your rocket for you. Looks aren't everything.

## Drama but not melodrama

Drama of any sort works because it makes us feel alive. It plays on our feelings and senses. Anything that is even slightly exaggerated and larger than life will have a sense of the dramatic.

Over the top — even camp — gardens crammed with theatricality can be great

*Gardening should be as much about fun as it is about fashion. Over-the-top corners crammed with theatricality like this 'shrine' in Peter Brady's Auckland garden tickle our senses.*

fun with architectural plants, colour and trickery at every turn. We can't help but feel stimulated. But drama needn't be bizarre or excessive. Often the emotional manipulation works best when it is subliminal. Dan Pearson, a renowned British garden designer, rightly said, 'The best gardens are where the senses are teased and tickled, not commanded to attention.'

When we think of drama in the garden it is easy to think in terms of excess: hard landscaping, over-the-top fountains, lighting and larger-than-life statues or urns. It all sounds like a lot of money and perhaps a bit too Hollywood for our tastes. But even if your style is less extrovert, don't shy away from adding something to tickle the senses. All gardens need dramatic plants that make you sit up and pay attention. I remember meeting my first-ever *Dietes robinsoniana* hanging its pristine white blooms over a path — it blew me away. I love plants because, of all garden 'features', they are by far the cheapest way of injecting life and drama and, being natural, the visual stimulation is easy on the eye. You may tire of your glazed pot or your mirror or mosaic but you'll never fall out with a dietes.

You might think that a relaxing garden is the opposite of a dramatic garden but in fact it is not the case. The simplest and most soothing of gardens, such as a green leafy glade or the sweep of gravel in a Japanese courtyard, are often highly stylised landscapes. In highlighting and exaggerating the elements of simplicity and calm, they are working in a dramatic way to heighten our sense of peacefulness. These places, though subtle, are still playing with our emotions — and we thank them for it. We will look at using simplicity in a dramatic way in Chapter 7.

## Ways to create drama in the garden

Here are nine ways to raise the temperature in your garden.

### 1 Use exaggeration and repetition

Drama is an inflated version of reality so when we repeat anything in our planting we are drawing attention to it. Take a trip out to a field of sunflowers or lavender for the ultimate effect of drama through multiplication. In the garden there are limits but if you can repeat plant some of your favourites you will both heighten the drama and increase a feeling of unity. That's two for the price of one. More of this in Chapter 8.

### 2 Plant with confidence

The worst gardens always feel like they are limping along — a hotchpotch of half-baked ideas and indecision. Get off the fence!

Gardening needs to be approached in the same way you hand over an apple to a horse; you need to go at it with confidence or you might find the consequences are painful. Even if you put together awful plant and colour combinations, done with boldness you will, more often than not, get away with it. So don't buy three narcissus; order a sackful. Don't prune back that tired pieris; fling it in the skip!

Confidence means deciding what plants you are going to use, whittling your choice down to a bare minimum and planting in bold groups and drifts. I don't believe in never planting anything singly as some designers advocate. A single specimen can be a fantastic detail or surprise in a scheme, but confident gardeners don't make single-specimen planting a habit. The more dramatic moments in a design are often the simpler parts where exciting elements stand out against a plain backdrop and are juxtaposed against contrasting forms. The exciting bits are where you go for it and don't hold back.

### 3 Highlight contrasts

Contrasts bring the thrilling clash of opposites. Sugar and spice, black and white, yin and yang; call it what you will, in the garden you need a bit of friction to produce flames.

The more stark you can make any contrast the bigger the effect. The great danger, however, is to overdo contrasts and end up with a restless soup of over-stimulation. Again it can be likened to an exciting movie — we love the goodie versus baddie tension but you also need to have some scenes where the guns aren't constantly blazing to develop the plot and give us a break from all the noise and tension. A good rule of thumb is that shapes and textures can be contrasted more often than colours. Don't forget that even the sense of space in a garden can be manipulated to bring about dramatic

*A bit of friction produces flames. Sandra Arnet throws unexpected ingredients together, such as cottage garden roses and funky aloes to produce a fusion of styles linked by a strong colour theme.*

changes. Something as simple as walking from a large lawn into a small hedged room can get the hairs standing up on the back of your neck. So don't see that dark, narrow passage down the side of a house as a drawback; see it as an opportunity to create an atmospheric tunnel of gloom from which to emerge into somewhere completely different — it's a journey of pure theatre.

It's worth noting that there are a few contrasts that don't work well:
- Large plants don't sit happily next to very small plants.
- Bright, intense colours don't look so hot in company with soft, muted shades.
- Random wiggly bed shapes clash with formal lines and curves.

Otherwise let your opposites attract.

## CONTRASTS

Here's a summary of some of the classic contrasts to exploit that are covered in this book.

- **Design:** formal design with informal planting; minimalist structure with exuberant planting.
- **Plant shapes:** leaf sizes and shapes; flower sizes and shapes; horizontals with verticals; ups with downs; blobs with spires or spiky plants.
- **Contrasting textures:** rough with smooth; glossy with dull; stringy with strappy.
- **Mood:** busy planting then simplicity; lots of colour then quiet and green; sunny then shady.
- **Finish:** pristine lawns and shaggy beds.

### 4 Bring clarity

Maximise special effects by clearing away anything superfluous to what you want to achieve. In a particular part of the border, for example, the drama might come from large grey macleaya leaves grouped behind a smooth, green piece of topiary. If the effect works, remove any scruffier plant material that may be blurring the sharpness of the contrast. Control your plants like you would a playground punch-up: make the crowd of bystanders stand back so that everyone can get a good look at the action!

The principle of 'less is more' is useful but while simplifying and 'sharpening' any part of your planting, consider how other plants that don't look essential at the moment may become stars in the drama at other times of the year. If they are, then their presence can be tolerated and you can spare them the chop. Creating a sense of clarity in the border comes as you identify those plant partnerships that are most effective. Then you can do something as simple as a little selective weeding and snipping to draw more attention to where the action is and to bring out that contrast.

### 5 Inject colour

As effective at drawing a crowd as putting Nicole Kidman's name to a movie, colour sells. Bright hues grab our attention but colour, like money, is a great servant but an awful master so use it wisely and don't become addicted. Sometimes a complete lack of colour can be as intriguing as the 'exploded paint box' approach. In Chapter 10 we look further at the pulling power of colour.

### 6 Celebrate age

Plants which tend to become the stars in your team of players might do so simply because they are full of age and character. That's why Gran gets the best seat at the dinner table when she comes to visit. Drama is not always young and glamorous (despite what the soaps might suggest). Plants with a sense of age — even when they are as ugly as hell — contribute a sense of permanence and magic to the garden. So if you can lay your hands on a fabulously old tree with a crazy, gnarled trunk and a sagging backside you've got a star on your hands. Before you dig out that old bay tree lurching over the path or curse the neighbour's Moreton Bay fig that seems to unload half of its canopy into your garden every summer, take another look and try to see the benefits such characters are bringing to your section.

Old timers deserve a bit of respect and breathing room so if you have inherited a particularly large and ancient old tree don't try and outshine it with dramatic planting. Instead celebrate it as the main attraction and play down the surrounds with a stage of sympathetic planting such as ghostly astelias or lush clivia, which will form a simple hors d'oeuvre for the main event. Fiddly planting next to large trees never works so keep your cool — a single planting grown well will speak volumes in such a setting.

### 7 Do the unexpected

Surprise is essential in any piece of theatre. When a plant is growing in the way you'd expect, it is comforting, but when you get it jumping through hoops that's when we sit up and take notice. Try and stage plants where you will notice them best. Raise small plants up to eye level where they will be in your face and where you will notice their details and any scent. Let the drooping bells of fuchsia or forlorn faces of hellebore sit along a wall where you can tickle their chins and poke your nose inside. Bromeliads are gymnasts and are fun to work with as they will balance in branches, perch along a fence in mounted baskets or metal containers and even hang around glued to a tree trunk.

Succulents too are well suited to urns and containers especially if you set them on pedestals or stack bricks underneath to further elevate their status. Such a multi-layered approach is especially useful in tight spaces where gardening in three dimensions is important.

**Above**
Topography always adds drama to any garden. This modern knot garden with scallop shells and hedges of grey teucrium, box and gold euonymus takes full advantage of the fact that it can be viewed from an elevated deck. The crisp focus of the design adds impact.

**Right**
Undoubtedly a prima donna plant, this hibiscus knows that colour sells and is milking the fact for all its worth.

Design is like feeding a horse: it is done best with boldness and confidence. The clarity of this scheme — blue fescues and *Pachystegia insignis* bounded by hebe hedges at Christchurch Botanic Gardens — has instant appeal.

Unusual training can bring its own particular surprises. A tree doesn't have to be a tree at all; it can be maintained as a bush. Species like catalpa, paulownia, eucalyptus and willow can be cut to the ground each year (coppiced) to stimulate bushy growth that is endowed with gigantic leaves. Train them and tie them onto iron frames and you can mould some trees into almost any shape. *Sorbus aria*, the whitebeam with felty undersides to its leaves, for example, can be trained into an arch or alcove where the bold, silvery young leaves create a sumptuous hood.

Climbers are especially malleable. We look at their gymnastics later, but an unexpected way to use them is as groundcovers, where dinnerplates of clematis can sprawl between your daylilies and daisies.

In contrast groundcovers like ajuga and pimelia need not spread their blankets flat but can be used to colonise artificial mounds and steep banks to add a three-dimensional aspect rather than allowing them to run on the flat.

Each time our preconceptions of a plant are challenged there is an opportunity for surprise and delight. Turn an unexpected species of shrub like dwarf kowhai (*Sophora microphylla* 'Dragons Gold') into a piece of topiary or treat a clipped coprosma or pyracantha like a climber, leading them along diagonal wires on a wall to create (after a year or two) a lattice effect in two dimensions.

## 8 Avoid tall poppy syndrome

A trap to avoid when using plants with strong personalities is to forget to link them into the border as a whole so they look like an integral part of everything else that's going on. Strongly variegated plants and those with brightly coloured leaves or flowers are especially prone to suffering from tall poppy syndrome, and it's a particular challenge to make them look at home with more mundane neighbours. Even when a key plant is repeated it needs to be acknowledged by the plants to either side. Coloured trees like golden gleditsia and copper beeches can be especially problematic because the colour is so intense and so plentiful. Even cabbage trees and palms can look high and dry after a few years when they have got to a height where they are becoming visually detached from the planting beneath.

The answer is to provide stepping stones of similar colours and textures which will echo the look of the star plant and stitch it into its setting. These stepping stones need to be in proportion to your star plant. For example, a pool of purple *Ajuga reptans* 'Catlins Giant' under a vast copper beech repeats the colour of leaf but does not acknowledge and echo the scale of the tree enough to be of any value. However, by underplanting the beech instead with some well-sized Japanese maples and then the ajuga below that, the dominating drama of the tree is diffused — out and downwards through the maples and down to the groundcover. Thus you will have created a scene rather than a random assortment of unrelated plants.

Bold variegations can be surprisingly domineering in a border and can often look out of place. From a distance the tone can vary greatly from creams to pinks and coral to strident yellows. Stand back and look at all variegated plants from a distance to get an idea of the overall colour tone so you can intelligently echo and acknowledge it in the surroundings. For instance, a white variegation can look surprisingly yellow from a distance, which might mean using creamy companions like variegated flax (*Phormium* 'Tricolor') or lemon sisyrinchiums rather than white flowers to develop a link.

These plants will anchor your star plant into the scene and avoid the 'tall poppy' detachment. This is what plant teamwork is all about — the supporting cast helping the star but not trying to take over the show.

### 9 Create set pieces

Any movie is a mixture of turbo-charged set pieces like a car chase or an explosion and then quieter scenes that develop the characters and the story. In the garden too we need moments of high drama and quieter contrasts — for without any hollows between the highs of drama there would be no exciting 'roller-coaster' effect. Set pieces are what gives your planting spice and add the high notes along the way.

Indistinct planting can be relaxing on the eye but at certain points, especially along lengthy stretches of border, it can be a good idea to create bite-size 'scenes' or grouping of plants to grab the attention and bring a sense of focus. If repeated along a border, these especially well thought out areas can act like punctuation marks or as distinct focal points in a scheme.

Corners where a garden changes direction, and spaces opposite important windows of the house are ideal places to create an area of heightened drama. Though the centrepiece might be a feature such as a piece of sculpture, a group of rocks or a sitting area, man-made features can become tiresome if used too obviously. Often a grouping of dramatic plants, a particularly arresting set up of contrasts or a peak of colour will provide all the drama that is needed.

A set piece doesn't have to be completely separate from the planting all around but there should be a sense in which the interest reaches a peak. If plants are the main drawcard, whatever species you use should differ from the other plants in the general border so that a set piece feels like a distinct entity in the design as a whole. You might frame a particular area in a theatrical way with a low hedge or highlight it with a background trellis screen, clipped greenery or a feature wall that is different from the rest of the boundary. Instead of the usual soil surface, break the floor texture between plants with a mulch of glass

Purple, gold, cream and even grey foliage can sometimes over-dominate a planting.

Acknowledge the presence of these gutsy colours by reflecting them in the planting around. These plants could be a purple banana linked to the border by using a coloured flax and flowers of ribouching.

beads, pebbles or shell or draw attention to the area with a massing of striking groundcover.

Whatever idea you use it should stand out but also tie in with your overall theme and not look entirely like something that has crash-landed in your garden. For example, where surrounding planting is restful and subtle you might want to stay with the colour theme and instead alter the mood by creating a zesty wake-up call with bolder textures and shapes.

Look at the rest of the border and try to identify a texture or shape that is undeveloped — you can use this for your theatrical peaks. For a tropical garden you might arrange three feature nikaus placed close together and set them in pale lime chip or a pool of creamy caladiums. For a more Mediterranean feel it could be an oil jar nestled in a carpet of gold marjoram and surrounded by lemon trees.

Extreme simplicity is most dramatic when in the context of exuberant planting. In a textural succulent garden crowded with foliage and rocks the level of drama is already high so as a break you might create a minimalist interlude as a refreshing lull in proceedings — perhaps just a stunningly simple lawn of blue helictotrichon grasses or a clipped bank of green.

Not only was the movie *Titanic* visually stunning but it had a good story too on a human level and the added spice that it actually happened. We may not want our gardens to be quite so 'Hollywood' but we certainly need to create a sense of drama. Often our problem is more that of being too conservative rather than too over the top, so don't be afraid to launch out — hopefully your journey into drama won't go the same way as the ship.

Though the planting style and rocks relate to the rest of this border, this corner with its three palms encircled with *Agave attenuata* has the feel of a distinct 'set piece'. A bold, simple sweep of *Echeveria* 'Chocolate' helps to draw the eye in.

## FOOD FOR THOUGHT

☆ In any part of your border what would you call your stand-out stars and which are the supporting cast?

☆ Do you have a shortage of one group or the other?

☆ Do a check up round the garden to see which of the 'Drama Boosters' you are employing?

Chapter 7

# Breathing Space

*less is more ... but more is nice too*

Above

Like the 'rondel', this circle of green in a forest of magnificent *Echium pininana* at Winterhome near Kaikoura provides the perfect restful pit stop for our eyes amid all the drama.

Below

The 'rondel' at Sissinghurst: calm in a circus of flowers.

'WHAT THEY NEED in here is a fountain in the middle to finish it off.' The American tourist whom I overheard was right in a way — the 'Rondel', a plain circle of lawn wrapped up in yew hedging, is a bit of an anticlimax in such a prestigious garden as Sissinghurst. But in a way the nothingness is perfect in its setting. Just greenness and sky amid the buzz of a busy flower garden is just what you need to gather your thoughts before moving on.

Even when you go to real theatre you have an interval where you can catch your breath and grab a drink, and a garden needs breaks too. At Sissinghurst the Rondel (whether it was designed for such a purpose or not) is the 'half-time interval' — a stylishly hedged 'rest room' where we can unwind and take a sensory breather from the colour overload all around.

For me, my time of sensory rest comes at the end of a hard day when I love to soak in a hot bath with the lights off. It's a time to reflect and in the best gardens too there should be hot-bath experiences, or at least their horticultural equivalents. They can be places where colours are muted or removed all together — where we are enveloped in green, in simple shapes and easy lines.

It might be a woodland glade, a wide lawn or a dark tunnel of evergreens. On a much smaller scale it might be something as simple as a quiet stretch of greenery amid the flowers. Whatever device you choose, these still pools of nothingness are an antidote to the excitement and stimulation of busier areas.

## Less is more ... but more is nice too

Simplicity needs to be balanced with our temperament. The world is split into those who are tidy and orderly and those who want to be tidy and orderly but never quite make it. If you happen to have untidy drawers, chaotic children and socks on the bedroom floor the chances are your garden is not going to be a Zen Buddhist enclave of rigid minimalism and calm. To some extent we need to fight our natural tendencies to achieve a balance in the garden. If you are a bit of a hoarder your planting will benefit from a good clean out. On the other hand, if you hate fuss you might look at how you can introduce variety and looseness into the garden without causing chaos.

Both busyness and simplicity are best enjoyed in the company of each other. Neither is wrong or right. There's a balance to be struck between the intricately planned areas and the simple parts. The drama often comes at the point where they meet and the contrast is sharpest.

Minimalist gardens, after all, can seem a little dull after the first hour (rather like my hot bath) and landscapers are especially guilty of using the old adage 'less is more' to justify what boils down to unimaginative planting. To those who claim that less is more I would say that, yes, less *is* more ... but more is nice too.

Ironically, gardens packed with detail and interest can also fail to satisfy because in their confusion and restlessness they leave us wanting to make some order from all the chaos. You go home after visiting a busy garden with a dissatisfied feel — it's the feeling one gets on climbing into an unmade bed.

The answer is to incorporate both busyness and simplicity at different points in a garden.

Experiencing the planting round your garden should feel akin to riding a rollercoaster. The experience is textured with moments of high drama and then great lulls of calm. The order in which plants flower has a part to play in how this mood flows — as certain areas of the

---

For the colour addict the journey towards restful simplicity can be a tortuous one. At least the lawn provides some sort of interlude in this wild party.

garden burst forth and others wait their turn and hold back until later in the year. But we can also create a more permanent series of ebbs and flows in our planting by creating areas of intricacy alongside much simpler groupings of repeated plants.

## Some ways to avoid busyness

It is easier to enrich a minimalist planting but often harder to simplify a busy planting — to cure a plant collector of the hoarding instinct. As a hopeless plantaholic myself, I know that a love of plants can often be more of a hindrance than a help in the search for satisfying design. Here are some practical steps to help us overcome our busyness addiction.

### 1 Don't be afraid of gaps

Some people can't stand to see a length of bare fence or bare soil in a border — they nervously rush off to the garden centre for a pot to plug the gap. But in the border, stretches of bare earth or pebble mulch can provide an effective and neutral setting for specimen plants and can create a satisfying feeling of uncluttered space. If we make our backdrops attractive then we shouldn't feel the need to fill up everything in front. On a practical level, space helps us get in to work in a garden bed — to deadhead or just to sniff the flowers without being poked and prodded. A clean mulch of bark, pea straw or pebble will keep any gaps manageable and attractive.

Gaps and spaces are what help to give a border its dramatic topography, especially in the low light of morning and sunset when shadows set everything into sharp relief. So use gaps as positive elements in the design and don't think of them as places where the ideas ran out.

### 2 Hire a skip

An obvious but difficult way to simplify your planting is to rip out the non-essential ingredients. It's difficult because most of us hate the idea of throwing plants away but once you begin — it's like eating olives — the habit becomes an addiction and you'll be constantly surprised, after removing a bit of this and that, how much better the border looks. It's one of the great paradoxes of gardening that one of the most creative things you can do to your planting is to remove much of it. By sorting the wheat from the chaff your planting design will become crisper and firmer.

Hire a skip and do the job on a 'bad hair day' when everything's gone wrong and you need some way to vent the anger. That way you will be far more

*Any mass planting, especially if it is green and subtle, can enhance a design. Here an island of mondo grass nicely offsets the busyness of patio furniture and pots.*

ruthless. Here are some common plants that might be on your hit list.

### The time wasters
These plants eat up hours in maintenance and are a constant thorn in the side. That pittosporum that went bare at the base years ago and is constantly being chopped back to stop it turning into a tree needs to come out and what about the lonicera hedge that you are out cutting religiously every week? Show no mercy.

### Over the hill
A lavender bush as it falls apart can, in the right light, be an object of great beauty when you don't need a smart look, but more often than not lavenders die badly. Put them out of their misery along with anything else that is obviously over the hill and constantly on the brink of demise.

### Hypochondriacs
These plants are never quite at death's door but they are always at the doctor's — you are forever dosing them with concoctions of trace elements, seaweed and bananas steeped in old tea water. It might be the pieris which always gets thrip, those daffodils that always fall over just as they flower or the expensive cycad that has never liked you. Don't keep blaming your soil. If it isn't exactly sick but has never grown either — give it the boot.

Japanese acers are on my current hit list. Maples are grown primarily for their foliage but where I have mine sited in full sun and too much wind, they get scorched leaf edges every year and it is only laziness that has stopped me moving them to a better position to make room for something more suitable.

### Careless colour
If you are a colour addict, the search for simplicity in your planting will be a tortuous journey and many a beloved bloom may have to be laid to rest along the path to perfection. A simple or even monochrome colour scheme is a good start, but somewhere in the garden it is nice to have a complete break from flowers and enjoy instead the cooling and soothing effect of unadulterated green. In mild Auckland (my neck of the woods), busy lizzies have a lot to answer for,

---

A gap is not always a failure or an anticlimax. Spaces are powerful allies in the garden. At Ayrlies Garden bare ground under swamp cypress trees (*Taxodium distichum*) shows off their unusual knobbly aerating 'knees' and a duvet of autumn leaves.

Large, simple plantings are particularly appropriate beside large trees. After these magnificent clivias have flowered they'll form a soothing green walk under the native trees.

sprinkling distracting shocking pinks and oranges like floral graffiti. Out they go. Without the distraction of colour, the pleasing shapes of leaves, shrub outlines, even shadows, become more defined and a more soothing and harmonious garden emerges.

## Deathly dull

Some plants lurk quietly in the shadows hoping we won't notice them. They have neither good leaves nor especially pretty flowers — they are just there like those tins of old paint you keep under the house. Rip them out and make space for something that will light your fire.

## Attention seekers

You wouldn't want a town crier in a library and neither do we always want plants which leap about as if crying, 'Look at me!' Variegated plants and anything dressed in brightly coloured leaves in silver, cream or gold are the worst attention seekers. Herd them into busier parts of your scheme where they can shout until they go hoarse, and keep some parts of the garden with a restrained feel.

As mentioned earlier some types of foliage are more restless than others. Small, fine foliage and rounded plant forms are ultimately the most restful but that doesn't mean you have to exclude spiky foliage or architectural plants — these can still be used simply in bold groups and drifts to give a more lively feel but with a pared down and restrained flavour.

## ACHIEVING SIMPLICITY

Here are more ways to add to that all-important sense of simplicity:

○ Drastically reduce your planting palette.

○ Use plants with small, fine leaves, which give a smooth look from a distance.

○ Go for rounded plant shapes rather than lots of spiky and architectural plants.

○ Make sure that adjoining areas such as decks and lawns are kept free of clutter.

○ When using flowers choose those that are quiet and simple — the nodding tear of a snowdrop or the newer dahlias bred with single flowers in preference to the overblown hybrids that look like ballroom dancers on Ecstasy.

○ Green is the most calming colour — use it generously.

○ Concrete the garden over (only joking).

After all this initial cleansing you will be feeling refreshed in the mind and exhausted in the body. It's a good idea to live with the results for a good while. It takes time to notice the strengths and weaknesses of the bones that remain. Ask yourself which plant shapes are working and whether there are any major shapes missing that you want to include. Remember that two or three contrasting shapes are often enough. For a really radical sweep of simplicity consider going with just a single plant form. In a cleared border, ask yourself whether the foliage is restful enough and whether the colours are working together better now with fewer ingredients. Enjoy also the new gaps created that may reveal a new side to plants previously swamped in the confusion or may give useful glimpses to other parts of the garden that you will want to keep.

### 3 Replant cautiously and boldly

With an existing border thinned out, it is time to embellish the plants that remain. Don't be in a hurry to fill all the holes; you might want to keep some permanently to give a more dramatic topography to the border. The primary process of creating simplicity is to group your plants together. Any scattered shrubs or perennials can either be moved together into comfortable groups or added to with new plants of the same type to simplify the fragmented look. Be wary of adding any new plant species to the existing mix for fear of heading back to that busy look, but if there is very little interest remaining you will however need an injection of life. Again plant any new arrivals in groups or drifts for these simpler parts of the border.

### 4 Include anchor planting

Even in busy borders try to introduce at least one large slab of simple foliage as an anchor to the busyness all around. It's surprising how something as simple as a hummock of choisya or drift of acanthus can calm and enhance a part of the garden where there is lots going on.

### 5 Create a curiosity corner

Often it's hard to throw away plants and clutter. If you have the room, create a corner in which to throw your odds and ends – those plants that maybe have sentimental value or were presents or remind you of a holiday in Timaru.

Sometimes the violent clashes which ensue as you herd your rejects together will encourage you to give them the final heave ho or, conversely, there may be happy accidents that will fire you up with new ideas for combinations in the main garden. I find it healthy to have at least one part of the garden where I can garden unselfconsciously and throw plants together. When I stop thinking and let nature and the laws of chance get to work it always makes for some exciting revelations.

*If your tastes are eclectic there's nothing like throwing in a hilly oasis of green (clipped* Coprosma *x* kirkii *here) to settle things down and provide an interval in all the action.*

---

### FOOD FOR THOUGHT

☆ Take a super-critical look at those plants in the garden that often get forgotten about or taken for granted. Do they really pull their weight for the space they take up?

☆ Get an honest friend to come and cast their critical eye over the garden to give you a fresh perspective on which plants are not contributing to the all-round look.

☆ Do you veer towards extreme chaos or acute simplicity? Does the garden reflect this?

☆ Where in the garden have you used simple blocks of bold planting? Do such groups satisfy all year?

Chapter 8

# More of the Same

## reassuring rhythm and repetition

IT'S NOT SO bad that builders whistle. At least they can usually hold a tune but it is the timing that is usually a bit dodgy. What builders need is something like my grandmother's clock to keep pace. It always kept me awake with its deep boom when we went to stay. We've lost all that now we've gone digital — OK, it was annoying but it was strangely reassuring at the same time too.

## A comforting order and predictability

Whether it's the reassuring tick-tock of an old clock, waves piggybacking one after the other onto the beach, or the arcing of the sun and moon, the world pulses within a framework of rhythms. It's the comforting predictability of repetition we like — order and security in the face of life's uncertainties. In gardening, repetition creates the reassuring sense of cohesion that draws together the natural spontaneity of plants. Indeed, the sense that nature has been tamed or at least tickled by human hands is the very thing that distinguishes a garden from a wilderness.

The basic design of hard elements, such as paths, lawn and walls, imposes the most obvious order in the garden, but it is in the planting that rhythm and repetition continue to form a structured framework in which the more chaotic plants can play and seed. How you use these concepts depends on how formal or informal you want to be.

Look down your planting and see which plants are repeated (if any) and how they are repeated. Self-seeders like annuals and biennials will often crop up through an entire border. Like gravy they weave around larger plants, making everything feel comfortable but unless they are in full flower, they only provide a tenuous linking element, without strong form or impact. How about the perennials and shrubs? Are you the sort of gardener

More in time than a builder whistling a tune: these nikau palms (*Rhopalostylis sapida*) create a sense of rhythm in a wonderfully relaxed and curvaceous design by Xanthe White. By repeating the planting small spaces like this look elegant and uncluttered.

who has one of everything? Many of us are; we buy a single plant at the garden centre meaning to bulk it up and propagate at a later date and then we forget about it and buy something else a month later and before we know it we run out of space.

One of the most important tricks you can learn in taking a dull border and making it stylish is to pick out a key plant and to repeat it through the border. If you visit large gardens you'll see this done again and again and it works just as well in small gardens too. You will notice how gardeners choose linking plants often in eye-catching but neutral colours that will look good with a broad spectrum of other plants. Lime green and greys will fit into most colour schemes so gardeners take plants like grey lamb's ears (*Stachys lanata*) and lime *Alchemilla mollis* and repeat them in patches down a border. Our eyes seem to be drawn to these repeated elements especially; we notice the nearest first then our eyes bounce on to the next and to the next. It's almost as if the lamb's ears and alchemilla are beckoning our eyes, leading us down the border or round a bend. Designers often talk about plants 'leading the eye' and this is what they mean — repeated, high-impact plants that draw our attention and carry us along. Of course there's little point leading the eye if there is nowhere to lead it to, so try and create a focal point: a seat, the front door of a house or just a specimen tree to wrap things up.

Imagine a border full of a wonderful mixture of plants as if it were a loose collection of jewels. By taking one particular plant and repeating it between all the others it acts like a piece of thread stitched through the jumble and the result is that what began as a random assortment of jewels becomes a necklace.

It becomes something with a sense of purpose and of greater beauty than the sum of its individual elements. If you thread plants with regular precision it has a strong rhythm, but if you string them together randomly you still enjoy the linking effects of repeated plants but the effect is more natural.

## Repetition:
### simplicity and boldness

Boldness always adds drama to a garden and even if you like your planting busy, if you can repeat at least one plant element through your other planting it will add both simplicity and boldness to your border. For bitty gardeners, learning the beauty of repeated planting is a key step towards more satisfying results. Any plant that is repeated has more impact and ties the other planting together. It creates a firm matrix and a feeling of unity, which will hold together more erratic planting should you want to include that also.

You can arrange your planting in a formal or informal style but whichever way you choose there are five main ways of arranging repeated plants.

### 1 Diffuse

Recently there has been a huge move towards planting in a way that more closely resembles natural plant communities, especially those found in open grasslands and prairie. These communities typically lack strong, architectural elements like shrubs and bold foliage plants and instead rely on tough bulbs, annuals and perennials that form shimmering sheets of colour. In reflecting nature, each species is not planted in large groups for mass effect, nor is each plant dotted about half-

---

A diffused sort of repetition looks light and charming seen here in a wildflower meadow rich with orchids and hawkweed. In conventional borders it best suits fine annuals and bulbs sprinkled around or through larger groups of plants.

heartedly; instead, species are repeated again and again, scattered and interwoven with all the others to give a diffused effect — rather like an intricate tapestry.

The mix has to be carefully thought out so that one plant species doesn't overrun the others. The beauty of meadow-style planting is that the plant mix works as a team for its effect; as one plant type is going over, another is coming into flower to take its place. Furthermore, plants dying down get to hide their fading foliage in the crowd, whereas if mass planted such a plant, once over, would stand out and spoil the look.

Another feature of this diffuse approach is that, with the right plant choice, plants grow in close proximity to one another and there is little room for weeds to get a foothold. With plants intermingled in a random mass rather like leaves tossed in a mesculun salad, you'd think the effect would be ultra bitty. However, because most of the plants have soft and indistinct forms and are not grouped but multiplied throughout, the massed effect can be surprisingly soothing and harmonious viewed from a distance, while close up there is still plenty of variety and interest.

The weakness of meadow planting is that it works best only in wide open spaces where individual pinpricks of scattered plants like cosmos or purple *Knautia* give the effect of dreamy sheets of colour. In a narrow garden bed with a wall or fence behind, you don't get quite the same 'wow' factor. Diffused, meadow-style gardening is also only useful where you want flat sheets of planting. When you need height and screening you will still need trees, shrubs and the gymnastics provided by bolder plants.

---

### DIFFUSE PLANTING

Advantages:
- Soothing and harmonious to view.
- Provides variety and interest.
- Dying plants are hidden.
- Weeds are kept out.
- A light and uncontrived simplicity.

Disadvantages:
- Needs careful plant selection.
- Works best in open spaces; not suitable for narrow borders.
- Creates only flat sheets so will not hide fences.
- Lacks structure to anchor it down.

---

*Simple blocky planting is perfect where you don't want to distract from a view of the wider landscape. It relies on using reliable year-round plants like these lavender at Ohinetahi in Governors Bay.*

### 2 Blocky

Big chunks of planting herded into one mass gives an air of simplicity and confidence to a border. Plants that spread, such as asters or monardas, tend to grow naturally into ever-swelling colonies anyway. Large groups of one species add weight and solidity to a border, and bright colours if massed together can be dynamite.

But blocky planting if overdone can look clumsy and formulaic and it relies on plant material that will perform well all year. If the plant chosen for block planting dies down or looks shabby at any time the ugliness is magnified, faults will look obvious and it will let down the whole border.

Blocky planting works well with structural shrubs that, if grouped, add a sense of solidity and weight to any subsidiary planting. Groundcovers like ajuga and dianthus also tend to be effective and grow naturally into large duvets of leaf. I find the front edges of a border can get especially busy and restless. If this is the case throw in a good block of a single plant like lavender or *Salvia nemorosa* and see how the bold grouping helps to anchor down the busy planting all around.

## *3 Drifts*

If a plant is repeated in snaking drifts or ribbons woven through the border rather than massed in a big block you can layer planting, one band behind the other, so that as one plant fades or takes a rest another plant swells up and takes its place. Gertrude Jekyll was a great proponent of planting perennials in naturalistic drifts for a richly layered effect rather like a large cake. In a formal scheme drifts can become straight lines or concentric circles of planting. Plants in flowing drifts winding through more static planting create a sense of movement and flow in the garden as our eye follows along. The beauty of plants that weave and trickle between more substantial players is that they act like gravy poured onto a meal — knitting together all the other ingredients and making everything taste that much better.

## *4 Scattered*

Feature plants can be threaded through other planting so that each plant or group of plants links visually to the next but there are gaps and breaks in the chain. Strong architectural plants like cabbage trees or aloes, for example, look exciting if arranged in family groups of differing sizes. There are gaps between the groups but they are small enough so that even from a distance each group relates obviously to each other. Designing this sort of effect can be tricky. Think of your plants as a group of friends gathered informally chatting in a room — there will be different huddles of people but all are in earshot of one another. Often in an informal planting there may be a 'parent' clump, which is the biggest cluster, and away from this several satellite groups of varying smaller sizes. Some designers insist you use odd numbers; seven, five, three is a good recommendation but I find that any numbers work so long as there is variety between each group.

---

Like gravy poured on a meal, drifts of plants can help knit together your other ingredients. Planted across the contours, these santolinas are forming an effective bridge between upper and lower levels.

A mixture of planting styles often works best. While the main star plants like aloes are here planted in scattered clusters, icy *Echeveria elegans* is dribbled between to knit the scene together.

## 5 Rhythmic

Like punctuation marks that split up groups of words into digestible packages certain key repeated plants can give a border a sense of rhythm and order. This repetition can be very exact and orderly or it can be more casual; it can run down a border or it can zigzag from one border to another across a narrow lawn or path. Because the space between one plant and the next is often quite big, to create a recognisable sense of rhythm you need to use plants that grab the attention so the eye is drawn and bounces from one plant (or group of plants) to the next.

Repeated down a border a good rhythm plant will lead the eye along and create a good sense of movement and perspective while at the same time dividing the other planting into digestible chunks. Because repeated plants are like magnets to us, we can use them to take us in any direction and not just along a long border. Often, in that cramped wedge of land down the side of a house, we want to get away from the long thin look and not accentuate it. If there are two narrow borders either side of a central path try repeating a key plant, not long ways, but diagonally across the path so your linking plant zigzags down the space. In this way our eyes bounce from side to side and the space can actually feel wider and larger. In large gardens where there are adjacent beds either side of a lawn or path you will often see key plants repeated randomly from one side to the other. Again like the thread of a necklace the repetition seems to be knitting all the visual elements of the scene together and creating a sense of unity.

The gaps between each repeated planting can vary and the size of each separate planting can vary if you only want a relaxed and subtle sense of rhythm but for the formal look more care is needed.

The five main ways of arranging plants in a garden bed. Often a combination of these styles works best.

| Blocky | Drifts | Scattered | Diffuse | Rhythmic |
|---|---|---|---|---|
| Good for structural shrubs. | Good for perennials. | Good for architectural plants. | Good for annuals and bulbs. | Good for shrubs and topiary. |

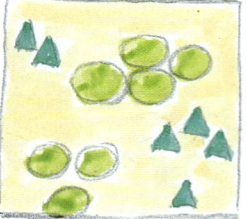

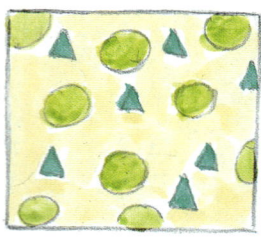

Each of the five ways to deal with repetition above are valuable, and it is nearly always best to take a number of different approaches to planting within the same border to avoid a formulaic look. Often there isn't space to repeat a tree (there may be no space for a tree at all) but you might plant a large block of structural shrubs to give weight to the border first. Around these you might add a scattering of architectural elements in family groups and beneath these there can be drifts of softer perennials. Popping up throughout there may be a random sprinkle of spring bulbs and annuals.

In all these cases there is a sense of repetition that will knit the border together as a whole and give it a sense of unity, rather than it looking like a botanical broom cupboard stuffed with all manner of curiosities.

## Formal rhythm

Especially near the house, in tight spaces and anywhere we want a clean and ordered feel, a formal approach works well. Here regular repetition of certain key plants is a great tool but it can easily be overdone. We tend to either shun formality altogether or we embrace it so wholeheartedly that we overplay it.

Gardens can get predictable and boring if we go overboard with repetition. We start with good intentions, with a low hedge down the drive perhaps, even a row of well-spaced standard roses to give a nice sense of rhythm; and then we spoil it all. Between the roses we add alternating weeping silver pears. Between these we line out regimented rows of lupins with sedum in front and, finally, to drive the point home that we are in control, we top it all off with alternating blue lobelia and white alyssum along the front, changing colour with traffic light precision.

Formal repetition is effective and easy to achieve but it needs to be used with discretion, whether it's marching avenues of trees or pots placed symmetrically round a pool. Along narrow beds and borders, which are such a challenge in today's small gardens, this approach is the obvious way to break up a long length of wall or fence into manageable chunks and also to create an instant sense of style. But resist giving everything in the garden the formal treatment, otherwise the sense of reassuring order we were aiming at becomes as jittery as the dots and dashes in a Morse code message.

### Avoiding too much repetition

One way to avoid fiddly repetition is to enlarge dots of planting into longer, more restful groups, which reduces the number of repetitions in any given space and settles things down nicely. Don't think that a small border needs small, numerous repetitions to be in scale; often the opposite is true and large groups of repeated plants actually create an illusion of space, giving a more confident and bold look to your planting. If you look along any metre strip of your border, whatever its size, and are repeating any plant within that space, then chances are your planting is starting to get way too fussy.

Another way to avoid over-repetition is to cut down the number of different plants that recur. One repeated element, perhaps a row of trees at the back of a border, is effective. Add a formal hedge at the front or a repeating shrub and you have two repeated elements. This is OK, but once you introduce a third repeated planting you might start to overplay the

---

#### Opposite
One simple element repeated formally is all that's needed to produce a pleasing hint of order and formality in this well-balanced subtropical entrance. It features grassy liriope, tall *Yucca elephantipes* and a large-leafed bocconia.

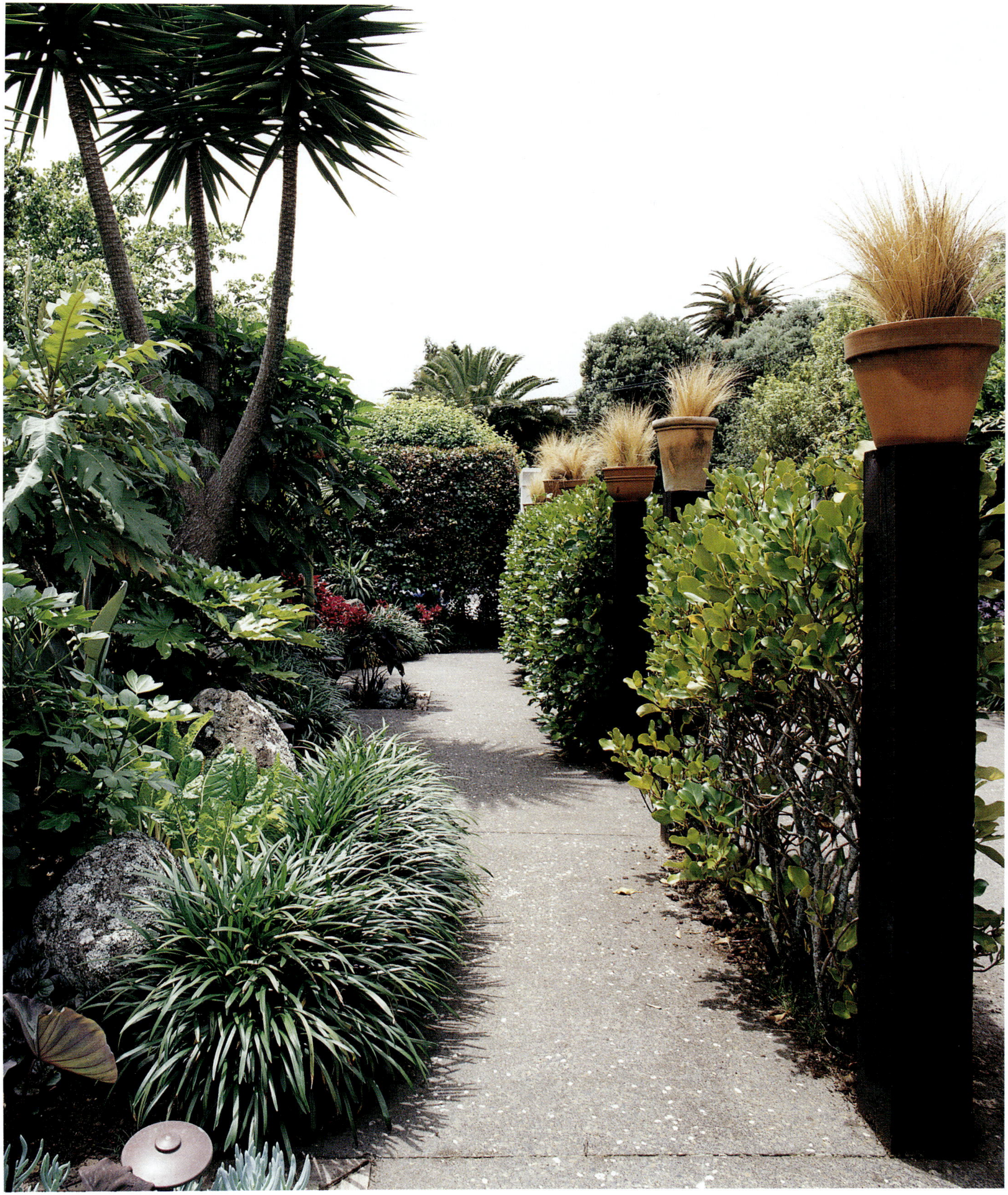

Four different ways to repeat the same plants down a narrow border. By planting in multiples of the same species a calmer type of rhythm is created.

whole rhythm idea. If we over-emphasise rhythm or formality with too many different elements we kill the power of those initial repeated elements and make our design muddled and not crisp.

Repetition may not come from plants at all. You may use wooden or steel poles as pieces of architecture through your planting or neatly spaced urns in formal features. Often the repeated sections of a fence or wall at the back of a border impose an immediate sense of formality and rhythm. In this case you can either go with the rhythm and accentuate it for a formal scheme or screen the backdrop out for a looser look.

### Mixing formality with chaos

In looking at the formal effects of rhythm and the looseness of informal repetition it's important to realise that we can use both effects together for the two-fold virtues of exuberance and order. Together they make a potent mix.

---

Repeating plants diagonally across a path leads the eye along and effectively unites the garden on either side. Blue *Senecio serpens* and silvery gazanias are used here in a clean, blocky planting style.

For example, a border may have an overall formal feel with a box hedge at the edge and, say, a line of pencil cypresses marching regularly through the centre, but planting in between can be free and easy. Whether it's a thread of hot paeonies or euphorbias and then in late summer drifts of Japanese anemones, these exuberant plantings will look fantastic held within the ordered framework.

It's an age-old trick, but if you combine your stronger formal elements with looser style planting between, the sense of formality is accentuated because of the associated contrast.

Remember that formality is not limited to straight-line layouts. Gardens with sweeping curves and bends can be given the smart treatment with a plant (or architectural features such as pots or tripods) repeated at regular intervals or a low hedge run along the front. It is really the spacing of the plants that implies the formality and not whether they are placed straight or curved. On a large scale you can bend the rules a little if you are trying to achieve a very formal look. Our eyes are bad judges of distance so, in laying out a tree avenue, for example, if your trees aren't exactly the same distance apart it is not a problem. Unless you are viewing them from side on, you can get away with a slightly fluid approach to the spacing if you need to fit a set number of trees into an awkward space. A bit of crookedness and wobble in even the most uptight garden gives it that slightly human touch anyway and adds to the charm. Control freaks will just think this is crazy talk!

### *Bigger plants create more rhythm*

Rhythm has a definite pecking order. The biggest plants have the most potential for creating rhythm — large shrubs and trees. Edging plants have the least clout in the game. If you try to suggest formality and order with your smaller edging plants but your shrubs and trees are dancing to a different beat — planted haphazardly behind — then your planting gives off confusing visual signals because the heavyweight elements are not playing the formal game. Down the side of a house in a tight space smaller plants can step out a beat effectively but in wider places you should create a rhythm with your larger planted elements first.

---

A play on repetition and rhythm: colours and shapes echo one another as elegant Irish yews ballet dance along a hedge and their counterparts (silvery verbascums) make similar moves in the room beyond.

## Plants to use to create rhythm

Plants that create a sense of rhythm need to be easily identifiable but sympathetic with the border as a whole. Colour always grabs our attention but it is easy to overdo strong colours as punctuation marks. Remember that gardening is about teasing and tickling the senses and not hijacking them. In a written sentence you need to take note of the punctuation marks but they are only there to make sense of the words between. Some people get so carried away with their commas and full stops that they neglect the planting in between. A bright gold *Cupressus sempervirens* 'Swayne's Golden' poking its finger at the sky is one exclamation mark with an ego problem!

### *Use dramatic forms and strong foliage*

Instead of strong colour use dramatic forms or strong foliage shapes to add rhythm. Plants with a strong form and outline always stand out. Topiary is the obvious example giving the classic, hard-hitting outline that is a powerful type of punctuation. After that large leaves and architectural plants with spiky or dinner plate leaves can work. Gertrude Jekyll, the icon of good planting in Edwardian times, always loved to use bold plants like bergenias and yuccas in great wedges like full stops at the ends of her borders. They nicely hemmed in her looser planting like bookends propping up a row of novels.

Using bold foliage plants for your punctuation creates a gentler effect that can be useful in more low-key places where topiary would look too contrived. Subtlety is a great ally in the garden and often formality is best when hinted at rather than rammed down the throat. The more architectural the plant, or the more brightly coloured, the more severe will be the sense of formality you impose. While a line of marching pencil junipers will stamp an ordered impression, billowing euphorbias will give a looser effect — even if they are repeated with the same regularity. Though subtle, euphorbias will still provide a distinct sense of order and, what's more, their effect varies with the seasons, adding another dimension to the picture you are painting. When flowering in spring the lime bracts will really punch out the rhythm but in other seasons the effect will be more subdued.

The best way to choose plants for

Often we associate repetition with classical formality and symmetry but this arresting combination involves both neatly staggered chamaecyparis conifers and a more relaxed matrix of helictotrichon grasses in front.

## FOOD FOR THOUGHT

☆ What plants do I repeat round my garden at present, if any?

☆ What existing plants do I enjoy that could be repeated round the garden?

☆ What is my natural way to group plants: are they in blocks, drifts, scattered or totally random?

☆ Are there places I can zigzag the same plant across a lawn or path to tie the two sides together?

☆ In my formal areas have I gone over the top in repeating plants to suggest too much rhythm and create a 'judder bar' effect?

## PUNCTUATION PLANTS

○ Punctuation plants stand out from a distance.

○ They are good doers that grow well.

○ They provide year-round interest.

○ Strong shapes are more effective than loud colours.

punctuation is to seek inspiration first from your own garden. You probably already have the right plants but have not yet put them to work in a meaningful way to tie together more chaotic planting. Potential punctuation plants are often evergreen so you have the effect all year. If not evergreen, then in winter they should still call the shots with a sense of style — perhaps dense twig structure in the case of shrubs or the dramatic bleached foliage of dormant perennials such as miscanthus grasses. Punctuation plants are also those plants that are going to look happy and healthy all year, so go for the plants that you know love your conditions. It's good to try new plants in the garden, but for this crucial tying together you need candidates that won't let you down.

Punctuation plants with a strong vertical aspect, from pencil junipers to clipped columns of coprosmas, are particularly arresting and need to be used carefully. They have the useful effect of 'pinning down' looser planting and that's why in soft, informal plantings, foxgloves or verbascums are so effective. Spires and spikes used formally are powerful tools too; they are indeed the exclamation marks, enlivening the garden, but if overdone, they can make a border begin to look as attractive as a hedgehog's rear end.

# Chapter 9

# Seasonal Symphony

## creating seasonal interest

SUNDAY AFTERNOONS used to be the highlight of the week. As kids we sat fidgeting while Dad watched the agonisingly long football match on the TV. We knew that after the final whistle had blown it was off to the 'Green Shop' for our weekly scoff. A week of planning and intense debate went into this fleeting trip. How would we spend our 50 cents this week? Would it be a bag of snakes and Coke bottles or pineapple chunks that cut your tongue with the sugar frosting? Would we blow the lot on a sherbet fountain or a monstrous chocolate 'wagon wheel'?

These days I shoot down to the garage or dairy whenever I want. Gone is the build up — the mounting thrill as Sunday approached, the excitement as Manchester United slipped in a last-minute goal and I knew I was only minutes away from my own winning moment: a ride in the car and the first bonbon slipping over my eager lips.

## The element of time in the garden

We live in a world where we want everything and we want it NOW. High-speed internet, instant noodles and in the garden year-round colour and foliage. But with everything to hand we miss out on the magic of waiting and anticipating. Nature, thankfully, has other ideas; she still likes to hand out her gifts at a leisurely pace and in seasonal order and if we play along we won't get fat and spoilt. In fact we might even rediscover something of the joy of delayed pleasures.

### A work in progress

A garden is as fluid as an unset jelly. With most works of art a single creator moulds and sculpts a distinct end result, but in the garden the creative process is always a collaborative effort between three very different creators, each having their say. It's also a work in progress with no completion date in sight. The gardener

The anticipation of new arrivals in spring is unbearable. Overnight, hostas explode from bare earth. While they will provide texture and colour for months, the blue *Corydalis flexuosa* that is there to greet them will fizzle out before the heat of summer to be nicely hidden by their expanding leaves.

comes along first with our clear-cut ideas — our paths and buildings and our tidy little thoughts. But as soon as plants are included nature gets involved. If you haven't noticed, nature loves to upset the apple cart. Nature won't be put in a box and, despite all our efforts to the contrary, it bursts out at inconvenient moments, seeds itself unpredictably and spreads out just when we wanted it to sit politely with its arms folded. The third member of the creative team, and the element about which this chapter is centered, is time. Plants burgeon, they break apart and collapse and often there is beauty at each stage of the process from youthful vigour to middle-age spread to the twilight years.

## Creating seasonal interest

If you watch too many garden makeover programmes on television you might have totally missed the important qualities time adds to a garden. One of the greatest qualities of plants, especially herbaceous plants, is the dynamic way that they reflect the rhythm of the seasons. To say that we don't want a garden to change is like saying we want to have a baby but we don't want it to grow up. On TV or at a flower show a garden is planted to look good at a particular moment. But in the real world each season brings its special flavour and nuances, painting a dynamic picture. As some flowers fade and others enter the stage the textures and mood of a planting shifts and flows.

Unfortunately, garden borders are often portrayed as a kind of fashion accessory. In reality plants are more than static fixtures you can bolt into a bark-chip bed. They are dynamic, living entities with changing rhythms and moods, much more akin to owning a pet or playing a piece of music.

Even when we live in a subtropical climate, and the passing of the season is less pronounced, certain flowers still mark with their arrival particular moments in the year. In so doing they connect the garden (and us) to the rhythm of the seasons — the bigger picture beyond the fence.

It's the way that gardening as an art form is sculpted by time that makes it so dynamic and satisfying. But today, the obsession with low-maintenance gardening and privacy, especially in urban gardens, has caused a shift away from seasonality. We want either colour all year or no colour at all. We seem to prefer plastic-looking plants with tidy, evergreen foliage that will neither change with the seasons nor develop and mature over time. Those new to gardening might understandably be nervous of a plant that threatens to double in size in a year and require an annual prune. However, instead of learning how to care for such plants many opt for more static alternatives that will be more predictable — a geriatric camellia or an impotent mondo grass. They miss out on plants like philadelphus with their explosion of sweet blooms in late spring in preference to the conservative predictability of an evergreen like griselinia, which will do nothing out of the ordinary and will look the same all year.

### Keeping a sense of surprise

If we fill our gardens only with the safe and predictable plants we will lose all sense of surprise. Surprise is essential. For me, one of the greatest arguments for a busy garden crammed to the gills is that at least it is easy to be constantly surprised — by old friends popping up for a visit, by flash-in-the-pan snowdrops or when you discover your runner beans are beaning and have stopped running.

Yet in today's back yards, every plant has to justify its place in the scheme and provide more than a froth of flower for two weeks of the year. So how do we create seasonal interest without creating evergreen dungeons that cut us off from the magical symphony of the seasons? Here are some ideas.

## 1 Box clever:
*enclose the garden*

Investing in quality walls and fences to enclose your garden is one way to avoid relying on evergreens to do your screening for you. This approach means you are free to choose all manner of varied plants that can ebb and flow in front of a reliable backdrop.

## 2 Build in a framework of all-round performers

Plan your garden with its clothes off. Imagine it in the depths of winter and ensure that at least half of your plant ingredients will look presentable for most of the year. These will be your foundational plants. Not all will be evergreens but many will, and in the bare months they should relate well together and should screen unsightly parts of the garden and provide much needed lushness and bulk.

As well as the obvious evergreen natives and shrubs, consider perennials like hemerocallis and dietes, which will provide structure with rather more style. Beyond year-round greenery there are other charms to be discovered. These include shrubs and trees with lively bark such as stewartias and lagerstroemias, and plants that look good even after they have died, such as grasses like miscanthus and hakonechloas, which prove that there is life after death with their seed heads and parchment-coloured winter leaves. Though a sorbus tree is deciduous you could say it has nearly year-round good looks from the spring flowers to autumn colour and berries which persist well into winter.

No plant will give you everything so, wherever possible, choose plants with several attributes that will provide maximum interest and at least one attribute that can be enjoyed over a long period, be it the plant's general shape, bark or foliage.

Don't be tempted to fill every nook and cranny with year-round interest. This is just your reliable framework of stalwart all-rounders. The space you leave will allow you to weave in your seasonal surprises.

Above
With good hedges and topiary, the planting in front can ebb and flow. This garden becomes a tall jungle of plants by summer but begins as a carpet tapestry of spring jewels — including wallflower and aquilegia.

Below
You don't need an evergreen garden but include a proportion of year-round interest. Aloes like these *Aloe ferox* and *Aloe arborescens* hybrids give permanent form and a seasonal climax.

## 3 Include luxury plants

With some space to spare you can now turn to those plants that will complement both your theme and the plants you have already included. These luxury plants may not dazzle for a whole 12 months but with a good framework in place you are no longer tied to that particular prerequisite. The luxuries will provide seasonal highlights to the mix.

Luxury plants provide the glamour element — those finishing touches and details that take a good border and make it fantastic. When James, our first child, was recently dedicated we unearthed the champagne glasses to wet the baby's head. The fact that we barely ever see or use these lovely objects makes the event more of an occasion and that's the crux of the argument for seasonal luxuries. These plants are not just added extras. At certain seasons they will become your cherished stars.

*Lilium speciosum* is a perfect example of a luxury plant; it flowers only briefly but at a time when colour is in short supply, and then it knocks you out with the scent. This lily could never be considered an all-round plant but at certain times it defines the character of the garden. Similarly giant cardoon (*Cynara cardunculus*) is a perennial grown primarily for its gargantuan silver leaves. In winter it disappears but from early spring to mid-summer it is a show-stopping fountain without a rival in the garden. (See the list of jack-in-the-box plants mentioned in Chapter 12 for some more ideas.)

## 4 Place plants so they disguise each other's flat periods

You might be forgiven for thinking a cotinus in winter is a non-event. But I make sure that mine — indeed all my deciduous trees and shrubs — have a backdrop that brings out the best in them even in winter. With the cotinus, like with many deciduous plants, a simple canvas of evergreen foliage is enough to set off the bare twigs, which have a lovely sense of octopus-like movement on a cold winter's day. In addition, underneath I plant evergreen groundcovers and spring bulbs, which become the stars in the lean months. Even the pruned old framework of knuckles, created when I pollard them back in mid-winter, are a feature I look forward to each year — sculptural shapes to enjoy and the promise of the spring explosion.

In context with a team of other plants each phase of the cotinus' yearly cycle becomes an occasion. Sometimes the enjoyment in the garden is as much about the anticipation as it is about what's in front of your eyes. Once you cast off the tired concept that year-round interest means 'evergreen' you begin to find all sorts of fantastic textures and forms. Take a clump of gunnera in winter; even in death it is a magnificent beast — leaves folded in on one another like the

Opposite

Siberian iris are luxury items only performing briefly but their moment of glory is stunning and provides the seasonal peak in this bog garden. Pickerel weed will give a blue 'encore' performance later and for the rest of the time shrubs and ferns will keep things interesting.

This page

The interest in the bog garden at Ayrlies reaches a peak in spring with the flower power of bog primulas (*Primula helodoxa*) and dwarf arums (*Zantedeschia childsiana*) which are architectural all year. By summer (below) the atmosphere becomes more subtle with fewer flowers but great textures from glossy farfugiums in the foreground and Bowles' golden sedge (*Carex elata* 'Aurea') beyond.

crumpled wreck of a rusting old aircraft, with fat buds poking their noses out waiting for warm weather.

Many trees are perfectly lovely just enjoyed against a blue sky but often it is in the company of evergreens that deciduous plants really come to life in their quiet season. The contrast of fresh foliage with bare twigs and seed heads always makes a richly satisfying partnership.

### Emphasising strengths and hiding weaknesses

In the considered border, as one player bows out the next is rising up to hide the hole left and to carry on the show. This is where teamwork between plants needs to be brought out most. Emphasise the strengths of each plant and hide its weaknesses. For example, plants like acanthus and zantedeschia are great structural plants in the border but have the unsociable habit of leaving large holes in mid-summer when they die away. By planting them behind permanent structural shrubs like artemisia or weaving in a summer bulb like tigridias near the base you can carry the interest forward.

Woodland plants like violets, woodruff (*Galium odoratum*) and ragged robin (*Lychnis flos-cuculi*) form welcome pools of colour in early spring but often little interest through summer. I let these weave around the crowns of later perennials, which emerge as the woodlanders have done their dash and add their own layer of interest later in the year. This close association of plants works well because the earlier plants appreciate the shade afforded by the late arrivals.

## 5 Vary your plant material

Plants are grouped broadly by the way that they grow. Each group brings not only its own shape and textural qualities but also very different ways of marking the seasons. By putting your eggs in many baskets you can be assured of something the whole year through.

### Trees and shrubs

The great seasonal strength of trees and shrubs comes not just in flowers and fruit but often attractive bark and the wonderful autumn effects of the deciduous types. The likes of pieris, photinia and acers even dazzle with a surprise show of brightly coloured spring foliage too. No one tree will give you everything, though some genus like lagerstroemia and sorbus do a good all-round job with a well-stocked bag of tricks. Remember that even in winter, deciduous trees provide some level of interest with that all-important sense of structure that will cast shadows on a lawn or come alive with the occasional hoarfrost or snow shower.

### Softer elements

Biennials often make attractive rosettes of leaf in the first year and often send up spectacular flower spikes by year two before setting seed and dying. Along with annuals, perennials and bulbs they form the softer plant elements in the garden. In general they don't bring tinted foliage in spring or autumn colours. Instead, their great strength lies in marking the seasons with flowers and the way their form changes and they weave between larger plants.

While bulbs spring up and dazzle in brief but dramatic bursts, annuals provide intense displays of colour, often for longer periods and are especially useful in summer. Most annuals take a little more work in sowing fresh each year but perennials come again and again, bringing a diverse mixture of form and flower throughout all the seasons — some evergreen and some dying down to take a nap.

I have a weakness for biennials. They have a particularly acute sense of the dramatic, often producing impressive mounds of leaf by late summer and exploding energetically the following

---

Because this low-maintenance border is varied and is planned for an autumn peak it will still look good in earlier months. While miscanthus grasses, purple tibouchina and sedums steal the show now, evergreens like phlomis, osteospermum and blue wattle (*Acacia baileyana purpurea*) will provide a permanent framework.

summer into architectural spires of flower but each plant group brings its own strengths and weaknesses to the seasons.

## 6 Reach for autumn

It is easy to make almost any garden look interesting in spring, with fresh leaves, and an abundance of bulbs and blossom before the bugs and dry weather kick in. Often you find gardeners cover over a multitude of sins with a blanket of aquilegia, foxglove or forget-me-not that dissolves to bare earth after Christmas. The litmus test is March when the best gardens are still going strong.

At this time there's nothing like late perennials to keep the garden fresh and exciting. The great advantage of late-summer perennials is that they still play their part in spring, with expanding leaf shapes and soothing greens among all the early season festivities. Then just as the hype is over and the garden is taking a siesta, plants like Japanese anemones, liriopes and sedums carry the torch toward autumn. Of course there are those generous souls — the salvias, hemerocallis, cannas and dahlias — which have been performing for months but the latecomers ring in high summer especially clearly.

Should you use old stalwarts like chrysanthemums and Michaelmas daisies, choose self-supporting and non-suckering types or lookalikes such as *Ajania pacifica*, which is more compact than a true chrysanthemum with wonderfully silver-edged leaves that look as though they have been cut by a pastry cutter.

## 7 Group seasonal interest

I've mentioned the danger of letting a garden become purely a spring garden. However, there is something to be said for grouping seasonal effects so that you get a symphony of colour at certain times rather than a scattering of solo performances. Allow parts of the garden to climax together for maximum impact.

Sometimes it's easy to lose all sense of drama and impact because we try too hard to have a dash of colour here and a dash of colour there every month of the year. In a smaller garden it just isn't possible to maintain constant sheets of colour all of the time and with carefully chosen foliage plants and strong forms in the border we shouldn't have to rely on colour to maintain the interest.

Pick a main season to focus on and group plants so three or four overlap in their flowering and relate together as a scene at that time. I often find inspiration for this process by taking existing favourite plants or shrubs and finding seasonal companions to make a scene. If it is a winter-flowering *Viburnum* x *bodnantense* you might choose similar winter flowerers like a mound of evergreen *Daphne odora* and a pool of

*Above*

Bedding is so often scattered about to little effect. Instead, make special pockets in prominent corners for a shot of seasonal colour that can be changed regularly.

*Below*

Short but sweet: pop-up lobelias grouped with *Rudbeckia fulgida*.

helebores with bold, hand-shaped leaves. As well as setting off the viburnum these plants will contribute year-round appeal with their attractive leaves.

After planning for a succession of seasonal symphonies in different corners of the garden, if there is room, build in a secondary season for a smaller encore performance. For example, if one corner looks its best in early spring I make a point of finding one or two plants that will shine in autumn. This way I can be sure that when the spring performance is looking its worst there will be at least something to take over.

## 8 Deadhead, water and feed

There is no substitute for regular maintenance in helping plants perform for longer periods. Good feeding and watering will always produce results, especially for annuals and perennials like dahlias, which produce a long succession of flowers and need extra sustenance. For plants like geraniums and tradescantia judicious cutting back after the first flowering will produce successive flushes that will extend the season. If you're not sure what to cut back, do a sample corner one year — after flowering is the obvious time. Sometimes a plant will not re-flower but might produce a tidy new flush of leaf to last the season.

## 9 Enjoy the quiet periods

We all want our gardens to look good for as long as possible but once we stop expecting everything to be firing on all cylinders all year we can relax, enjoy the quieter moments and look forward with anticipation to what's ahead. It is in those lulls that we notice the subtle pleasures.

The beauty of dormancy and decay are as much a part of a garden's atmosphere as the springing to life.

Many plants have an uncanny way of making an art out of falling apart at the seams. After the last shrub and tree has dropped its leaves many perennials are gently lowering their sails. Some produce attractive seed pods if we delay the cleaning up of the garden and wait to see what ferments.

In our mild climate, there isn't a clean-cut end to the growing season. Plants slip away piecemeal. It's like a pack of cheap fireworks: you get the duds and the surprises. A dahlia is a comic tragedy — frost transforming it to mangled black wreckage. In a painfully drawn-out performance, salvias fall to their knees and crawl off the stage over a period of months but a hosta goes off with a bang and a crash: fantastic butter yellow leaves for a few days before all turns to slushy custard. Many plants leave goodies behind. With astilbes, it's stiff little spears, a bit like charred kebabs stuck into the ground and sedums transform into flat-headed skeletons; they are incredibly architectural even into spring when fresh growth is bubbling up below. In winter, when colour is scarcer, these stark seed heads and dying foliage create silhouettes and outlines that are a dynamic contrast to the evergreen elements of the garden.

Gardening is all about balance. You don't want everything to collapse into a heap come winter so evergreens are an essential part of the recipe, but in the search for lushness don't forget the beauty in a drawn-out demise.

---

### FOOD FOR THOUGHT

☆ Is your succession of flowering either very boom and bust, or an ineffectual dribble of colour through most seasons?

☆ Look at any plant that is flowering on its own. What other plants could you team it with to make more of a 'scene' at this time of the year? Write their names down.

☆ When is the best season in your garden? When does it look its worst? How could you change this?

☆ Look at the garden in late summer and late winter — how is the framework of year-round interest at these times?

☆ In winter is there a satisfying mixture of deciduous and evergreen elements?

☆ Do you cut down perennials too soon in winter? Could you leave them longer and try to enjoy more year-round effects from dead leaves and seed heads?

☆ When the garden is looking its worst take a walk round the neighbourhood. Are there plants looking good that might help boost your seasonal effects?

Chapter 10

# Using Colour

WHAT IS IT about cars? Studies reveal that while the blokes look at engine size, performance and speed, one of the main determining factors for a woman in buying a car is its colour. Do women really appreciate colour more than men? Should they really care about the paintwork over the performance?

In our colour preferences there are some strange dynamics at work. While guys go for conservative greys and blacks in clothes and women take more risks, in the garden the roles are often reversed. Men set to shock with loud, clashing colours and pushy textures while the women play safe with pastels and prefer a softer look.

## Colour:
*a powerful element*

You might object to such glib generalisations but the point is we all care about colour — and more often than not we have firm ideas about what we like and what we hate. This passion is what helps us to be purposeful when we think about the colours in our garden. Some clients say to me, 'You can give me any colour but yellow.' It later emerges that as well as yellow they don't like pink much either and only orange if it's a deep, burning sort! When we talk about colour it is such an emotive issue and sometimes we don't know what we like or hate until we see it.

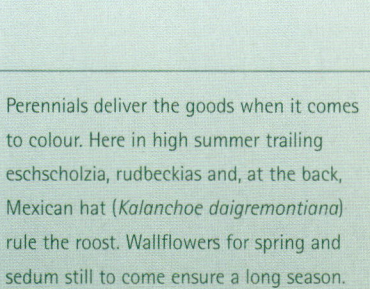

Perennials deliver the goods when it comes to colour. Here in high summer trailing eschscholzia, rudbeckias and, at the back, Mexican hat (*Kalanchoe daigremontiana*) rule the roost. Wallflowers for spring and sedum still to come ensure a long season.

Colours affect us deep down and, because of that, we should use them wisely to affect our senses in the right way — to soothe or to stimulate; to fire us up and to settle us down according to the mood we want to create in particular corners of the garden. This play on our emotions is part of the important process of adding drama to drab gardens.

Colour is one of the most powerful elements in the garden. At first glance in a shop window it is the colour rather than the shapes or forms that first attracts us, and our planting is the same. While whites and the hot colours shout, the cooler blues, purples and greens are more subtle in their charms. So use your brightest colours where you want to draw most attention. Often in front gardens, bright summer annuals are not grouped purposefully to draw a visitor to the front door but instead are poked into any available space where their impact is diffused and lost.

## Is colour king?

Though colour is the most immediate element in our garden, is it the most important? Though we tend to notice colour before textures and even plant shapes it is a mistake to put colour as the top priority when planning a border because often the effects are ephemeral as flowers ebb and flow with the seasons.

Yes, colour is sweet and intense and wonderful but it is the quieter, more enduring qualities of form and texture that undergird and hold everything together and ultimately provide the lasting pleasures.

The traditional herbaceous borders you see looking so magnificent in books were planned primarily for colour and such images don't show the full picture; for example, in winter when everything dies down to a flat, formless soup — all icing and no cake beneath.

By planning primarily a framework of pleasing forms and exciting textural contrasts we can then have fun with the colours to complete the picture.

## Marshmallows and flamingos:
### colour intensities

Each colour comes in many different intensities. The stronger a colour is the more it will stimulate, and the softer or more pastel the hue, the more relaxing it will be. Pink, for example, can be creamy and dreamy — the colour of a marshmallow — or as it becomes brighter and more intense and saturated the very same colour can turn into a shocking flamingo shade, which can be notoriously hard to place. Bright primaries are especially effective in harsh sunlight where they aren't bleached out like softer shades.

In each area of the garden it is important to decide whether you want to soothe or to enliven the space; it is hard to do both in one area. Pastel shades and crisp primary colours often look uneasy together so if you want a planting based on orange, for example, decide if it is to be the zesty impact of a mandarin or the more mellow shades of apricot.

---

*Left*

The white garden at Sissinghurst before everything explodes. When using a high proportion of colourful perennial plants, a good framework is essential so that when they retire for winter you aren't left with a formless void.

*Opposite*

Terracotta can be a tricky pastel shade to reflect in your planting but this cunning scheme uses yuccas for structure, blue echeverias for foliage and *Achillea millefolium* 'Salmon Beauty' and scented *Brugmansia* 'Noel's Blush' for flower.

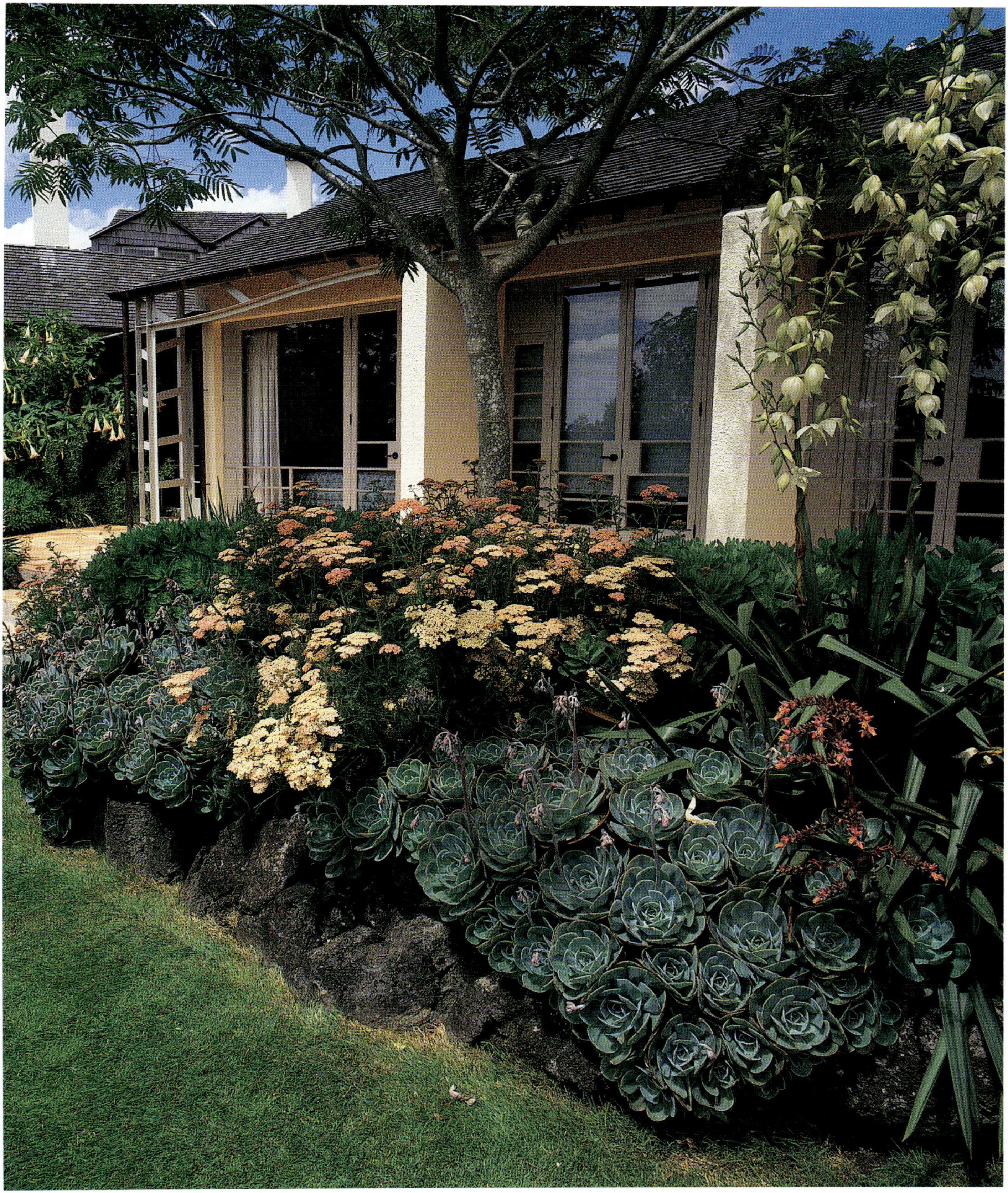

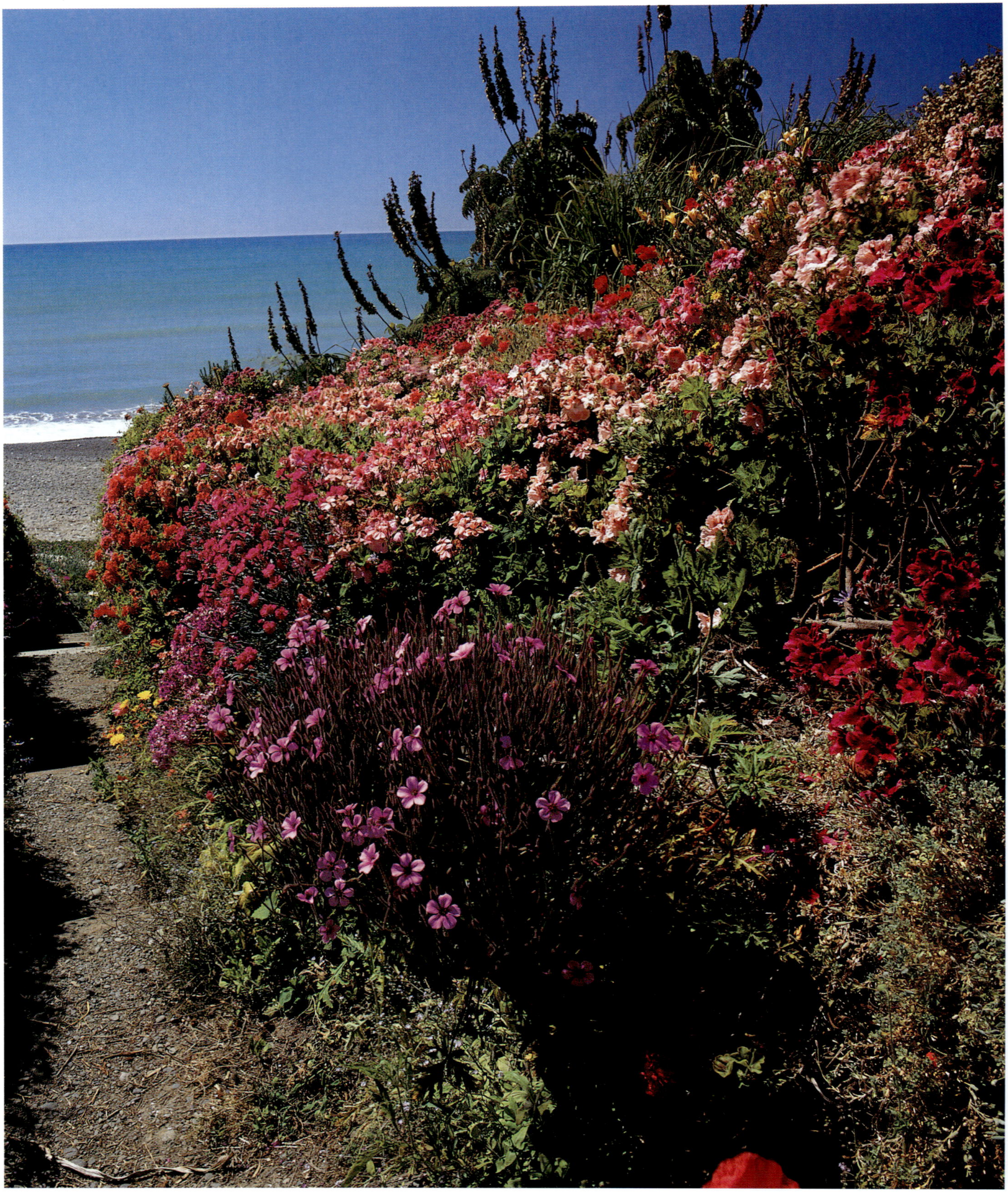

Very few flowers come in pure colours; most have traces of other hues. It is worth taking a second look when you choose and arrange plants to see if you want them to relate together and be telling the same story. That lupin you thought was whiter than white might turn out to be a dirty cream when you put it alongside the virginal dazzle of a gaura or osteospermum. Pink is often imbibed with either blue or red. As the blue element increases pinks tend towards an aggressive puce and eventually head toward purple. These tones naturally mix well with blue or purple flowers. In contrast as pinks get redder they head toward coral, which is a tricky colour to use anywhere in the garden.

That's the trouble with colours: you just can't pin them down, but it's certainly fun playing. By looking closely at flowers and seeing what other tints and tones exist within each bloom, you can get a clue as to what other flowers will make suitable companions.

## A spot of colour to cheer things up?

Gardeners either become colour junkies and forget foliage and form or go the other way and abandon the joy and drama of colour for more subtle pleasures.

In the latter case, people see colour as almost amateurish — a cheap circus trick for effect. Instead these people prefer to stick to tasteful, soothing greens and only

#### Opposite
Liquorice allsorts: with its bright light and getaway atmosphere the seaside bach is not a place to get all up-tight about clever colour combinations. Sometimes there is a place for an outrageous explosion of brilliance.

venture into inoffensive white to brighten things a little. The attraction is that this is a safe way to garden. No one hates white and you can hardly have a garden without green so who can possibly accuse you of bad taste? The trouble with this approach is that it is sensible and healthy but rather dull all the same time — like eating boiled cabbage when you could have a crunchy stir fry instead.

At the other extreme are the colour addicts who see colour's ability to lift our spirits as an inexhaustible resource; more colour equals more cheerfulness ad infinitum. Their catch phrase is 'You can never have enough colour' and they set out to cheer themselves up with all manner of garish variegated leaves and psychedelic flowers in a chaotic kaleidoscope that takes you not on a flight to cloud nine but to the sick bag instead.

### Colour to complement a border
The idea that colour is a magical panacea for all ills is incorrect. You can't just patch up the boring bits of your border with a dash of red or pink — you need to look at the border as a whole and ask whether the problem is a lack of colour or, as is more often the case, a lull in good texture and form. Colours should always be working to complement a border's structure and not to steal the show.

In any part of the border it's a good idea to ask what the main focus is. Is colour working to draw the eye to that place or is it leading our eyes on a merry dance all over the place?

## Contrast or harmony?
The world of colour use is a minefield of controversy. As well as the argument about how important colour is at all is the issue of whether to choose colours which harmonise or clash.

Colours that blend easily together are undeniably restful and easy on the eye. A flower bed devoted entirely to red shades or a blue border if done well can look incredibly effective in its striking sense of unity, but if we go overboard the effect can get predictable, staid and monotonous.

Harmony strokes our senses — it's like grooming a dog: smooth, relaxing and non-confrontational. But as much as dogs

Colour has a powerful effect. It can pull a planting together or fragment it.

Strong colours dotted along a border will give a fragmented feel.

By changing the overbearing tree and pulling the colours together so they relate to each other, the border looks more like a team effort than a series of solo perfomances.

Using Colour

like to be stroked they also relish a good scratch behind the ears. Contrasts, even clashes, provide us with the visual scratch – they wake us up and inject life and vitality into our planting. Even single colour schemes incorporate contrasts of one sort or another to provide drama – whether it's in the form of lively foliage, contrasting flower shapes, or often by the introduction of neutral colours like greys and limes as a break in the theme.

Often it's good to move beyond a conservative monochrome approach to something more dynamic. Nature, after all, rarely arranges her wares in carefully graduated schemes. Once the clash of yellow and pink was scoffed at by garden designers but in nature buttercup meadows sing with the hot pink of ragged robin (*Lychnis flos-cuculi*) and moors are awash with purple heather and chrome yellow gorse as well as a hundred other hues. Today the pendulum has swung and bold contrasts are fashionable.

### Contrast in complementary colours

While a clash can be made by throwing any two colours together for dynamic effect, in the garden a total disregard for considered colour schemes can lead to planting that looks as hectic and sickly as a bag of liquorice allsorts when it could look like a wholesome meal. Rather than random combinations it is better to go for tried and trusted contrasts of what are known as complementary colours. Orange, for example, is a colour that looks good on its own but comes alive in the presence of blues or purple. Most complementary pairings have a softer pastel counterpart. For the example above, because orange goes well with blue or purple we can be sure that apricot will look good with powder blues or lilac colours too.

In planning a planting, as well as a good foundation of essential greenery I often start by choosing a primary colour theme as a background against which any other colours can play. This provides an overriding sense of harmony, giving a relaxed and unified feel. I then might overlay a less frequent, complementing thread of colour and lastly throw in a few surprises to make you blink and to avoid an overly contrived look. The last, experimental layer is often where we get the most sparks.

### Coloured foliage

Leaves as much as flowers are important in the adventure of mixing colour. It is tempting to use lots of coloured foliage, knowing that the effects will last longer than flowers, but don't underestimate the importance of green as the great foundational colour in any planting. Add in too much coloured foliage and the background of green starts to break up and things can begin to become unhinged and restless looking. A single block of coloured foliage is good to spell out your colour theme in no uncertain terms but then just echo this with occasional coloured foliage effects in the neighbouring planting rather than overplaying the theme.

Flowers tend to carry colour in a more elegant manner and are more forgiving of mistakes. Whether it's flowers or leaves, however, colour can be studied over a lifetime and still not mastered. Here there is only room to touch the surface but what follows are some of the more important players in the colour game.

*It's become a cliché but in its harmonious approach, a single colour theme has a great sense of focus and draws our attention to the enjoyable qualities of contrasted shapes and textures.*

## Enjoy your greens

The most essential colour in the garden, green, emanates life and vitality and is the universally soothing colour. In a shower of flowers it's easy to take green for granted and forget what an important part it has to play as it weaves its magic spell through louder hues.

Green acts like an arbitration service helping other colours to live together happily. Even if we stick just to green there is opportunity to create a tapestry of different shades.

### Dark greens

The darkest shades present a beautifully sombre backdrop to any other colours and increase the sense of depth in a border. A plant dressed in deepest green is like gold dust in the border. Suitably dark plants to use include bay trees, rhododendrons, camellias, daphnes and ericas or New Zealand natives like pseudopanax and macropiper, but mix them with lighter greens or the effect can become rather funereal.

### Mid-greens and lighter greens

A large proportion of plant foliage is an inoffensive mid-green that is essential as a neutral background, diffusing harsh blocks of colour. Against this it is effective to throw lighter, fresher greens like dusky sage tones and zingy limes. Sage greens are a pastel swing on the norm and are especially prevalent in Mediterranean plants adapted to dry soils.

Lime green leaves, which suggest the zing and life of a beech forest in spring, are especially valuable. Lime, whether in a leaf or a flower, is one of the great mixer colours that enhance a wealth of brighter flowers without taking the spotlight. Whether it's a shrub like golden philadelphus, mounds of gold marjoram or the flower bracts of euphorbias, lime lights up and freshens any planting in a more subtle way than white would and brings the essential quality of freshness to sombre plantings.

---

### PLANT PICKS: TOP GREENS

**LIME GREEN**

★ **Flowers:** *Alchemilla mollis*\*, euphorbia (most), *Helleborus foetidus*\*, *Hydrangea arborescens* 'Annabelle', moluccella (bells of Ireland), *Nicotiana langsdorffii*\*, *Viburnum opulus* 'Sterile'\* (now 'Roseum'), *Zinnia elegans* 'Envy'

★ **Leaves:** *Lavandula viridis*, lettuce, *Lysimachia nummularia* 'Aurea'\*, *Malvaviscus arboreus*\*, *Origanum vulgare* 'Aureum'\*, *Paesia scaberula*\*, *Pittosporum tenuifolium* 'Gold Star', *Salvia microphylla neurepia*, *Santolina* 'Lime Fizz', *Sedum spectabile*, *Solanum quitoense*, *Stachys byzantina* 'Primrose Heron'

**DEEP GREEN**

★ **Leaves:** *Alectryon excelsus*\* (titoki), *Aucuba japonica*\*, buxus\*, camellia\*, ceanothus, clivia\*, *Daphne odora*\*, erica, garrya\*, *Ilex altraclarensis*\*, *Itea ilicifolia*\*, *Jasminum mesnyi* (primrose jasmine), *Laurus nobilis*\*, *Ligustrum japonicum* 'Rotundifolium', *Macropiper psittacorum*\*, *Michelia yunnanensis* 'Velvet and Cream', pieris\*, *Prunus lusitanica*\*, *Pseudopanax* 'Forest Gem'\*, *Raphiolepsis indica*\*, rhododendron\*, strelitzia\*

**SAGE GREEN**

★ **Leaves:** *Agave attenuata*, *Ajania pacifica*, *Ajuga reptans* 'Silver Carpet', *Aloe ferox*, *Aloe petricola*, *Carex comans* 'Frosted Curls', *Echeveria elegans*, *E. imbricata*, *Euphorbia obtusifolia regis-jubae*, iris (bearded), *Lepechinia salviae*, *Leucadendron salignum* 'Mrs Stanley', *Phlomis italica*, *Pittosporum tenuifolium* 'Little Squirt'/'Silver Sheen', *Stachys byzantina*, *Zauschneria californica*

*\* suitable for shady conditions*

---

Like oil lubricating the cogs of colour, plenty of green perfectly sets off and 'settles' awkward colours like these violent crimson roses growing wild in the Coromandel. When you get brave with colour, pour on the green.

## Bright white

Inoffensive, pure and sparkling, white is elegant and sophisticated. As cool and fresh as an iceberg, it brings a peaceful note to our planting. In shade it is essential to offer highlights in the gloom but in the sun white can give you headlight dazzle and send you rushing for the sunglasses, especially when it is planted in indigestible blocks, so go easy and diffuse the colour. Cool things down with plenty of refreshing green, which never goes amiss.

Despite its dominant nature white's saving grace is its ability (like grey) to mix with just about anything and to bring sparkle and life. So when next you get the blood lust (most gardeners do from time to time) and flood a corner in heavy maroons and gothic plum shades, let a sprinkle of white bring some light relief — as welcome as cream drizzled over a dark chocolate cake.

White gardens are a bit of a cliche but always arresting if done with panache. When white gardens fail to get the blood racing it's because they incorporate too much grey foliage and not enough dark green. White and grey gives a washed-out and tired look while rich greens soothe and punctuate the brightness. Another word of caution about white in such a purist setting is that it shows up the slightest imperfection whether it be fungal spots on a petal or golden stamens clustered in the middle of a flower. So forget any ideas of a virginal scheme — nature is corrupted through and through.

---

Whether it's foliage or flower or both as in this honesty (*Lunaria annua* 'Alba Variegata'), white lights up gloomy corners. Here the mundane underskirts of the cabbage tree are given some icing-sugar dazzle.

### PLANT PICKS: TOP WHITES

★ **Leaves:**: *Acer negundo* 'Variegatum', *Cornus alternifolia* 'Argentea', *Cornus controversa* 'Variegata', *Farfugium japonicum* 'Aureomaculatum'*, *Lamium maculatum* 'Beacon Silver'*, *Miscanthus sinensis* 'Variegatus', *Phlox paniculata* 'Norah Leigh', *Pisonia brunoniana* 'Variegata'*, *Pulmonaria* 'Majeste'*, *Salvia argentea*

★ **Flowers:** *Agapanthus* 'Snow Queen', *Allium tuberosum*, *Ammi majus*, *Anemone* x *hybrida* 'Honorine Jobert'*, arabis, argyranthemum, arthropodium*, *Clematis paniculata*, *C.* 'Huldine', etc., *Convallaria majalis*\* (lily-of-the-valley), *Convolvulus cneorum*, cornus*, eg, *C.* 'Eddies White Wonder', crambe, cydonia (quince), davidia (handkerchief tree), *Echinacea purpurea* 'White Swan', *Eryngium giganteum*, galtonia, gardenia, *Gaura* 'So White', *Hosta plantaginea*\*, *Luculia grandifolia*, *Olearia cheesmanii/phlogopappa*, *Romneya coulteri* (tree poppy), *Sedum spectabile* 'Stardust', spiraea, *Trachelospermum jasminoides*, *Viburnum*, eg, *plicatum* 'Mariesii'*, *V.* x *burkwoodii*\*, yucca

★ **Fruit and bark:** *Betula jacquemontii* (utilis), *Eucalyptus pauciflora* (snow gum), *Melaleuca linarifolia*, *Lagerstroemia subcostata*, *Onopordum nervosum* (Scotch thistle), *Rubus cockbunianus*

*\* suitable for shady conditions*

Grey power: pinks and silvers aren't just for geriatrics. In this scheme cottage meets contemporary and instead of the usual lamb's ears or artemesias the soothing grey comes from steel loungers. The purple spires belong to the annual *Lysimachia atropurpurea* and variegated sisyrinchiums (bottom) provide some foliage interest.

## Gentlemanly grey

Gone are the days that tasteful ladies swam blissfully in gardens of tissue-pink roses and swirling grey artemisias — we all seem to turn up the heat these days but grey is still an important mixer on the colour scene. As a neutral tone it creates some worthwhile breaks in foliage colour without interrupting any more dominant colour schemes. Like lime green, grey mixes and mingles like the most adept of party hosts. It goes with anything, drifting dreamily with the pinks and powder blues and equally at home soothing and cooling the more volcanic colours.

Moderation as ever is the key with this tone. If overdone grey can make a border look ghostly, pallid and tired — especially in strong sunlight. Those pale, cotton lavenders (santolina) and *Tanacetum ptarmiciflorum* can be the trickiest of grey plants to incorporate as the hue is so close to white and the foliage so dense that it can easily dominate a planting — you are left trying to diffuse the brightness by using white flowers planted around. Often it is far easier to throw out the offending shrub so you can take off the sunglasses and enjoy what else is on offer.

I particularly enjoy the subtle interplay of grey with yellows, oranges and the dark chocolate brown foliage of many New Zealand natives. Grey and blue is an all together calmer affair which works well, especially if you chip in a touch of pink or magenta to rock the boat a little.

### PLANT PICKS: TOP GREYS

★ **Small plants:** agave, aloe, artemisia, astelia*, *Cynara cardunculus*, dianthus (pink), echeveria, *Erysimum* 'Bowles Mauve', *Festuca glauca*, *Helichrysum petiolare*\*, *Hosta* 'Big Daddy'/'Halcyon'\*, etc., *Kalanchoe pumila*, lavandula, *leptocarpus similis*, macleaya, melianthus, *Plectranthus argentatus*\*, *Salvia chamaedryoides*, *Santolina* 'Bowles lemon', *Sedum* 'Vera Jamieson'

★ **Trees and large shrubs:** *Brachyglottis* 'Otari Cloud', *Cassinia leptophylla*, corokia, *Elaeagnus* 'Quick Silver', *Euryops pectinatus*, *Hippophäe rhamnoides*, *Leucadendron salignum*, *L. argenteum*, olea (olive), *Pachystegia insignis*, *Phormium tenax*, *Pyrus salicifolia* 'Pendula', *Salix alba*, *Sorbus aria*, *Teucrium fruticans*

*\* suitable for shady conditions*

## Brown

I always secretly hoped that my seventies shag-pile carpet would come back in fashion and, at last, rich chocolate and tawny shades are all the rage. Earthy, rich chocolates relate perfectly to New Zealand rustic gardens incorporating railway sleepers, rusted iron or copper and drifts of native grasses reminiscent of the highlands of South Canterbury.

Tawny foliage is easier to find than the very few true brown flowers like rich chocolate bearded iris or the foxglove *Digitalis parviflora*. New Zealand is also particularly blessed with exciting structural plants coloured a deep bronze, from strappy flaxes to grassy carex and libertias. But, as with all coloured foliage, don't overdo the theme as, in excess, brown can look very dead and lifeless.

---

This bronzy planting with native flax, carex and *Pittosporum tenuifolium* 'Tom Thumb' is saved from becoming dull by rich textures and an injection of brighter hues from the gate and a yellow choisya.

Like grey, brown is quite a neutral colour that will combine with most colours (although the jury is still out on pink). However, unlike grey, this ability to mix is largely due to the fact that brown absorbs light rather than reflecting it. Because of this receding nature, brown can easily become gloomy and lacking in impact so use it carefully. Add in plenty of rich greens and warm flower colours to bring life. Try chocolate foliage with warm apricot and peach flowers as well as brighter oranges and yellows, which provide the exuberant shot of warmth brown often needs. Enjoy also the quieter effect of tawny shades mixed with pale grey foliage and sky blue flowers like ageratums or annuals such as *Didiscus caeruleus*, the lace flower, with its flat umbels of bloom.

### PLANT PICKS: TOP BROWNS

★ **Flowers:** *Arisaema sikokianum*\*, *Arisarum proboscideum*\*, *Aristolochia elegans*\* (Dutchmans pipe), *Digitalis ferruginea/parviflora*\*, *Ferraria crispa* (Starfish lily), iris (bearded — many types), *Salvia africana lutea* 'Kirstenbosch'

★ **Leaves:** *Astelia* 'Westland', *Carex buchananii/flagellifera*\*, *Coprosma acerosa brunnea*, *C. virescens*, *Corokia x virgata* 'Frosted Chocolate', *Echeveria* 'Chocolate', *Eupartorium rugosum* 'Chocolate'\*, *Hallogurus erecta* 'Wellington Bronze'\*, *Neolitsea sericea*, *Olearia nummulariifolia*, *Phormium tenax* (purple form), *Phormium* 'Chocolate Fingers'/'Surfer', *Pseudopanax discolor* 'Rangitira'\*, *Uncinia rubra*

★ **Fruit and bark:** *Acer griseum*, *Lagerstroemia fauriei*, *Luma apiculata*, *Prunus maackii*, psidium (guava)

\* *suitable for shady conditions*

## Roaring red

As arresting as a stop sign, red is the rag that attracts the bull and likewise it pulls us towards it just as aggressively. Passion, heat and danger — you can't relax with red around. Despite the lack of subtlety, red is the loveable extrovert — confident, warm and passionate. If used in moderation it can ignite just the right amount of spark in any drab border and turn a quiet party into a fireworks display. As with all colours the size of flowers you use determines the atmosphere of the end result. Big gutsy poppies, paeonies or dahlias will be uncompromisingly in your face while dainty geums and salvias hold their heat with a little more delicacy.

Red sparks in an obvious and stimulating way with the other hot colours, especially yellow. Using it with orange is a wasted opportunity, however, because the two colours are almost too similar and don't set each other off well. Instead give red flowers a rich bed of green. Greenery acts like an ovenproof glove setting fiery flowers off perfectly. Plenty of lime thrown in will add some suitable zing to the cooler smouldering crimsons and a dash of deep purple foliage is another classic complementary shade to sound a base note.

The molten fire of red seems to leap out of the border, searing itself onto the back of the eye, so don't use it in small spaces where you want to increase a sense of depth. Here recessive blues and purples would be much more effective.

Red with blue is almost too overpowering a contrast but with white you get a refreshing energy, especially if the two colours are diffused and intertwined. Dazzling crocosmia with feathery gaura on a summer's day are as mouthwatering as a bowl of strawberries and cream.

### PLANT PICKS: TOP REDS

★ **Flowers:** *Alstroemeria* 'Red Baron', *Canna* 'America'/'Parkes', *Clianthus puniceus* (kaka beak), *Crocosmia* 'Burning Embers', *Dahlia* 'Bishop of Llandaff'/'Ayrlies', *Euphorbia pulcherrima* (pointsettia), gazania, *Grevillea* 'Gaudichaudii'/'Fanfare', *Hemerocallis* 'Kent's Favourite Two'/'Scarlet Orbit', hibiscus, leucadendron, *Lobelia tupa*, *L.* 'Fan Scharlach'/'Queen Victoria', *Metrosideros carmineus*, *Papaver commutatum*, *P. orientale* 'Goliath', pelargonium, *Rosa* 'Eyeopener'/'Flower Carpet Red'/'Phantom'/ 'Trumpeter', *R. moyesii-geranium*, *Salvia confertiflora*, *S. microphylla neurepia*, *Tropaeolum speciosum*\*, *Tulipa sprengeri*, Vireya Red Rover/Ne-Plus-Ultra\*, *Vriesea poelmanii*

★ **Leaves:** *Imperata cylindrica* 'Rubra' (blood grass), *Phormium* 'Dazzler', photinia, pieris\*, *Vitis coignetiae*

★ **Fruit and bark:** *Cornus stolonifera*\*, cotoneaster, *Crataegus* x *grignonensis*, *Gunnera prorepens*\*, *Idesia polycarpa* (wonder tree), *Ilex aquifolium* 'Golden King'\*, *Rosa rugosa*, *Viburnum opulus* 'Compactum'\*

*\* suitable for shady conditions*

The lurid border at Ayrlies: while *Alstroemeria* 'Red Baron' and *Canna* 'Parkes' provide the volcanic action, foliage plants like purple fennel and *Aeonium arboreum* 'Schwarzkopf' provide textural interest.

## Yellow

From the daffodils of spring to the flutter of buttery-leaved tulip trees in autumn, yellow seems to hem in the year first and last and imbue it with light and warmth. Good yellows are easy to find in the plant world, especially in daisy form, with heleniums, coreopsis, anthemis and the broad smile of a sunflower. Perhaps that's why some find yellow a vulgar and common colour. The name like the colour certainly sounds a bit brassy and harsh, but think of it as gold, and yellow is instantly wrapped up in regal respectability. Yellow brings the warmth and friendliness of sunshine into our gardens — something that's especially welcome in cold, shady corners and on a frosty spring day when the first primroses have poked their heads up to give us a boost.

The wealth of golden foliage plants adds to the fun to be had with this colour, but because foliage is often there all year it is easy to produce an indigestible glut of gold in a border at the expense of fresh green foliage, which is essential in cooling and calming all the brightness. You may not be able to stomach a domineering tree like a golden robinia (like a truckload of popcorn crash-landed in the back garden) but even the most snobbish of gardeners have a soft spot for a touch of soft lemon tones to add just the right note of acidity in a bed of girlie pink roses.

Put together yellow and blue and you cannot fail — it's as inevitable as sun and sky. The deeper the blue and the brighter the yellow, the more arresting the contrast. Pink with yellow used to be off limits as noted, but now everyone is getting reckless and running verbascum spires through their patches of phlox. Yellow puts a zing into cloying pinks but it also turns up the heat on volcanic reds and oranges, giving them that extra lift. But it is with rich purples that yellow forms perhaps its most dramatic partnership. When 'Black Parrot' tulips prance over duvets of yellow wallflowers or pale anthemis pile up against *Salvia nemorosa* 'East Friesland' it's a sight as heart-warming as plums and custard, and as dramatic as a storm gathering over a desert.

### PLANT PICKS: TOP YELLOWS

★ **Flowers:** *Achillea* 'Anthea'/'Cloth of Gold'/'Moonshine', *Anthemis* 'E.C. Buxton', *Arum creticum*, *Brachyglottis* 'Leith Gold'*, *Camellia nitidissima**, canna, cassia, *Centaurea glastifolia*, coreopsis, euryops*, gazania, *Genista* 'Yellow Imp', helianthus, hemerocallis (many), *Inula magnifica*, *Kniphofia* 'Little Maid'/'Sunningdale Yellow', *Lysichiton americanus*, mahonia*, narcissus*, *Pomaderis kumeraho**, primula*, *Reinwardtia indica**, *Rudbeckia fulgida* var. *sullivantii* 'Goldsturm', *Solidago* 'Cloth of Gold' (goldenrod), *Sophora* 'Dragons Gold', sternbergia, *Thalictrum flavum* 'Glaucum'

★ **Leaves:** *Berberis thunbergii* 'Aurea', *Carex elata* 'Aurea'* (Bowles golden sedge), *Choisya ternata* 'Sundance', *Ginkgo biloba* (autumn colour), *Gleditsia triacanthos*, *Helichrysum petiolare* 'Limelight'*, *Ilex crenata* 'Golden Gem', *Philadelphus coronarius* 'Aureus'*, *Pseudopanax lessonii* 'Gold Splash'*, *Robinia pseudoacacia* 'Frisia', *Sambucus racemosa* 'Plumosa Aurea'*, *Sedum mexicanum*

★ **Fruit and bark:** *Malus* 'Golden Hornet', *Cornus stolonifera* 'Flaviramea'

*\* suitable for shady conditions*

Left

Varying flower shapes as well as colours will always maximise your contrasts and add drama. Here the whorls of *Phlomis russeliana* team up with *Campanula latifolia*.

Opposite top

When we allow plants to mesh together, colours associate not in indigestible blocks but in diffused blends. Here the yellow/purple formula finds its softer equivalent in lilac phlox drizzled through lemon hemerocallis.

A sophisticated tapestry by Pauline Trengrove with a good spread of qualities: rounded *Santolina* 'Lemon Fizz' for evergreen structure, thalictrum for architectural form (right) and violas for flower power.

Hot penstemons like *P.* 'Drinkstone' or 'Garnet' love to quench their thirst in a sea of purple/blue — here provided by violas.

## Ice cool blue

Cooling and calm, blue conjures up the easy arc of a summer sky or in its deepest inky depths the mystery of the sea. Like purple, blue is a 'receding colour', which means it tends to sink into the background and create a sense of depth to the garden. This diminutive quality can be unhelpful if you hinge a planting scheme on blue as the primary colour. Seen from a distance, the blue can get lost in green foliage and lose impact. Blue schemes are also tricky to pull off because true blue flowers are not always easy to find and many shades head off in divergent directions towards purples and lilacs. But blue is a good team player and it supports and adds depth to more vibrant schemes.

You can use the cooling qualities of blue to quench the fire in hot colours like magenta, red and orange where it is as welcome as 'after-sun' cream on a sunburnt back. Or for more of a harmonious look, team clean blues with brilliant white for a refreshing scheme reminiscent of ice, water and sky. This is an especially effective pairing in the evening when pale blues are not so bleached out; rather they seem to buzz with an electric energy while whites similarly glow.

Intense, saturated blues are best paired with equally strong hues like yellows (blue water iris and kingcups, for example) while softer baby blues work well with equally gentle lemon yellows and, in the case of an orange contrast, with apricot shades. That blue/orange combination at its most faded extent still creates excitement as found when faded denim ageratums rub shoulders with buff-coloured grasses.

Blue foliage often works even better than flowers, perhaps because it contains a proportion of neutral grey. Such foliage relates well with brightly coloured swimming pools as well as with slate-coloured stonework and pebbles but, like all coloured foliage, use it sparingly.

---

### PLANT PICKS: TOP BLUES

★ **Flowers:** aconitum*, agapanthus, ajuga*, *Amsonia tabernaemontana*, anchusa, *Browallia americana*, brunnera*, *Campanula* 'Mystic Bells', *Caryopteris* x *clandonensis*, ceanothus, *Ceratostigma willmottianum*, *Cerinthe major* 'Purparescens', delphinium, *Dichroa versicolor*\*, echinops, *Eryngium alpinum*, *E. oliverianum*, *Felicia amelloides* 'Santa Anita', gentiana, hydrangea, *Iris sibirica*, *Lithodora diffusa*, *Meconopsis grandis*\*, nigella, *Omphalodes cappadocica*\*, *Orthrosanthus multiflorus*, *Pulmonaria* 'Bertrum Anderson'/'Beths Blue'/'Roy Davidson'*, rosmarinus, *Salvia patens* 'Indigo Spires'/'Blue Enigma'/'Blue Hills', *Thunbergia natalensis*, veronica

★ **Leaves:** *Cuppressus glabra*, *C. arizonica*, *Festuca coxii*, *Helictotrichon sempervirens*, *Juniperus squamata* 'Blue Star', *Senecio serpens*, *Echeveria elegans*, *Eucalyptus pauciflora*

★ **Fruit and bark:** *Elaeocarpus reticulatus* (blueberry ash), mahonia (berries), *Viburnum davidii* (berries)

*\* suitable for shady conditions*

---

Playing pool: this planting cleverly brings the blue of a swimming pool into its surroundings. Icy *Agave parryi*, *Echeveria elegans* and, as a looser form, trailing *Acaena caesiiglauca* nestle between the rocks.

## Purple

Like blue, purple recedes, creating the illusion of space. Purple is decadent and sumptuous — the opulence of aubergines and the richness of damsons. In bright plantings it creates pockets of shadow that throw other colours into three-dimensional relief. The darkness makes an arresting and tasteful contrast with shimmering grey foliage — often an effect achieved within the same plant as in *Lepechinia salviae* — a stately, salvia-like perennial.

Within purple there are a host of shades and tones from claret and burgundy tones, which are infused with red and therefore associate well with true reds, to the blue-infused bells of a campanula. Again like blue, purple cools hot colours effectively, particularly orange and yellow. Team deep, saturated purples with bright yellows or use the paler, pastel shades of purple such as mauve and lilac with apricots, peaches and lemon.

Dark and brooding, purple foliage is so deep that it almost becomes a non-colour and thus will combine with anything, adding a useful sense of shading to pale schemes. In soft pink plantings this shadowing — using perhaps, purple berberis, heucheras or tropical iresine — is just the ticket to add texture to the canvas of flowers and provide breaks in the brighter colours. If overdone, however, purple foliage can be as cumbersome and smothering as a shroud and will snuff the life out of your brighter colours. As always it's a case of bring on the green or, in this case, a touch of creamy variegation too.

---

Plums and custard: rich purples are not that easy to find but verbenas are happy to oblige. *Anthemis tinctoria* 'E.C. Buxton' stops things becoming too sombre.

---

### PLANT PICKS: TOP PURPLES

★ **Flowers:** *Allium sphaerocephalon*, *Angelica gigas*, *Aquilegia* 'Ruby Port'*, *Aster frikartii* 'Mönch', *Astrantia major* 'Claret'*, *Echinacea purpurea*, fuchsia*, jacaranda, *Lobelia* x *gerardii* 'Vedrariensis', *Knautia macedonica*, *Liatris spicata*, *Osteospermum* 'Tresco Peggy', *Papaver orientale* 'Patty's Plum', *Penstemon* 'Raven', *P.* 'Purple passion', *Petrea volubilis*, *Rosa*, eg, 'Chiante', *Salvia nemerosa* 'Ostfriesland', *S. vanhouttiae*, *Sedum* 'Purple Emperor', tibouchina, *Tulipa* 'Black parrot', *Verbena bonariensis*, viola

★ **Leaves:** *Acaena inermis* 'Purpurea' (piripiri), *Acer palmatum* 'Bloodgood'*, etc., *Ajuga reptans* 'Catlin's Giant'*, *Atriplex hortensis*, *Berberis thunbergii* 'Atropurpurea', *Brachyglottis repanda* 'Purpurea', *Cercis canadensis* 'Forest Pansy'*, *Cimicifuga simplex* 'Atropurpurea', *Cordyline* 'Red Star', *Cotinus* 'Grace', *Eucomis* 'Burgundy', *Euphorbia cotinifolia/dulcis* 'Chameleon'*, *Foeniculum vulgare* 'Purpureum' (purple fennel), heuchera, *Loropetalum chinense* 'China Pink', *Perilla frutescens*, *Phormium* 'Merlot', *Pittosporum* 'Tom Thumb', *Salvia gauranitica* 'Black Knight', *S. officinalis* Purpurascens (purple sage), *Sambucus nigra* 'Black Beauty', *Vitis vinifera* 'Purpurea'

★ **Fruit and bark:** *Callicarpa bodinieri*, *Colocasia esculenta* 'Fontanesii', *Davidsonia pruriens* (Davidson's plum), dianella (berries)*

*\* suitable for shady conditions*

Ever the socialite, white can gate-crash any party: here it's *Nicotiana sylvestris* with late-summer cannas and *Salvia elegans*.

## SOME CLASSIC COLOUR PARTNERSHIPS

**Green**
with all colours

**White, grey, lime green, deep purple**
with most colours

**Red**
with yellow, white, purple

**Blue**
with orange, yellow, white, pink, magenta

**Brown**
with grey, orange, yellow, pale blue, apricot

**Purple**
with pink, yellow, orange, cream, grey, peach, apricot

**Yellow**
with pink, orange, blue, red

**Coral pink**
with deep blue, mauve

**Pastel blends**
Pale blue with fawn, apricot

Lemon yellow with lavender, pink

Mauve with apricot, coral pink

## FOOD FOR THOUGHT

☆ Which colours do you like and which do you hate?

☆ Does your present garden reflect a thoughtful or chaotic approach to the use of colour?

☆ Of the colours you like, think about the mood you want to create in different parts of the garden (cool and restful or lively) and pick a primary colour scheme for each area as a foundation.

☆ If you want, decide on a secondary, complementing colour you can run through as well.

☆ In less formal areas, there might be room to throw in a few shocks so things don't look too clever and contrived.

☆ Is your border all icing and no cake? If a bed is already strong on colour, look beyond the flowers and ask whether there are enough strong forms and leafy textures to carry things through the quiet months. Often adding just a few foliage plants will be enough to provide year-round satisfaction.

☆ Green is your friend. Are you using it in all its shades or are you hooked on coloured foliage for your effects?

☆ Is your colour formed only from uncompromising blocks or is there a sense of diffused intertwining of colours in your borders?

☆ Is there a strongly coloured plant dominating one part of the garden? If so can you consider moving it, dumping it or diffusing its colour by echoing the shade with companion planting?

Chapter 11

# Using Foliage

Whether ferny, strappy or spiky, leaves provide the perfect stage on which flowers dance. Under an old oak tree the contrast of silver fern and *Iris foetidissima variegata* make good companions for the architectural bulb *Scadoxis multiflorus* subsp. *katherinae*.

IT'S A SAD STATE of affairs but one of my first love affairs was with a chestnut bud or, rather, the unfurling of the bud. I had the best kind of start with a primary school teacher who loved nature. Miss Lister was a biology teacher of the old school: she kept a fungi table with a puffball the size of a football. With toadstools, a tank full of tadpoles and a collection of owl droppings, I was in heaven and every spring we lined the windowsills with jam jars and raced out to find branches to fill them. If you didn't go for fat, furry pussy willow then it was the catkins of hazel trees. But the prized exhibit had to be those horse chestnut buds. We watched, amazed, each day as those sticky toffee-apples cracked open in the warmth. Furry and ribbed, they crept out and unravelled with all the reptilian menace of a pterodactyl hatching from a 'Jurassic Park' egg.

The thrill of watching hasn't gone. Thirty years on and spring still takes me right back to thoughts of jam jars and high windowsills dappled with the greenness of new life bursting out with spine-tingling beauty.

## Foliage:
### the main course

It is often claimed that leaves are more important than flowers. Leaves flutter in your face for most of the year while flowers in general come and go. Even the deciduous types grace us with their presence for a good deal longer than any flower, often exiting in a spectacular finale of autumnal glory.

Gardeners used to be obsessed with flowers and colour, but today the pendulum has swung the other way. We paint our walls pink and our pots blue to get our 'fix' of colour instead of using flowers; and foliage has become the hip accessory, from the fat paddles of taros to whispering bamboo.

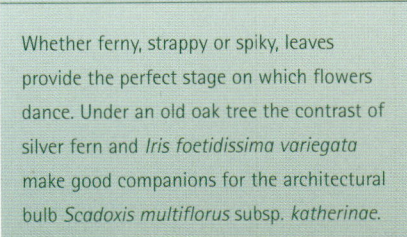

But there's a danger in assuming that foliage is more important than flowers. It is like saying the main course of a meal is better than the dessert when really we don't have to choose between one or the other — together they make the feast complete. In the garden we can, and should, have both our main course and a large helping of dessert.

When planning a border, then, think of it like a meal. Plan primarily the main course — your carefully contrasting foliage shapes and textures — and then you can save some room and have more fun and freedom with the dessert. If we plan our garden primarily around flowers its year-round appeal may prove to be unsatisfactory.

For me, the relationship between leaves and flowers is best mirrored in the richness of family life. Foliage is like the ideal parent — always there to reassure us — a comforting presence that can all too easily be taken for granted. The flowers, on the other hand, are like mad Uncle Gerald who bursts on the scene from time to time, popping up at Christmas, weddings and funerals with his red nose, his party tricks and his embarrassing laugh. Leaves form the comforting furniture of the everyday while flowers provide the seasonal entertainment. Both are essential in their different ways. Neither underestimate flowers as they emerge and fade nor neglect the art of crafting a border that is a rich tapestry of leaf.

---

Variegations that can look garish close up on an individual leaf may produce gentler effects from a distance. In this sunny border the lemony billow of a variegated agonis is reflected in the planting while a furcraea (bottom left) adds textural spice to the harmony.

## 'Evergreenitis'

In medieval times evergreen plants were credited with containing magical spirits because they seemed immune to the cycle of the seasons. Today we credit them with being the low-maintenance panacea to all our gardening woes and, unfortunately, this belief is just as much of an old wives' tale. Evergreen trees drop just as many leaves as deciduous trees — they just do it all through the year, which if they hang over a path is as annoying as a dripping tap. Similarly people seem to prefer evergreen perennials so they have interest all year and don't have to worry about cutting them down. But plants like dietes, flax and mondo grass still produce dead leaves and after a few years they get very clogged with thatch. With a deciduous perennial at least you cut them off cleanly once a year and that's it for maintenance. All the new growth is fresh and clean but with the evergreens you are left picking through the entire plant, teasing and grooming out the dead, which is far more fiddly.

Deciduous plants too bring the wonderful rhythm of the seasons to the garden. Obviously they would be unsuitable for a tropical theme and where you need year-round privacy and screening from neighbours. But if you can, try and weave a pleasing mix of both deciduous and evergreen plants into the border for a richer mix. Arrange the evergreen elements first so you will be sure they look good even in winter when the deciduous neighbours are less visible.

Try not to dot evergreen trees about but place them so that they relate without forming a heavy block. In a glut they can be as oppressive and gloomy as a funeral parlour — all those glossy leaves giving the garden a plastic look. In winter evergreens work best when they are broken up and form a backdrop to the delicate patterns of deciduous tree branches and to the dried and attractive seed heads of some perennials.

## Foliage from far off

Leaves can be enjoyed on many levels apart from the obvious qualities of colour and shape. Often the first impression we get is of how leaves relate together from a distance — all hung out like the washing on any particular bush or plant. Some shimmer and shine, some flutter and reveal underskirts in racy colours. Big leaves have a strong, individual character right from the start but small leaves make a collective statement. Take variegation for example. You might detest variegated plants, considering their flecks, spots and streaks to be as vulgar as a tattooed chest. However, if they are small and seen massed from a distance on something like a pittosporum or a berberis they provide a light and smoky effect that is not at all distracting or busy.

## Arrangement

How each leaf sits on the bush also affects the big picture. Some leaves like those of euphorbias are piled up on stems in layers as neat as stacked plates. *Phlox* 'Mount Fuji' is like this: each leaf spaced and splayed out in a wonderfully ordered arrangement as if someone has been through with a comb. The leaves in themselves are boring, but together, impressive teamwork lifts the profile of the plant from average to brilliant.

It's important not to write off a new plant simply because the foliage appears to be uninteresting. In a garden centre, a shrub might be clothed in only 20 to 30 seemingly mediocre leaves, but after a few years in the garden those humble few slices of green multiplied a thousandfold and dancing gracefully in a gentle breeze might form a dynamic arrangement. This is where a little background knowledge goes a long way before you shop. Visiting gardens and devouring books will help you anticipate the grand effects leaves can play en masse as your garden matures and individual shapes stack up into layered cathedrals of form and texture. Euphorbias, lilies and the fantastically ethereal perennial sunflower *Helianthus salicifolius* all hold their leaves in whorls that only reveal their beauty as the plant matures in the garden setting.

## Contrasting leaf shape and texture

The second way we enjoy leaves is up close — the more subtle qualities, as well as the shape of each leaf. Contrasting one type of leaf shape with another is one of the oldest design principles in the book, yet again and again landscapers seem to ignore it. Too often natives with similar leaves like libertias, flax and grasses are herded together in unimaginative plantings — often grouped with daylilies or dietes, which add even less by way of a contrast. All these spiky or grassy shapes together without some broader leaf forms for relief produces a planting drained of drama and impact. Leaves come in so many varied shapes that it's easy to set your plants up so that one leaf type contrasts with its neighbour.

Where we might choose to either harmonise or contrast colours, with leaf shapes, when we stick to a basic palette of greens, the rule of thumb is to go for contrast, contrast, contrast every time in both leaf shape and texture. The subtle colours of the leaves will provide a unifying thread while the clashing shapes will add zest to your planting.

---

With plants like *Euphorbia lambii*, it's low marks for content, high marks for presentation. The individual leaves aren't remarkable but they are stacked up in lively whorls.

## The nine lives of leaves

To effectively contrast leaf shapes and forms it is essential to identify at a glance the broad types of different foliage. Below is my version of how I group foliage mentally whenever I put a planting together. Nature, of course, hates to be put into neat boxes; a plant like a gunnera is simultaneously a hand shape and a grand dinner plate! My divisions are simply here to help you begin finding the broad differences in foliage shape so you can create our own contrasts. You will make up your own rough divisions and vary the model. Even if you keep it as simple as putting big leaves next to small you will be on the road to thinking about how you use leaf shapes to add power and purpose to your garden.

### 1 Dinner plates

Like sumo wrestlers, large roundish leaves add a richness and a sense of weight and definition to any border. The broad paddles of cannas give a vertical thrust but most leaves of this shape lie out flat to catch maximum light and in so doing they create useful planes of horizontal form to be contrasted with the upward thrust of spikes and spires. In the subtropical garden, leaves can never be big enough, from the paddles of Abbysinian banana to the muscular giant fig (*Ficus dammeropsis*) with perhaps the most dramatic leaves of any shrub, ribbed like sheets of corrugated iron. Colder gardens might rely on the umbrellas of giant rhubarb (*Gunnera tinctoria*) for shock tactics but with some gunnera now becoming a noxious weed it might be better to use bold alternatives like *Darmera peltata* and farfugiums. Use big leaves carefully. The larger a leaf gets the more it becomes a dominant element in the border and there is only so much room for prima donnas — you need the supporting cast too.

Beyond the usual tropical associations, even in traditional cottage gardens fat foliage is essential; it somehow pulls together and gives cohesion to any busy planting that is round about. In a classic country rose border see how mounds of bold bergenias can create punctuation marks at the edge of a border, anchoring more dainty plants. In woodland, hostas and smaller asarums and pulmonarias create similar, high-impact carpets of substance under the trees, but for low-maintenance options use large and tough plants like *Trachystemon orientalis* or big symphytums like *S. caucasicum* 'Emminence' or *S.* 'Hidcote Pink' (which is almost white) for strong, rounded carpets of foliage.

Acanthus, even though its leaves are serrated, presents stylish expanses of green that reflect the light and are a welcome helping of boldness among the usual array of timid woodlanders in dry shade. People avoid acanthus but I find that if it is deadheaded promptly it never becomes invasive. Though more arrow shaped, the paddles of zantedeschia are always welcome too for providing bold mounds of lushness in tough places.

The process of coppicing — cutting trees back to the ground each winter, can turn a forest giant into a herbaceous

---

### PLANT PICKS: DINNER-PLATE SHAPES

★ **Smaller plants:** *Acanthus mollis*\*, *Ajuga reptans* 'Jungle Beauty'\*, *Alchemilla mollis*\*, bergenia, caltha, canna, colocasia\*, *Darmera peltata*, farfugium\*, gunnera, hosta\*, ligularia\*, *Myosotidium hortensia* (Chatham Is. forget-me-not)\*, nelumbo (lotus), nymphaea (waterlily), pelargonium, rheum\*, *Salvia forsskaolii*, symphytum\*, thalia, *Trachystemon orientalis*\*, tropaeolum\*, zantedeschia

★ **Climbers:** beaumontia, *Vitis cognetiae*

★ **Trees and large shrubs:** brachyglottis\*, catalpa, *Ensete ventricosa* (banana), entelea (whau), *Eriobotrya japonica*\* (loquat), *Ficus dammaropsis*, *Macropiper melchior*\*, *Magnolia acuminata*, *Meryta sinclairii*\* (puka), paulownia, *Pisonia brunoniana* 'Variegata'\*, *Senecio grandifolius*

*\* suitable for shady conditions*

---

**Opposite**

Contrasting leaf shapes is not rocket science — the secret is finding the plants that enjoy your site and soil. In this textural melting pot natives like puka, tree fern and grassy chionochloa battle for leafy supremacy.

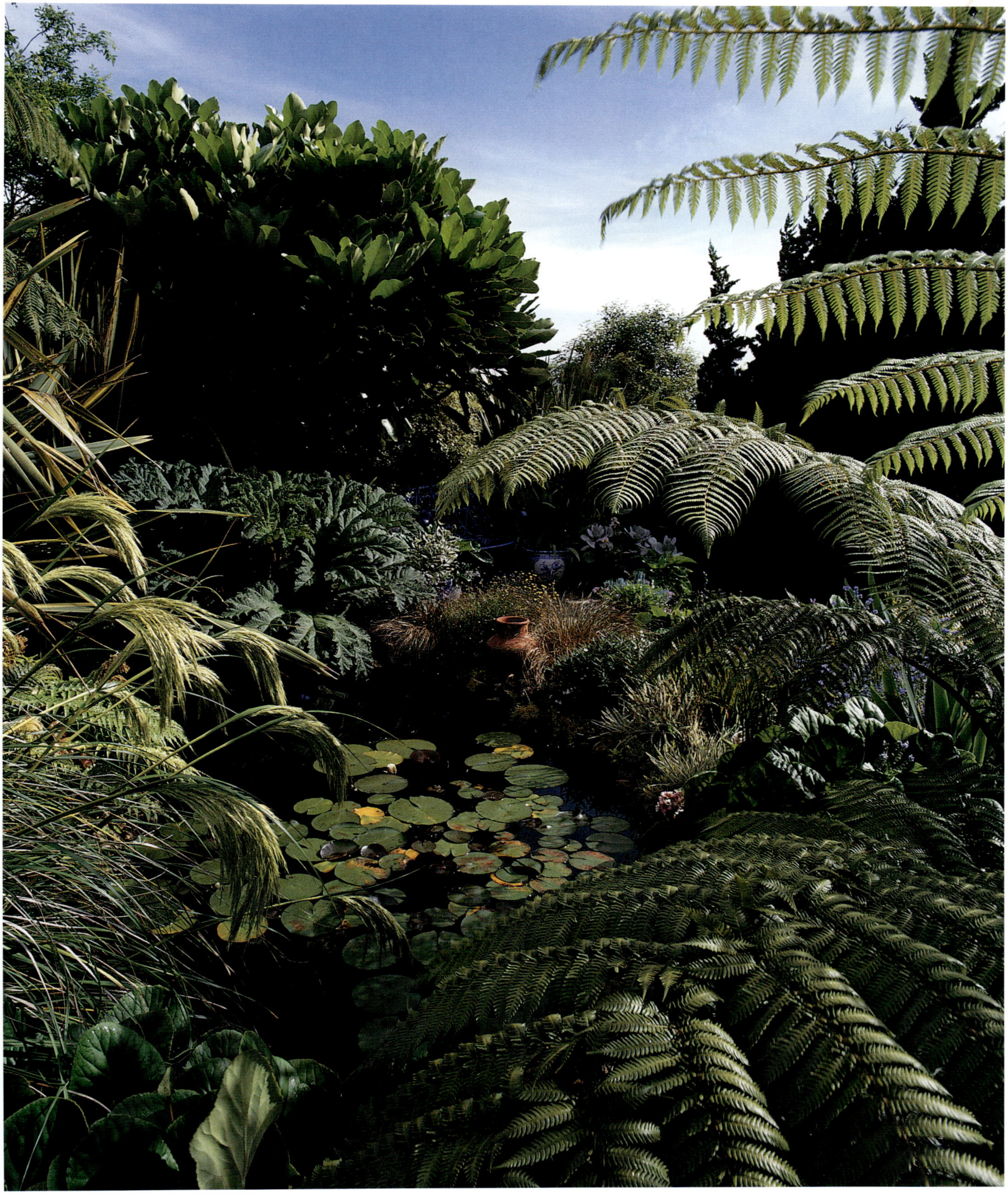

Like a bull in a china shop this muscular paulownia looks oddly incongruous beside a line-up of puny perennials. It's coppicing rather than steroids or working out at the gym that produces such elephantine growth.

plant with giant leaves. Large-leafed species like paulownia and catalpa produce regrowth up to 3 metres high, layered with the most sumptuous paddles. At Ayrlies golden catalpa looks especially good counterbalancing the upright thrust of *Phormium* 'Yellow Wave' and set against the hand-shaped leaves of a bank of choisyas.

Wherever you find them dinner plates have a nice, relaxed generosity about them that will contrast with any leaf shape. Being so simple they also carry variegations well, making a real feature of any streaks and splashes such as the dramatic variegated puka *Meryta sinclairii* 'Cream Edge'.

## 2 Strappy

More slimline than dinner plates, plants like New Zealand arthropodiums and many bromeliads form bold rosettes that contrast well with finer plantings in shady places. For more drama strelitzias and bananas can add useful height, and for

**Right**
Strappy billbergias hanging out together.

### PLANT PICKS: STRAPPY SHAPES

★ **Smaller plants**: agapanthus, *Aloe plicitalis*, *Arthropodium cirratum*\* (Rengarenga lily), aspidistra\*, bromeliads\*, *Carex siderosticha*\*, clivia\*, colchicum, crinum\*, cymbidium (orchid)\*, *Iris evansia*\*, *Limonium perezii*, *Phormium* 'Dark Delight' and weeping kinds, nerium (oleander), stokesia, veratrum\*

★ **Trees and large shrubs**: *Clematis armandii*, *Cordyline terminalis*\*, strelitzia

*\* suitable for shady conditions*

a softer scheme perennials with bold, strappy leaves include stokesias and statice (*Limonium perezii*) and noble veratrums with deeply pleated leaves.

## 3 Ferny

Ferns are like toilet paper (if we are to believe the adverts) for they contain in their lacy form that unusual combination of softness and strength. They deliver delicacy in a strongly architectural framework, which is such an arresting contrast with bolder and simpler leaves.

> **PLANT PICKS: FERNY SHAPES**
>
> ★ **True ferns:** adiantum, asplenium, blechnum, doodia, matteucia, paesia
>
> ★ **Smaller plants:** acaena, *Acanthus spinosus*\*, achillea, aciphylla, aconitum\*, *Ammi visnaga*, anemone\*, angelica\*, artemisia, astilbe\*, callicoma, cassia, cimicifuga\*, cycads, *Cynara cardunculus* (cardoon), dicentra\*, eschscholzia, ferns\*, filipendula, *Foeniculum vulgare* (fennel), galega, indigofera, melianthus, *Myrrhis odorata*, *Oenanthe javanica*, polemonium, tanacetum, thalictrum
>
> ★ **Trees:** *Acacia dealbata*, *Acer palmatum dissectum*\* cultivars, *Akama rosaefolia*, albizia, *Alectryon excelsus*\* (titoki), cycas (cycad), gleditsia, laburnum, palms, *Radermachera sinica* (Canton lace), robinia, *Schizolobium paraphyllum* (Brazilian fern tree), sophora (kowhai), sorbus
>
> ★ **Shrubs:** calliandra, indigofera, mahonia\*, nandina\*, *Sambucus racemosa* 'Plumosa Aurea'\*, sophora, sorbus (Rowans), wisteria
>
> *\* suitable for shady conditions*

It is not just the true ferns that provide lacy foliage to offset chunkier companions, though. At ground level there are dicentras and astilbes where the effect is rather more diminutive but good and fluffy all the same and combined with beautiful flowers as well. Taller herbs like polemoniums, cimicifugas, thalictrums and fennel are important for providing architectural veils of texture which, if placed at the front of the border, allow you to peer through to plantings beyond, creating a wonderfully three-dimensional effect. We sometimes class fern-like foliage as a rather gentle and feminine feature, but there are more substantial players such as angelicas, melianthus and writhing mounds of cardoon (*Cynara cardunculus*) for the softer garden.

In their own way palms and cycads also have a fern-like quality for subtropical schemes, overshadowed by the grandeur of the Brazilian fern tree (*Schizolobium paraphyllum*).

Pinnate leaves composed of smaller leaflets attached to a mid-rib often give plants, especially shrubs and trees, a ferny look. If they are relatively small in the case of rowan trees and members of the pea family like gleditsia, laburnum and robinia, you get a nicely light and delicate effect but if they are larger the foliage becomes much more of a feature in itself such as *Sambucus canadensis*.

Variegation on a fern-shaped leaf is rather a squandered luxury because the individual subtleties of colouring get lost in the intricacies of the leaf shape. It is

Delicate and detailed, yet structurally strong: the spiraling feathers of this cycad (*Cycas revoluta*) lead into a cone perched like a dinosaur egg in its nest.

Usually a glut of variegation is indigestible but carefully matched colouration and dramatic shape contrasts help pull off this arresting team.

very much the case of gilding a lily, and the unadulterated green version of the same leaf usually looks more satisfying.

### 4 Hand shaped

Like the spokes of a cartwheel the leaflets of the horse chestnut (*Aesculus hippocastanum*) spin a wonderfully dynamic design. A hand shape has a nice intricacy about it but at the same time a rounded completeness and a reassuring rhythm in the repeated leaflets. In the subtropical garden, examples like windmill palms and schefflleras are invaluable while in a cottage garden you might use choisya, rodgersias or astrantias and hellebores. While spiky leaves tend to accentuate the verticals in a border, hand-shaped leaves are useful for adding a layered horizontal sense of balance. But they can feel quite restless too so the two often don't sit well together. A good idea is to separate them with mounds of fine foliage and relaxed dinner plates of leaf.

### PLANT PICKS: HAND SHAPES

★ **Smaller plants:** astrantia, *Begonia luxuriens*, cyperus, fatshedera, galium, helleborus, hedera, heuchera, lupinus, *Pachysandra terminalis*, rodgersia, tiarella

★ **Trees and large shrubs:** acer, aesculus, aralia, brachychiton, *Cecropia peltata*, choisya, *Chorisia speciosa* (floss silk tree), fatsia, liquidambar, *Pseudopanax lessonii adiantifolius*/Cyril Watson/Trident, *Schefflera actinophylla/arboricola*/'Condor', tetrapanax, trevesia, palms like *Chamaerops humilis*, *Trachycarpus fortunei*, washingtonia

★ **Climbers:** akebia, parthenocissus, passiflora

### 5 Spiky

The gnash of fierce teeth: this is the effect of spiky leaves. Let a bold astelia or yucca loose in your borders and it's like releasing a crocodile — things will never be boring again. Spiky leaves enliven your planting. Like spire-shaped plants, spikes have more than a whiff of an exclamation mark about them.

A desert-style planting is the classic place to see swords drawn en masse with plants like aloes, doryanthes and yuccas all battling it out — often among harsh pebbles and rocks. Though spikes are visually arresting and provide dramatic impact, if overdone — as they often are — all those jagged edges can become restless and unsettling. But inject a few soothing hummocks of hebe or cistus and you will instantly achieve a better sense of balance.

Some spiky plants add dramatic form but in a softer way. The likes of crocosmias, dietes and the diverse iris family can be comfortably woven into a cottage style, adding punch without looking like they are getting the daggers out.

While most spikes add a sense of vertical thrust to a border, some like astelias and yuccas explode in all directions. Others, like phormiums, offer a diverse range of habit from those which stand to attention to those like the luscious *P.* 'Dark Delight', which begin purposefully enough but then weep seductively at the tips. The difference between the two habits is huge so it is best to see a mature plant before you buy. Erect forms wake us up, while relaxed strappy foliage is altogether more graceful and gentle on the eye while still being architectural.

### 6 Grassy

There is a merging where spiky foliage ends and finer, grassy foliage begins. Sometimes the difference is enough to make a successful contrast such as a flax/carex partnership but more often it is better to contrast grasses with more obviously different leaves.

Grassy foliage is stringy and light. Where most spiky plants are architectural many fine grasses contribute more to the garden by way of their general rounded form than the shape of individual leaves. The bronze *Carex flagellifera* is a classic example, making useful hummocks of soft stringiness — the perfect foil for glossy angelicas or round-leaved coprosmas and macropiper.

The prince and the pauper: two carex grasses; one (*Carex siderosticha* 'Variegata') is replete and showy, the other (*C.* 'Frosted Curls') is stringy, weepy and mean — both have their uses.

### PLANT PICKS: SPIKY SHAPES

★ See plant list in Chapter 2, page 29.

### PLANT PICKS: GRASSY SHAPES

★ **Smaller plants:** acorus, candida, *Eryngium pandanifolium*, hemerocallis, kniphofia, *Leptocarpus similis* (oioi), *Liriope muscari**, *Luzula sylvatica**, ophiopogon* (mondo grass), *Restio tetraphyllus*, *Russelia juncea*, zephyranthes

★ **True grasses:** *Carex hachijoensis* 'Evergold'*, chionochloa, cortaderia, *Festuca ovina coxii* (for flowering grasses, see page 34)

★ **Trees and large shrubs:** carmichaelia, casuarina, cytisus (broom), *Elegia capensis*, nolina, *Spartium junceum* (Spanish broom), tamarix, xanthorrhoea (grass tree)

*\* suitable for shady conditions*

Grasses tend to create softer effects than plants with spiky leaves. Instead of the teeth of astelias or flax, grasses make waterfalls and fountains to soothe the senses and therefore blend easily into traditional perennial gardens as well as more contemporary designs. In New Zealand at least, many grassy and spiky plants are considered low maintenance and are lumped together rather too often in dreary and amorphous plantings. Mass planting is a useful technique for grasses but they benefit from at least some form of contrasting foliage to produce a spark of chemistry.

With their fine form, grassy-foliaged plants (and I include here hemerocallis, kniphofia and fine iris like *Iris sibirica*) bring a useful sense of lightness to the garden. Perhaps it's why they blend so well with dainty meadow-style perennials and form such a useful counterpoint to heavy succulent gardens full of obese aloes and armchair agaves.

## 7 Fuzzy

The smaller a leaf gets, the less important is the precise detail of each leaf shape and the more important is the general look as seen from a distance. A host of plants have such small leaves that they create smooth and fuzzy effects that contrast nicely with any foliage that is bolder and more defined. Fuzzy plants include the smooth shapes of topiary like box, lonicera and yew as well as many conifers that all have a fine texture and smooth outline. Less formal are heathers, lavender, small-leafed hebes and the New Zealand divaricates.

Divaricating plants, with the wire-netting look, are often texturally more interesting than many small-leaved plants because their branch structure rather than the leaves becomes the point of interest. Divaricates range from billowing bushes like *Coprosma virescens* and *Muehlenbeckia astonii* to compact dwarfs like *Coprosma rhamnoides* 'Mangitangi', which can be clipped but loses much of its character if you do. *Coprosma* acerosa forms make earthy and fantastically stringy groundcovers. Because divaricates

> ### PLANT PICKS: FUZZY SHAPES
>
> ★ **Smaller plants:** *Coreopsis verticillata, Erica carnea\*,* lavandula, santolina, scleranthus
>
> ★ **Trees and large shrubs:** calliandra, *Coleonema album* (Breath of Heaven), *Kunzea ericoides* (tea tree), *Leptocarpus similis,* myrsine, pinus, podocarpus\*, *Salix matsudana* 'Tortuosa' (twisted willow), *Westringia brevifolia*
>
> ★ **Divaricating natives:** *Coprosma acerosa, C. brunnea, C. crassifolia, C. Mangitangi, C. rhamnoides, C. rugosa* 'Clearwater Gold', *C. virescens, Corokia cotoneaster, Muehlenbeckia astonii, M. divaricata, Pittosporum obcordatum, Plagianthus divaricatus\*, Sophora prostrata*
>
> *\* suitable for shady conditions*

Where hard landscaping is already highly textural and structured, plants don't need to work so hard to impress. Like a six o'clock shadow the fuzz of subtle divaricating plants adds just the right note of informality.

are so stark they blend well into arid-style schemes and make excellent contrasts to lush foliage.

When too many small-leaved plants get together things can start to look desperately drab — even when leaf colour and plant shapes are different. Often there just isn't enough textural interest to carry a planting and you start to get a huddle of 'blobs'. An example is a purple berberis planted with a pool of gold marjoram at its feet. The purple and yellow colours are a contrast and the berberis is large and the marjoram low — so far so good. The trouble is that even with these obvious contrasts both plants share similar small leaves, which drains the combination of textural drama. It's a bit like making a couple wear matching outfits for a date — certainly they are different in character but the cutesy clothes would surely kill the conversation. In the berberis/majoram pairing if we replace the marjoram and get instead something more textural like a gold-leafed hosta or a carex, you will create a far more dynamic partnership.

## 8 Leafy

Most plants have leaves, of course, but in this category I include any plant with simple leaves of a size where they become features in themselves when seen from a distance. Shrubs like *Camellia japonica*, laurels, rhododendrons, michelias and bay all have leaves of the classic oval or elliptic shape that are bold enough to be appreciated in their own right and produce textured shrubs. Perennials with strong leaves are harder to find, but here I would include textural plants like tall eupatoriums, the giant *Lobelia gibberoa* in which the leaves are the main event and the flower spike, though colossal in stature, is a bit of a damp squib. Salvias generally are prized for their flowers but those with beautiful leaves include types like *Salvia madrensis* and *Salvia confertiflora* and the ghostly grey salvia lookalike *Lepechinia salviae* with more

*Synadenium grantii* 'Rubra' is a leafy subtropical that keeps its purple-speckled livery even when in shade; as an upright shrub it is useful in tight spaces.

diamond-shaped (rhomboidal) leaves and rich burgundy flowers in late summer.

Leafy plants sit squarely in the middle of the scale of dramatic effects. They don't blow your socks off like a cartwheel of giant Queensland schefflera might, but neither do they cause you to doze off like a homely hump of heather might. So in some ways they actually provide a useful link between the larger and smaller leaves in your foliage tapestry.

---

### PLANT PICKS: LEAFY SHAPES

★ **Smaller plants:** brachyglottis, crassula, elatostema, hydrangea, kalanchoe, *Lobelia gibberoa*, *Salvia confertiflora/involucrata* 'Bethelii'/*madrensis*, *Smilacina racemosa**

★ **Trees and large shrubs:** *Alberta magna*, *Camellia japonica* cultivars*, gordonia, *Griselina lucida**, hibiscus, *Justicia carnea*, leucodendron, luculia, magnolias, michelia, *Petrea volubilis* (sandpaper vine), protea, rhododendron*, *Salix magnifica*, *Sorbus aria*, *Viburnum odoratissimum* 'Emerald Lustre'*

*\* suitable for shady conditions*

*9 Indistinct*
A whole truckload of plants have mediocre leaves that are instantly forgettable – you just don't notice the foliage at all. It doesn't mean we should resign such plants to the skip; they may be team players that contribute other valuable talents. For example, there isn't a single philadelphus with an interesting leaf, but what philadelphus do have (and have it by the truckload) is scent. They also have attractive flowers. Behind a 'feature' plant like a strappy phormium or ferny-leafed melianthus, a philadelphus might be just the thing – a low-key curtain of green to show off the drama in front with the burst of scent in spring as a nice bonus.

Old-fashioned spring shrubs are often weak in the leaf department and have been unduly forgotten in the rush for the show-stopping architectural plants. The likes of deutzias, chaenomeles, weigelas, kerria, ribes and good old forsythia are an invaluable supporting cast, so long as you don't fill your beds with them to the exclusion of more exciting foliage effects. A host of brilliant bulbs, annuals and perennials also lack show-stopping leaves but our gardens would be sunk without their fleeting blasts of colour, their flower form, seed heads and berries.

You really have to weigh up everything in the context of where a plant is to be fitted into a border when deciding if that particular plant makes the grade. A garden really is like a football team. If your bed already has team players with good leaves and architectural form, then there may be room to slip in something with no obvious leaf appeal but with other surprises up its sleeve. Covering as many bases as possible without losing focus will produce a stronger design.

## Beyond shape

In addition to leaf shape, there are stacks of other aspects of foliage to consider when combining leaves. Here are a few more things to get you revved up about leaves and the way you combine them.

*Colour*
Plants come in such a range of leaf shades these days that it is hard to resist going for streaked, splashed and coloured varieties rather than for 'boring' old green. When using our native plants, which often lack dazzling flowers, contrasting such leaf colours is an excellent way of providing drama. Generally, however, foliage carries bright colours with less grace than flowers and it is best to avoid mixtures of different leaf colour beyond shades of green, except of course in autumn when any tree is forgiven should it catch fire in a blaze of glory. Bright clashes are enjoyable in flowers, perhaps because we know the clash won't last for long but, with leaves, any uncomfortable or restless combinations you include are with you for most of the year. We look more closely at leaf colour in Chapter 10.

*Dew drops*
*Alchemilla mollis* is renowned for the way the scalloped leaves capture rain or morning dew in a glistening ring round the edge of the leaf. The effect gave it the traditional name of lady's mantle. Lotus leaves trap a single globule of rain in their central dimple where it perches on the waxy surface like a bead of mercury. Many other leaves capture rain or frost in peculiar and intriguing ways, so run out after a shower to see what's shimmering.

*Jekyll and Hyde: leaf undersides*
Turning over a new leaf is a great habit to get into quite literally because some plants that appear dull and staid above often dazzle and surprise when you get them belly-side up. On top some leaves can look pretty average but there might be underskirts in a shocking array of colours. Red ginger (*Hedychium greenei*) has rich, liver-coloured backs to the leaves that are really striking as the plant emerges in spring. In colder areas the same effect is achieved by the dark medallions of *Ligularia dentata* 'Desdemona' or the newer 'Britt Marie Crawford', which flashes burgundy when the wind flips the leaves over. The colour looks especially good if echoed in nearby plants like *Aquilegia vulgaris* 'Ruby Port'.

Trees like *Sorbus aria* and several poplars are renowned for their silvery backings, which bring the trees alive on a windy day when what lies beneath is exposed. For best effect place trees like this against dark background foliage for added contrast (or a stormy sky if you can orchestrate it). In smaller spaces try shrubs like *Loropetalum chinense* or plants like macleaya for a silvery shimmer that will bubble up from below. Many rhododendrons wear wonderfully bizarre 'chest wigs' on their bellies. Lift a dark, glossy leaf and you might be surprised by a mat of furry hairs (indumentum) in white or rusty fawn.

*Rough and smooth: texture*
The texture of leaves is as important as their shape. Take hosta leaves, for example: most are a similar shape but some can be smooth, some are ribbed like a concertina and some are puckered like alligator skin. Texture is a subtle quality. Unlike colour, you can pack a lot of contrasting textures into your planting without it looking busy. A textured border has a depth and richness that doesn't detract from the overall picture.

One of the most obvious and striking textural differences we can use for dramatic effect is the glossy/dull contrast. It is based on the principle that opposites attract and, whenever they do, you get an exciting visual dynamic. Glossy leaves add a sparkle that will enliven any dull corner. In shady places this light reflection is especially good at brightening things up, but it doesn't mean you should opt only for laurels, box, rhododendrons and camellias. The popularity of such evergreens can easily lead to a glut of gloss. Furnish your garden entirely in plastic-leaved plants and the high-lacquered look can begin to look artificial and even seedy, like the walls of a public toilet or the shimmer of dirty raincoats huddled round the deck.

The solution is to provide matt relief with dull foliage that will provide a dynamic contrast. Think of it like you would a meal — every glistening banger has its dollop of comforting mash; or entertainment — every star has their stooge (Dame Edna and Madge, for example). So, we also need leaves with a matt finish to counterbalance the gloss. Put a dull brown carex against a slick clump of arthropodiums or the lacquered sheen of a pepper tree (macropiper) and both are transformed — you've got a sweet and sour thing happening; the liveliness of one is tempered by the stringiness of the other. It's a symbiotic relationship, and both plants benefit.

In shade, furry-leaved plants that absorb the light might include duvets of helichrysums, plectranthus and *Eupatorium megalophyllum* — old-fashioned shrubs with bold leaves as velvety as snooker tables — and all dull in the nicest of ways. In sunny places, New Zealand natives provide a wealth of light-absorbing options from billowing tea trees and corokias to the fuzz of all those wire-netting plants — the divaricates listed on page 116. These will all melt quietly around your high-gloss specimens — as sweet a partnership as a hollandaise sauce melting around squeaky asparagus tips.

## Sound

You can't really plan how your garden beds will sound but every plant makes some noise or other when the wind gets up and it adds that extra dimension to enjoying the garden. Palms and evergreen magnolias clatter like dustbin lids being banged together — there is a sense of menace in the harsh rustle. Altogether more smooth and relaxing are the grasses and bamboos, which whisper even in the slightest breeze. Aspen trees have long been appreciated for their leaves, which have flattened stalks (petioles) that hinge gently so that even a whisper of a breeze is captured and amplified as the whole canopy picks up on the movement. Nearer the ground enjoy the construction of giant taro leaves (colocasias). Like leathery drum skins, the leaf surface is stretched over a muscular scaffolding of veins and it booms reassuringly whenever you give it a bang on passing.

## Spring greens

The way some leaves stretch out and unfurl in spring can be as entertaining as any flowers. It is hard to beat the sheer vitality and freshness of an oak or beech tree, fresh in leaf, seen against a blue sky

---

Back to basics: reliable plants like dryopteris fern, arums and comfrey are the meat and veg of the garden with simple, satisfying shapes. No gimmicks, no razzmatazz, just light and chlorophyll — magic!

Sitting in a nest of *Carex* 'Frosted Curls', this liver-leaved rhizomatous begonia is placed to catch the low morning sun and positioned where it is easy to look under its skirts.

## FOOD FOR THOUGHT

☆ Looking at your garden, would you say you plan with foliage or flowers as the main consideration?

☆ In any particular bed, what main leaf shapes are present?

☆ Are there places where you are missing an opportunity to contrast two leaf shapes?

☆ What effects does your foliage have when seen from far off?

☆ Do parts of your garden suffer from 'evergreenitis'?

☆ Are you over-using variegated and coloured leaves?

☆ What other aspects of leaves do you particularly enjoy beyond leaf shape?

but, for others, before green chlorophyll has formed, different pigments shine through and provide fleeting drama.

Many Japanese maples begin each season almost as dramatically as they end it with limes, purples and pinks. My favourite is a form of *Acer palmatum* with lilac shoots, which perfectly complement the scented panicles of a neighbouring wisteria. The toon tree (*Toona sinensis*) is chameleon-like as coral pink shoots expand and turn cream before settling down to a conservative summer dressed in green. Other fiery spring tints are encountered in pieris, royinas and photinias, which all enjoy an initial fiery flush to start the season. Perhaps the most dramatic is *Neolitsea sericea*, which arrays itself in a golden gown. The new leaves have a silky shimmer — fantastic for stroking, which deservedly earn it the nickname spaniel's ears.

### Lanterns: translucence

Placed strategically so early morning or late evening sun streams through, some larger leaves are translucent when lit from behind. When this happens you get that extra 'X' factor that takes an ordinary corner of the garden and turns it into something to blow you away. I love the tender plectranthus for this; several have purple backs to the leaves and as these are ignited as the sun sinks lower each bush becomes a glowing lantern.

Like many of these leafy subtleties we cannot exhaustively plan to include every facet in our planting — that way we would drain the garden of its ability to create its own surprises. Instead just keep your eyes open for foliage effects and your enjoyment of the garden will only grow deeper.

Chapter 12

# Personality Plants

IN BEV MCCONNELL'S Arylies Garden there has been a scuffle going on for years — and no one is in a hurry to resolve the issue. The fight is high in a tree where two banksia roses, one yellow and one white, are struggling for supremacy. They intertwine and push ever upwards, searching out sunny strongholds to conquer. The weeping conifer that is the playground for this particular battle is struggling itself. Swamped under the blanketing roses it thrusts its threadlike growth further out over the pond each year, trying to avoid its unwelcome guests. There will be no happy ending. One day the whole lot will come crashing down, but for now the playing out of this drama makes a magnificent spectacle, especially in early spring when the entire battleground is awash with flower and alive with bees.

## Adding spark and spontaneity

We can get so carried away looking at plant shapes, colour and textures that we can forget that plants are living things;

The one that got away: plants dance to the beat of their own drum no matter how hard we try to train them, coerce them, win their trust or just beat them into submission with a blunt spade.

they have definite personalities, strengths and weaknesses, boastful giftings and bad habits. Some are well-behaved friends and some are downright rebellious; there are the plodders, the athletes and the show-offs who creep up on us and then explode into life.

Plants dance to the beat of their own drum. However, as much as we try to clip and train, coerce and nurture them, they seem to take a mischievous delight in surprising us. In fact, it's an unspoken rule that the ones you desire to grow the most often turn their toes up, while the plants you hate seem to thrive in the shadow of your displeasure — especially the weeds and the scoundrels.

*No talking to your neighbour — hands by your side — sit up and behave! Sometimes it's a hard and regimented life being a plant in someone's minimalist paradise.*

### *The virtue of unpredictability*
In the analogy of our garden as a shop window there is really no parallel for the animated habits of plants which, in having a life of their own, add that essential spark and spontaneity that makes gardening such a unique art form.

Instead of seeing the unpredictability of plants as irritating and inconvenient the challenge is to see it as a virtue — in fact it is the most exciting aspect to garden making. In allowing plants to express themselves, we have to learn to step back and allow nature to paint the final brushstrokes on our picture. Take aquilegias and violets, for example: their seeding habits can be seen as either annoying or charming. They will certainly require a bit of managing, but if you step back and let them seed where they will, you'll be inspired by the results more often than not. Annoying though it is, nature seems to be better at arranging things.

The individuality of every plant and the unique way in which each grows add the icing on our garden 'cake'. We can all plant a trailing rosemary down a wall but no two plants in no two gardens will cascade in quite the same way. Some will age with great beauty, lifting a hem to reveal a gnarled framework of flaky-barked limbs; others will reach to the floor and (if allowed) root into a gravel path then take off with a second wind across the driveway.

Managing your cast of characters to bring out the best in each is the gardener's challenge. But a good director doesn't keep interfering and meddling. He or she trusts his staff to make their own decisions — even make their own mistakes, and in such an atmosphere of trust and freedom the employees are happy and they thrive. In this spirit then, why not allow your pristine topiary to swell a little and dictate its own outline? Allow the prostrate juniper to creep over the path edge and see how it might soften a harsh edge. Plants love the freedom as we loosen the reins.

## Plant interaction
Appreciating the different characters of plants only comes with spending time with them. Just like children, if you put in the time, both parties benefit. Most plants fall into one of two personality types: those that like to stay put and keep to themselves (many shrubs and trees, for example) and those that love to go places — to mix and mingle — such as climbers and trailers. In the search for low-maintenance gardens it's easy to opt only for the well-behaved plants. After all, they may swell a little over the seasons or years but basically they are a known quantity; they won't go getting into trouble and fraternising with other members of the team.

### *Creating animation and exuberance*
The problem is that keeping all your plants at arm's length from each other when they are literally in the same bed can look a bit sterile and unfriendly. Leaving a bit of bare soil between plants may be appropriate in certain situations, perhaps when you want to discourage humidity and disease for example. But this style of planting leaves each plant looking alone and uncomfortable. In contrast, when plants are allowed to

## PLANT PARTNERS: MIXING PRINCIPLES

There are no rules about which plant personality to team with another. Trial and error is the best approach, but take your cues from natural plant communities you see in the wild. What makes sense about letting your plants get close and personal is that even in a town garden there is room for much more diversity and detail when plants are layered much as they would be in a natural plant community. Small bulbs can emerge from low groundcovers, which are themselves nestled under deciduous shrubs. In turn, on the shrubs climbers can scramble and feel their way into an overhanging tree — all this, in the space of a metre square!

When letting plants mix and mingle here are a few useful principles.

- Always try to balance vigour so that weak plants are teamed with weak and strong with strong.

- Underplant deciduous trees and shrubs with groundcovers and spring-flowering bulbs.

- Use bulbs and plants that seed like annuals and biennials; they will find imaginative crannies to nestle into.

- Try shade-tolerant groundcovers that flower early like violets and *Geranium phaeum* round the skirts of tough perennials such as paeonies and hostas. They will keep down weeds and provide colour at the start of the year.

- Species that are going to associate closely need a certain degree of shade tolerance as they share the same space. Leathery-leaved evergreens make good hosts for climbers.

- Spiky-leaved groundcovers like sisyrinchiums, sansevieria and libertia combine well with groundcovers that sprawl but which don't root as they go, such as *Sutera cordata*, *Campanula portenshlagiana* and scaevola.

- Climbers love to scramble through shrubs and trees, but only those that can cope with the shading and smothering.

- Underplant low groundcovers such as thyme and pratia with small bulbs like zephyranthes.

- Spreading perennials combine well with other spreaders of a similar habit. They also look good running through shrubs of an open and suckering habit such as *Indigofera decora*, old hebes or suckering clerodendrums.

Tough plants like the grass *Carex flagellifera* can cope with the nomadic likes of *Iris tectorum* passing through and flirtatious lobelia popping in when the mood takes her.

jostle and to throw their arms around each other you get more of a party atmosphere. Some plants might get squashed or shaded but at least there is animation and exuberance.

Not all plants play happily together though. In choosing those that can associate intimately, care needs to be taken that one doesn't dominate or smother its associate. An evergreen climber like *Clematis montana* will quickly smother a pittosporum, but choosing a less vigorous, deciduous type such as *Clematis viticella* will allow the host time out from the partnership during winter when this type of clematis is cut to the ground.

When plants get together the effect is often more decorative than the sum of its parts. An example is *Lithodora diffusa*, a bright blue groundcover, and *Libertia peregrinans*, a grass-like running native with an orange tinge. Individually they are great plants but put them together and the result is dynamite. Orange and blue is always a winning combination to start with, but this partnership is exciting, not just because of the colours but the way that the lithodora gets out of its comfort zone. Normally it forms a flat, boring puddle but here it is forced to snake and twine its way through the libertia in search of light and in scrambling it looks far more interesting. As a bonus it also helps to hide the libertia's unsightly dead leaves as it goes.

If you are nervous about letting your plants get close and personal just look at the natural world. Here they rarely grow in isolation but instead develop complex and tightly knit communities, which are relatively self-sustaining. Evolution has spent thousands of years getting these finely balanced mixtures right so we can't hope to throw a barrowful of plants together overnight and expect them to play 'happy families'. Often a bit of reducing, judicious deadheading and training will be needed to ensure combinations are relatively sustainable and sometimes we will make mistakes.

As vigorous plants fight it out together, after a few years one may begin to predominate and at this stage it might be possible to blow the whistle; step in and dig the whole lot out for a fresh start. This doesn't mean we have failed. Like the banksia roses mentioned earlier, it may have been a very beautiful battle while it lasted. What would you rather have: plants fighting battles and partying together or sitting quietly around like a bunch of pensioners in a rest home?

## Different plant habits

Although every plant has an inherent look that suggests a certain character (all cacti look stark and starved, for example) different plants move and grow in very different ways. It's this animated aspect that we can use to give our gardens more personality. Here is a sample of some of the different ways plants use the footholds we give them in our gardens.

---

Interaction needn't mean chaos. In this well-considered coastal planting grey *Euphorbia glauca* (top) and *E. cyparissias* 'Fens Ruby' run their rampaging fingers through more sedentary toughies like hibiscus, hemerocallis and *Aeonium arboreum* 'Atropurpureum'.

## The thugs: vigorous growers

Plants have definite preferences whether they like us or not — they either curl up their toes or take over our lives. The shrub labelled as 'compact' in the garden centre that is now tapping at the windows of an upstairs room is never going to endear itself and is best removed and replaced with something more suitable. But what of those over-affectionate perennials that quickly spread and run through your borders — are they practical or even welcome in today's low-maintenance world? The answer has to be yes, but only when grown in the right place.

Take Japanese anemones for example — they have million-dollar looks. Producing mats of attractive leaf from early in the season, they announce the end of summer with happy swags of white or pink. But anemones also have awfully bad manners. They are born to run and once you've got them it's very hard to remove them because every piece of root that you leave in the ground will resprout. But an anemone is more a rascal than a monster. All that's needed is a little training. Place an anemone with more delicate perennials and you are asking for trouble — its surface roots will compete with and strangle out the neighbours. But if put to bed with agapanthus, red-hot pokers or cannas your monster will be well matched.

Similarly if allowed to run around at the back of a wide border under deep-rooted shrubs like roses or philadelphus, it will furnish the ground with leaf and provide colour just when the shrubs are looking drab. Bear in mind, however, that it's not a good idea to underplant shallow-rooted shrubs like rhododendrons and hebe with rampant perennials as there will be too much competition for surface nutrients and water.

## Thriving in adversity

Vigorous plants are perfect too when you want to cover large stretches of soil with bold and simple planting that will cut out weeds. Because they are often tough and obliging I use them where my more fussy specimens will not grow, places like steep clay banks or in the dry shade under house eaves or in the poor soil under a large tree. These challenging microclimates often take the edge off the appetite of a thuggish plant and help it to behave in a more civilised manner.

Many wetland plants are natural thugs — the likes of Louisiana irises, *Zantedeschia aethiopica* and *Pontederia cordata*. In damp hollows these will happily fight it out together — the secret with rascals is to team them with similarly vigorous team-mates who also like to play rough. In spring enjoy carpets of woodlanders like *Saxifraga stolonifera*, *Viola labradorica* or the ever-flowering Australian violet *Viola hederacea*. Then combine these vigorous groundcovers with other tough perennials such as hostas, liriope and polygonatum, which don't mind jostling for space and will provide foliage interest through the summer.

## Containing spreaders

In smaller modern gardens, you might think there is no place for vigorous spreaders but the opposite is true. Often these modern designs require planting that is bold and simple, using plant material that performs well even under difficult conditions. Today, beds are often small, well-defined and bordered with hard paving so any spreader is easily contained and control is not an issue. Here tough, evergreen plants like acanthus, anemone and hellebores are perfect, providing lushness that will contrast nicely with box-edged beds and harsh path edges.

Another way to keep the reins on the rascals is to use them in island beds on lawns. There is no place to run so rampant plants like agapanthus, cannas, *Salvia uliginosa* and eupatoriums can be mass planted and kept in check by the mower. Well away from more delicate plants, these brutes provide striking architectural blocks of colour and texture that is perfect for breaking up the monotony of large lawns.

## The seeders

Many larger perennials that seed, such as acanthus and thalictrums, can be a nuisance. Coming up where we don't want them, they burgeon and elbow out their new neighbours, but if we are judicious with deadheading it's easy enough to stop this happening. As well

---

### PLANT PICKS: VIGOROUS SPREADERS

★ **Smaller plants:** acaena, agapanthus, *Alchemilla mollis**, *Anemone* x *hybrida** (japanese anemone), asters (some), *Campanula glomerata*, *C. takesimana**, chlorophytum* (spider plant), *Colocasia esculenta**/Fallax, *Euphorbia amygdaloides* var. *robbiae**, *E. glauca*, heterocentron (spanish shawl), *Imperata cylindrica* 'Rubra' (blood grass), *Iris* louisiana, *Libertia peregrinans**, lysimachia, ophiopogon*, *Pleioblastus variegatus**, pontederia, *Salvia forsskaolii*, symphytum*, *Thalia dealbata*

*suitable for shady conditions*

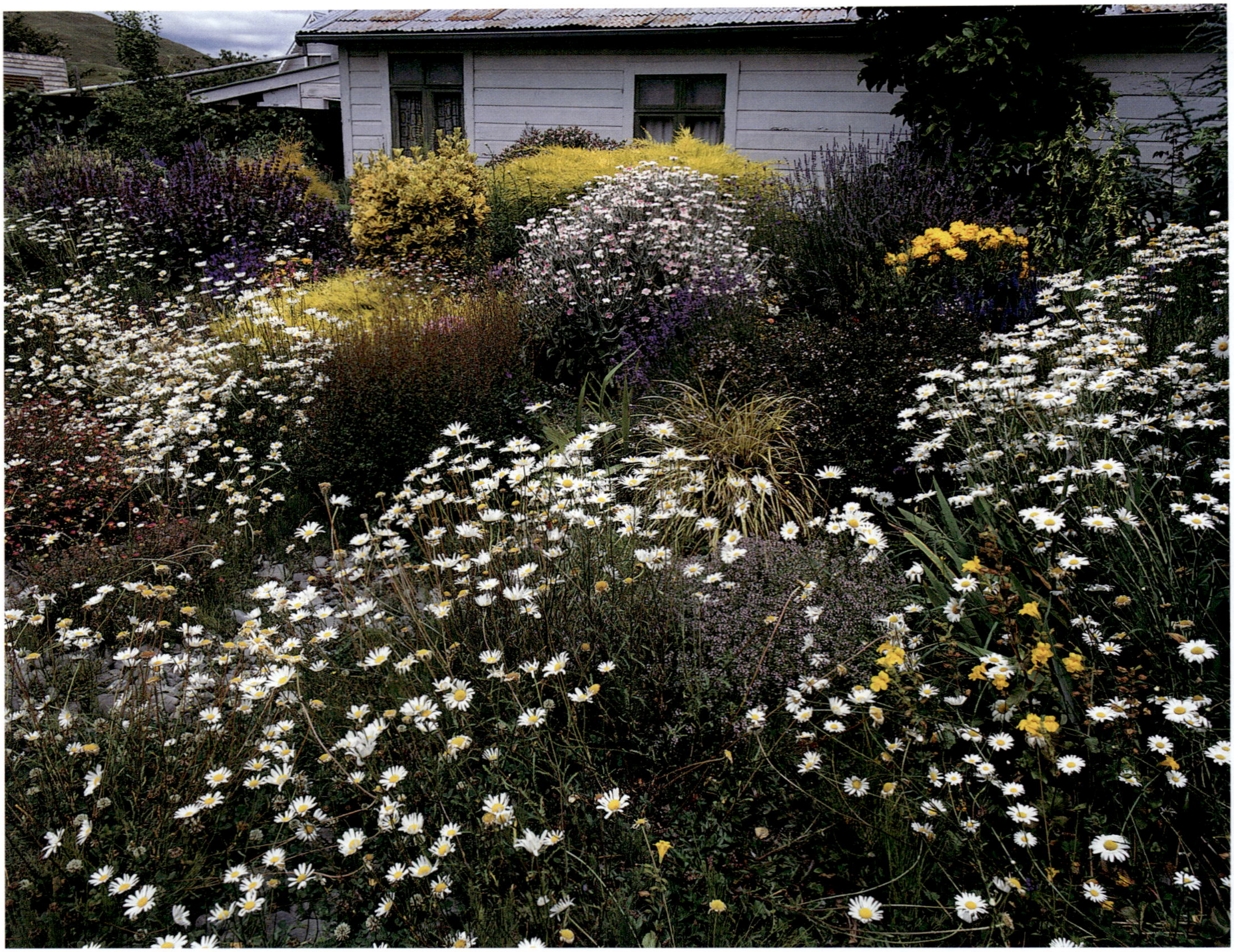

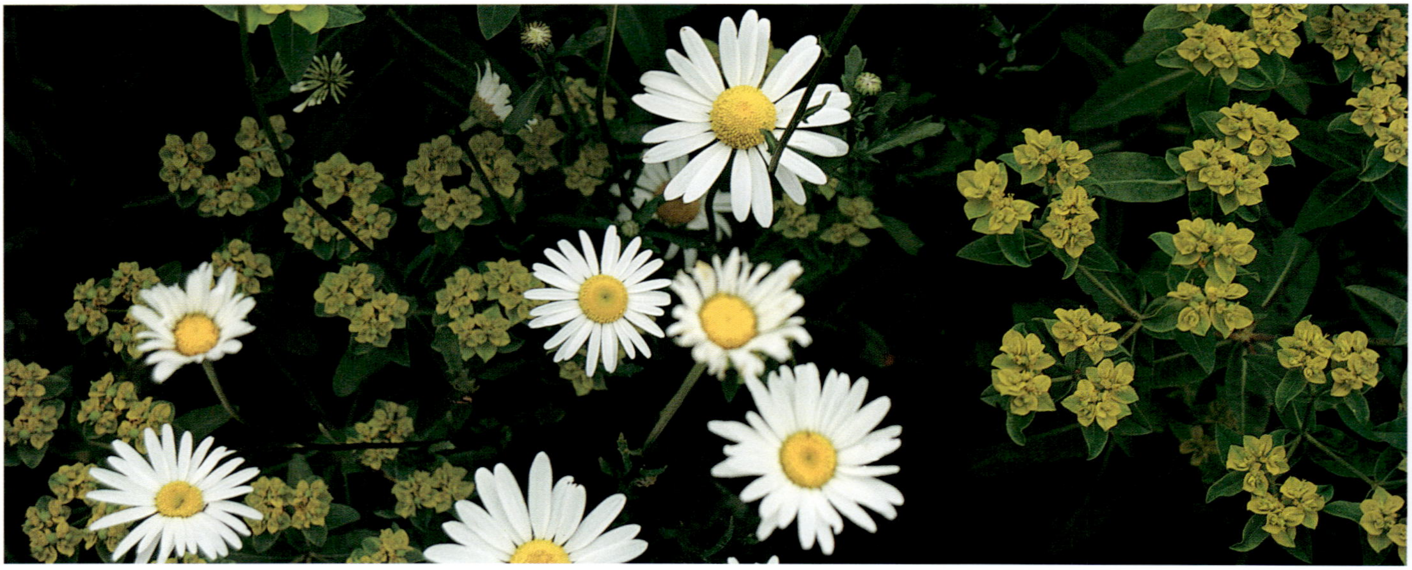

as these troublesome seeders there are promiscuous plants with more endearing qualities. Annuals and biennials can be invaluable for knitting together more blocky planting in a border. Along with a few light, perennial seeders like gaura and centranthus, these are the ballet dancers of the border, which tip-toe through, rather than trample upon, your other plantings. In weaving about, these less substantial plants can provide unifying threads of colour at certain times of the year that add a special magic and softness for a season while more substantial foliage plants will provide the year-round appeal.

Problems can arise when those of us with a yearning for the loose cottage-garden look allow seeding plants to dominate a border. Many, including the likes of forget-me-not, cynoglossum and poached egg plant (limnanthes), flower simultaneously in spring. They are often big on colour but when the flowers fade there just isn't enough foliage interest and form to hold things together through summer and beyond. Remember that usually annuals and biennials are the icing on the cake – and as such you still need a cake beneath. The beauty of these short-life seeders is the way that they slip in between more permanent plantings and pop up in different places each year adding a dynamic lightness to the border.

### Adding pep and zing

Annuals dance lightly over the garden and add a personal touch. If you have a defined colour scheme, these seeders are also useful for reinforcing and fortifying the theme without dominating. Just as a sprinkle of icing sugar is the finishing touch on a muffin so white annuals like *Omphalodes linifolia* or *Orlaya grandiflora* are great allies for pepping up a border with a dash of brightness. Similarly those lime green seeders such as *Nicotiana langsdorfii*, alchemilla or the often-used *Euphorbia polychroma* can add a zingy backdrop to more substantial slabs of colour provided by permanent planting.

Although a majority of seeders are happy to trickle in between other plants, watch out for the more thuggish types: biennials like foxglove and verbascum that can easily swamp smaller plants with their hefty leaf rosettes. With these, some intelligent thinning out early in the season will be needed.

Just because a plant seeds around doesn't mean we have to leave it entirely to its own devices. I like to shift around seedlings in winter and set them out in defined groups where they will create more impact as they flower the following year. Judicious 'editing out' of unwanted seedlings early in the game is another sensible habit to adopt to prevent a complete meltdown of law and order.

Seeders come with some stigma attached. Designers sometimes consider them to be only for cottage gardens. A few well-chosen species, however, will soften and add detail to any scheme, from tropical to desert. In nature every ecosystem has its annual opportunists. *Eryngium giganteum*, for example, is an architectural biennial that would look perfectly at home in a dry succulent garden alongside fizzing eschscholtzias and the skeleton-like arms of *Lychnis chalcedonia*.

Another myth about biennials and annuals is that they are without good

#### Opposite top
Seeders like lychnis and ox-eye daisies add detail and delicacy, but like icing needs a cake to wrap around, so they need more structural plants for when the flowers have flown.

#### Opposite below
Lime is a sociable colour and *Euphorbia polychroma* loves to mix and mingle – as it seeds itself among brilliant ox-eye daisies (*Leucanthemum vulgare*).

---

## PLANT PICKS: WELCOME SEEDERS

★ **Perennials:** aquilegia\*, *Asphodelus fistolusus*, *Centranthus ruber* (false valerian), *Euphorbia polychroma*\*, gaura, helleborus\*, *Lychnis chalcedonia*, primula\*, *Salvia forsskaolii*, viola

★ **Annuals:** alyssum, *Atriplex hortensis*, browallia, *Cerinthe major*, cosmos, *Dianthus barbatus*, eschscholtzia, linaria (toadflax), linum, nicotiana\*, nigella, *Omphalodes linifolia*, papaver

★ **Biennials:** *Campanula biennis* (Canterbury bell)\*, *Dianthus barbatus* (sweet william), digitalis (foxglove)\*, *Eryngium giganteum*, impatiens\*, lunaria (honesty)\*, oenothera (evening primrose), verbascum

★ **Bulbs:** anemone\*, galanthus (snowdrop)\*, galtonia, *Hyacinthoides hispanica* (Spanish bluebell)\*, ixia, lachenalia, scilla\*, sparaxis, tigridia

*\* suitable for shady conditions*

---

Personality Plants

form and foliage. The bold rosettes of foxgloves and verbascums or the huge leaves and strong presence of the giant tobacco plant (*Nicotiana sylvestris*) will add more than a trickle of impact for a season.

But form and structure isn't everything. Between cracks in paving and in gravel gardens where seeding plants really prove their worth, blurring the edges and shifting with the seasons as they dance in the wind and weave their magic.

## Sociable climbers

The trapese artists of the garden, climbers take interest to new heights. Climbers aren't just for draping over an ugly fence like an old duvet. When you allow them to interact with other plants they can look far more animated. The trouble is that we get so obsessed with having enough space, the upwardly mobile plants get shuffled off to the edges when what's needed is a bit of upward interest within our boundaries to divide the garden and make the spaces more interesting.

Climbers are roughly divided into three types:

- self-clingers such as ivy, which are great for covering walls and fences and for adorning tree trunks;
- twiners like clematis and vines, which need a twiggy support so they can get a foothold with tendrils and adapted leaf petioles;
- scramblers, which climb clumsily using sharp thorns to grab the branches of other trees. Climbing roses and bougainvilleas are examples of this last group. They usually need a firm framework on which to climb.

Posts and tripods are the perfect way to display climbers and create a vertical

### PLANT PICKS: CLIMBERS

★ **Vigorous:** bougainvillea, clematis, *Ficus pumila**, hedera* (ivy), *Humulus lupulus* 'Aureus' (hop), jasminum, lonicera (honeysuckle), mandevilla, passiflora, tecomanthe, thunbergia, *Vitis cognetiae* 'Purpurea', wisteria

★ **Less vigorous:** akebia, ampelopsis, clematis most types except *C. montana* varieties, dregia, gelsemium, lapageria*, *Lathyrus grandiflorus*, *Solanum crispum* (potato vine), *Trachelospermum asiaticum/jasminoides*, *Tropaeolum speciosum*, *Vitis vinifera*

★ **Annuals:** asarina, eccremocarpus, ipomoea, *Lablab purpureus*, *Lathyrus odoratus* (sweet pea), *Mina lobata*, *Rhodochiton atrosanguineus*, *Thunbergia alata* (black-eyed susan), *Tropaeolum peregrinum*

*\* suitable for shady conditions*

dynamic at the same time. These vertical accents break up areas of boring blobbyness in the border and act as 'space busters', pepping up the topography of your garden.

As well as smaller perennial vines such as *Vitis vinifera purpurea* and gentle sollya with blue or pink bells, there are annual climbers that are easy to grow from seed. Try fiery *Mina lobata* for hot schemes, and for a subtle look there are scented sweet peas.

Lighter climbers like gelsemium look fantastic trained up tripods or poles or draped into shrubs. The deciduous clematis are like gymnasts; they look insubstantial — but deliver a meaty performance. By cutting them to the ground each winter it is easy to keep them from going ballistic.

Growing roses into trees might be considered romantic; however, in practice it is highly impractical as roses love sunshine and heavy feeding. Anything climbing into a tree, however, is going to be heavily shaded all summer and will suffer from intense root competition so it is better to grow roses up stout supports out in the open, combining them with late-flowering clematis or vines to extend the season.

Vertical gardening is just as relevant in contemporary gardens where exotic bromeliads can be used rather than traditional clematis and honeysuckle. Wire them to ponga posts and add small self-clingers like *Trachelospermum asiaticum* with scented bloom or the native rata *Metreosideros carminea*.

### Frontline friends: front-of-border plants

'Going nowhere' is not a label many of us would want to get stuck with but for plants perched at the edges of our flower beds a reasonably civilised growth habit is essential. Here we want plants that aren't going to lurch out and block a path or

---

Opposite

The burnt-out carcass of a seasonal miscanthus grass (centre), suckering *Euphorbia glauca* (left) and blue *Echium pininana* seeding itself about, means this border moves beyond the usual 'safe succulent cemetery' scenario.

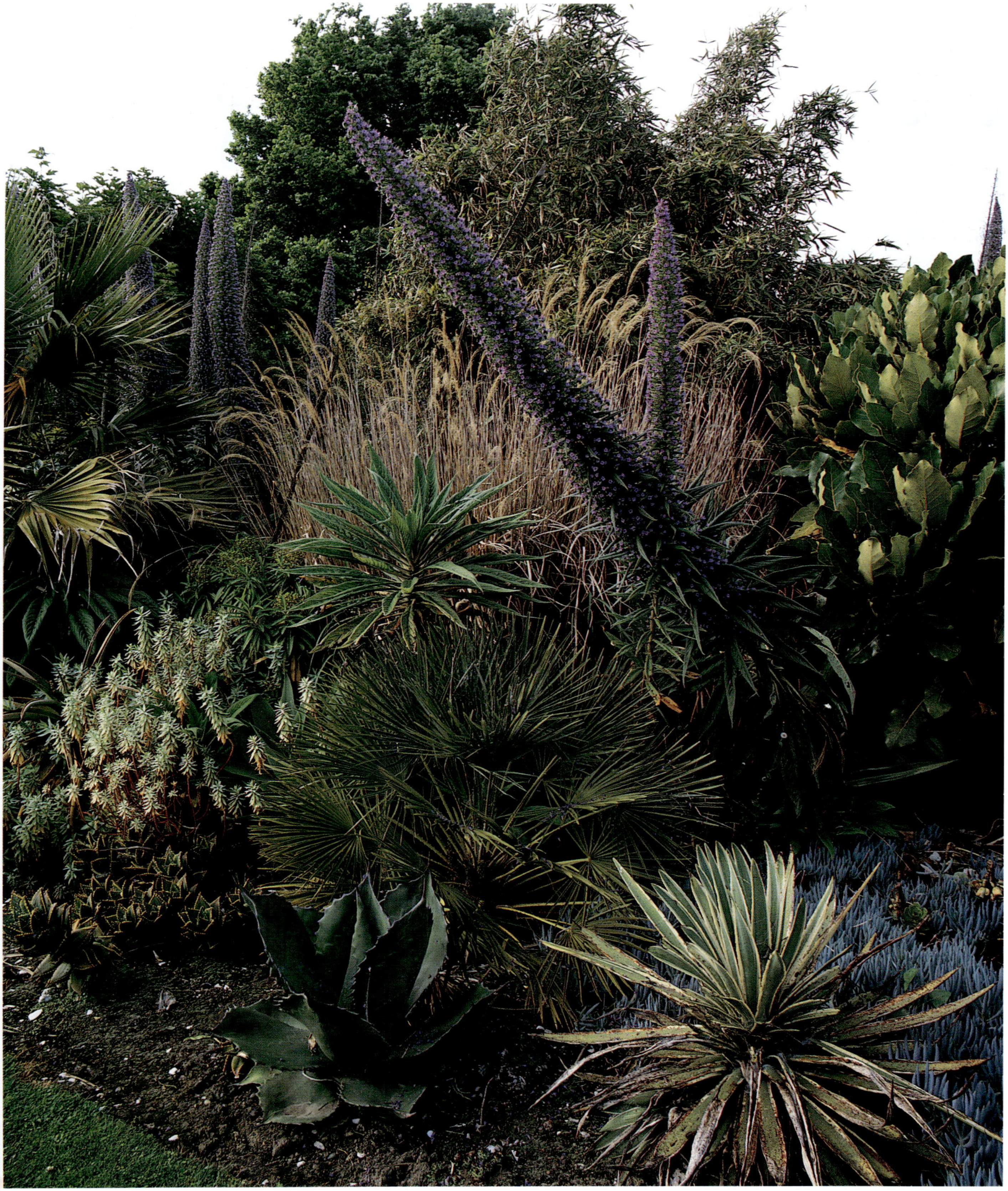

*Above*

Rather than containing roses, good pruning should help to set them free. This beautiful multiflora variety 'Cathayensis' at Ayrlies Garden is actively encouraged to get friendly with a neighbouring magnolia.

*Far left*

Flax makes a great playground for adventurous groundcovers like this *Campanula* 'Elizabeth' entwined with *Phormium* 'Platt's Black'.

*Left*

*Physostegia virginiana* 'Lavender' and, beyond, clouds of thalictrum make shimmering veils to break up blocky planting.

### PLANT PICKS: NEAT EDGERS

★ *Achillea* 'Moonshine', acorus*, armeria (thrift), *Aster novi-belgii* 'Pink Lace'/'Royal Ruby'/'Lo Jinx', *Campanula portenschlagiana*, *Convolvulus cneorum*, *Coprosma* 'Mangitangi', daphne*, *Coreopsis verticillata* 'Moonbeam', *C. rosea* 'American Dream', *Deutzia crenata* 'Nikko', dicentra*, erica*, *Erigeron glaucus*, *Eucomis zambesiaca*, gazania, *Genista lydia*, *Geranium sanguineum*, *G.* x *riversleaianum* 'Mavis Simpson', geum*, *Grevillea lanigera* 'Mt Tamboritha', *Hakonechloa macra* 'Aureola'*, heuchera, hosta*, nemesia, *Origanum vulgare*, *O. laevigatum* 'Herrenhausen', osteospermum, pulmonaria*, *Salix helvetica*, *Sedum* 'Ruby Glow'/'Vera Jamieson', stokesia, tiarella, tulbaghia (also see low hedge list page 144 and flat mat list page 27)

*suitable for shady conditions*

run about and swamp other small frontline plants. Usually the intricacy of planting will increase towards the front of the border so here, as things get busy, you need a large proportion of sociable plants that will perform well in close proximity to others.

Against a backdrop of plants that droop and spring up, seed and run about, it is necessary in a composition to have those plants that will sit pretty and behave themselves. A lavender bush is the perfect example, crisp and self-contained — for the first few years at least — there can be beauty even in its slow demise as the shredded bark within is revealed and annuals like nigella move in to fill the gaps.

Plants like tulbaghias, wall flowers, stokesia and perennial statice all sit tight and flower generously but give them something of an animated look by planting them in naturalistic drifts and flowing ribbons to loosen the effect.

---

*Lychnis chalcedonica* is a little luxury that pops up only briefly but in mid-summer this particularly clean red brings a welcome injection of life. The structural plant (left) is *Inula magnifica*.

## Jack-in-the-box plants: bulbs and explosive growers

I love those plants that arrive as if by magic — jet propelled from bare earth. If your climate is cold enough an eremurus is a magnificent beast rocketing up at a rate of knots. There's nothing like bulbs to add a sense of drama and locomotion. Many like nerines, colchicums and blood lily (*Haemanthus* species) come into flower before their foliage arrives. They look unearthly against bare earth like dazzling stars that have crash landed on a grimy asteroid. Bulbs are especially useful for dibbling into tight spaces as added extras in your scheme and some, like scadoxus, eucomis and crinum are bold enough and hang around long enough to become important architectural statements in themselves.

With smaller bulbs, if we devote too great an area for them they can leave an ugly hole as the leaves die down after the show, so it is best to drizzle them rather as you would dress a salad so they slip into crevices in the planting. In wilder parts of the garden if you have the room, mass planting in blocks is more acceptable as there the dying leaves are less obtrusive.

Spring bulbs can be integrated with later-flowering perennials such as phlox and Russell lupins, which as they burgeon will obligingly hide the fading leaves. But this idea doesn't work so well for South African bulbs, which prefer a more open aspect than that afforded in a crowded perennial planting.

## PLANT PICKS: JACK-IN-THE-BOX PLANTS

★ **Perennials:** aquilegia*, *Arum creticum*, echinacea, *Eupatorium rugosum*, *Geranium pratense*, heleniums, lobelia (perennial), lupinus, *Papaver orientale*, platycodon, *Ranunculus cortusifolius**, tradescantia

★ **Early deciduous bulbs:** allium, *Anemone nemorosa**, arisaema*, camassia, crocus, *Cyclamen coum**, *Dracunculus vulgaris*, eranthis*, erythronium*, fritillaria, galanthus* (snowdrop), ixia, lachenalia, narcissus*, ornithogalum, ranunculus, scilla, sparaxis, trillium*, triteleia, tulipa

★ **Late deciduous bulbs:** *Amaryllis belladonna**, colchicum, crinum*, *Cyclamen hederifolium**, eucomis, galtonia, gladiolus, lilium*, moraea, nerine, oxalis, sternbergia, tigridia

★ **Biennials:** *Alcea rosea* (hollyhock), *Anchusa capensis*, *Campanula medium* (Canterbury bell), *Cynoglossum amabile* (Chinese forget-me-not), *Dianthus barbatus* (sweet william), *Digitalis purpurea** (foxglove), *Echium vulgare*, *Eryngium giganteum* (Miss Wilmott's ghost), *Hesperis matrionalis* (sweet rocket), *Lunaria annua** (honesty), *Oenothera glaziouana* (evening primrose), *Verbascum adzharicum* (mullein)

*\* suitable for shady conditions*

### Volcanic growers

As well as bulbs being a powerhouse of dynamic growth other plants share their supersonic lifestyle. In warmer areas I eagerly await the arrival of spring when exotic evergreen perennials like doryanthes and beschorneria send out their flower spikes of volcanic proportions. Like agaves and furcraea, the doryanthes take many years to come to flower but when they do, you know about it. With all these monocarpic plants the individual flowers are a bit of a let down but the flower spikes are impressive and comical — you can almost hear them growing. The cycle ends as spectacularly as it began when the parent plant dies and takes on the look of a burnt-out car wreck before new pups emerge around the base and seed is set.

Once we get past the idea that all tall plants have to be sent into the corners of our gardens like naughty school children we can bring them out to the front to work their magic. As well as being architectural one of the great qualities of many flower spikes is the speed with which they develop. Echiums seem to go from nought to 60 overnight, and foxgloves, verbascums and evening primrose all erupt at a dazzling rate of knots. Though the flowering may be brief often the seed heads stay on to add form among more sedentary growers.

Still other plants — perennials like heleniums, perennial lobelia and tall annuals like mignonette and Bishop

---

Bulbs, like Christmas, are over all too soon but always worth the wait. As these outrageous tulips bow out, collapsing under their own weight, elegant alliums are waiting to carry the show on. A wide path is always useful to allow such slovenly plants some elbow room.

flower (*Ammi visnaga*) have little going for them except for a brief show of flower. But they take up so little room at ground level and deliver such a seasonal injection of colour that it seems a pity to leave them out. They rise as fast as condominiums in a crowded city scene where they always enhance the skyline.

## Lightweight whisperers: light, ethereal plants

While the wonderful virtue of water is extolled for the sound and movement it contributes to the garden, some tall and soft plants provide just as much action if the breeze is blowing the right way.

Light and ethereal plants — those which rise with a whisper and dance lightly over the garden — weave their own special flavour and magic and are to be highly treasured in a design. Kings of quiver have to be the elegant grass family but many perennials too spin misty veils of leaf and stem that add a lightness and delicacy to offset more sedentary planting.

The arching flowers from a clump of aptly named angel's fishing rod (*Dierama*) bob in the gentlest breeze but it takes a hearty gust to get the paddles of a leathery palm or banana palm to clatter together. It is not what you would want right outside the bedroom window but the sound is all part of the rich tapestry of effects. Veil-like plants such as cimicifuga, thalictrum and fennel (*Foeniculum vulgare*) will not only come alive in the wind but make great front-of-border plants that you can look through to planting beyond, which gives a greater sense of depth to a planting.

Of the grasses, bamboos have a wonderful sense of movement even on a still day but need some containing. The smaller grasses, however, can run free and

An open space is a great place to show off ethereal plants like the fishing rods of *Dierama pulcherrimum alba*. Away from a wall and up a tree the mushroom cloud of *Clematis* 'Perle d'Azur' becomes far more animated too (with a bit of help from some ties).

### PLANT PICKS: LIGHT WHISPERERS

★ **Smaller plants:** *Ammi visnaga* (bishops flower), *Anethum gravealens* (dill), anigozanthos, *Campanula lactiflora*, *Cephalaria gigantea*, cimicifuga*, cleome, cosmos, *Crambe cordifolia*, *Deschampsia cespitosa*, dierama (angel's fishing rod), *Eryngium pandanifolium*, *Filipendula rubra* 'Venusta', *Foeniculum vulgare* 'Purpureum' (bronze fennel), *Francoa sonchifolia**, gaura, gypsophila, *Helianthus salicifolius*, limonium (statice), perovskia, *Salvia haematodes*, thalictrum, *Verbena bonariensis*

★ See also most flowering grasses list page 34

★ **Trees and large shrubs:** alyogne, *Calliandra eriophylla*, carmichaelia (native broom), *Genista aetnensis*, lavatera, sophora (kowhai)

*\* suitable for shady conditions*

Personality Plants

Aptly named old man's beard, *Tillandsia usneoides* swings in the wind from an old villa verandah. This bromeliad is really a massed colony of tiny individual plants linking arms. All bungi jumpers need room to free-fall to their heart's content and, in this case, protection too from the birds at nest-building time.

## FOOD FOR THOUGHT

☆ Are your plants like Irish dancers with their arms firmly by their sides or are they having a party and interacting together?

☆ Could you weave climbers into existing shrubs or add shade-loving bulbs and groundcovers under larger plants?

☆ Jack-in-the-box plants take up little room but add seasonal highlights — how are you using yours? Does year-round planting cover their quiet season?

☆ Could you prune, trim and tidy more lightly to allow plants to mix, mingle and let down their skirts a little?

☆ If a plant is encroaching on a path consider widening the path rather than cutting back the plant to allow it to express itself.

☆ When plants are mingling, decide when you will have to wade in and put a stop to the fun and games to prevent a friendly wrestle turning into an all-out war.

are invaluable for adding grace and animation. Use all flowering grasses where evening and early morning light can set the flowers alight if you can and try to place them on a corner or at the front of a border so that, like the veil plants, you can again enjoy their translucent qualities. Native grasses like carex are excellent for texture but it's the chionochloas and toetoes and many introduced types with better flowers that are so useful at suggesting height in the garden without blocking a view. Of beefier grasses the miscanthus top the list. Though they need more room there is something to see nearly all year either alive or in death when they provide structural seed heads for winter.

### Bungi jumpers: trailing plants
Wherever there is a wall or a bank trailing plants come into their own softening a surface. We looked at trailing plants in Chapter 2.

### PLANT PICKS: TRAILING PLANTS

★ *Convolvulus sabatius, Coprosma kirkii/prostrata/*'Hawera', *Grevillea fasiculata, Helichrysum bellidioides, Lithodora diffusa, Lotus berthelotii, Pimelia prostrata, Scaevola aemula, Silene maritima, Sutera cordata* 'Snowflake', *tropaeolum**

★ See also weepers plant list page 22

*\* suitable for shady conditions*

Chapter 13

# Skirting Around the Issue

## dealing with edges and backgrounds

THE TROUBLE FOR my friends began when the decorators' van rolled up. Next-door's house had looked a bit rundown so they were excited about a makeover on their doorstep. But their delight crumbled when they realised the neighbours, obviously living in something of a time warp, had let loose with a glowing peach acrylic. Not a brick was spared. Just when it seemed things couldn't get any worse it did. Work began on painting the roof — purple. Rather than a newly painted phoenix rising from the ashes our friends woke the next morning to find a parrot of a house squawking at them over their (now) woefully inadequate fence.

Why in the gardening books do the flowers dance within film sets neatly bounded with regal yew hedges, antique brick walls and distant views of sheep-studded pastures when in the real world our plants have to perform in rather less salubrious settings?

## Framing the garden

Every shop window display relies not just on a suitable background but a sense of framing and our garden planting is no different. How we create a backdrop for our borders and what happens at the edges when they end and meet the rest of the garden is as important as the plants that form the heart of our planting.

## Backdrops

### Acknowledging the backdrop

The background incorporates not just the immediate things behind your planting like walls and fences but also the more distant environment if it can be seen. You may be more fortunate with your neighbours than my friends and your view over the fence might take in a snatch of greenery — a nice bit of neighbouring architecture or even a view. If this is the case then grab the opportunity. Don't

We can't all have a room with a view. By repeating key colours these keen gardeners have at least worked with their surrounds rather than fighting them. Full marks for enthusiasm!

automatically shut the world out; make the most of this 'borrowed scene' — it will blur the boundary between your property and the outside world and make your garden appear larger.

To use the views beyond your own garden it is best to somehow acknowledge them and reflect them within your own planting. A glimpse of softly rolling hills, for example, could be interpreted in your own planting with gently undulating mounds of shrubs indicative of the wider landscape. Even if you don't go a bundle on what's happening over the fence it is often best to work with it rather than fighting it. A copper beech in the distance might be 'acknowledged' by choosing dark cannas or cordylines on your side of the fence. With my friends' neighbours' mauve roof, I've suggested they abandon any urge for a hot border with reds and golds in favour of a scheme of soft yellows, which will look happy with the 'view' beyond.

## Screening

If things get real ugly over the garden fence, the best thing to do is to screen off the eyesore. Screening not only shuts out the outside world, it also conveniently hides your own boundaries. If your walls and fences are attractive then make a feature of them, but often we inherit a mixture of boundary styles and materials and it's just too expensive to consider replacing the lot when a few well-chosen bushes will hide a multitude of sins. Trees are usually a bad choice for screening.

A tree should be used for height, shade and a sense of scale but as a screen they invariably get just too large and greedy. The likes of palms or frangipani may look the part when you first plant them, but as they rocket up and lose the lower canopy you are left once again, staring out under the crown and over the fence.

Shrubs are the obvious choice for screening, they are often relatively quick and permanent, yet where space is a premium they can take up a lot of valuable room. Moreover, for instant effect, it is all too easy to opt for the fast growers, which inevitably get too large and demand regular clipping in a few years' time, after which they add insult to injury by going bare at the base. If you have room for good planting in front, this nudity at the base may not be a problem. Judicious pruning and feeding will also keep these shrubs well furnished from top to toe. If you can bear the wait, however, choose slower-growing species that will be less demanding. Keep your other planting at a slight distance away too, so that you can access the back and prune your chosen means of camouflage.

## Climbers

Climbers are so versatile. Some like native tecomanthe and parthenocissus have fantastic foliage and others dazzle with a show of flowers. Climbers are the perfect solution for covering up ugly boundaries, they are relatively quick and take up infinitely less space than shrubs. Often, however, they get overlooked as screening plants because we wrongly assume they won't grow any higher than the fence. It's true that while a clematis will just bend over and trail once it has scaled the heights, more woody climbers like mandevilla, podranea and gelsemium will keep going up. They readily form a sort of suspended hedge of upright, evergreen foliage, which can add up to a metre of screening on top of an existing fence or

Even the smallest view beyond the garden is an asset. The feel and colour of the hills glimpsed beyond are nicely acknowledged in this planting of gently rolling banks of natives such as flowering *Olearia cheesmanii*.

wall. If all else fails you can always add a layer of trellis to the top of a fence.

With all climbers it is important to keep them regularly trimmed so they don't balloon out into a haystack once they get their heads into the sun. On a sturdy wall this spread might be fine, but on a fence the weight of foliage catching a strong wind can cause everything to come crashing down. Good strong supports are the foundation of growing a satisfying blanket of climbers but often we avoid the time and effort of properly supporting our plants and wonder why they aren't doing the job.

One sneaky way out of this is to opt for the self-clingers like *Hydrangea petiolaris*, virginia creeper or ivy. But the problem with these wild rascals is what happens when they get through the fence into next-door's property? If your neighbours just happen to have painted their roof mauve you may not be losing much sleep over this possibility. Otherwise it is best to talk things through before you plant – often both properties will benefit from screening, and vines that are not self-clinging are a safer option for shared fences because if one party doesn't like the look they are easier to remove.

## Islands apart

Island beds present a particular challenge in dealing with the background to your planting as they have no obvious backdrop and their 'borrowed view' is your own garden. You might have seen those TV out-takes where, behind a news reader, someone is picking their nose or doing a 'Mr Bean' impersonation unaware that the camera is catching their every move.

By the same token, what goes on in the rest of your garden is usually helping or hindering the effect you are trying to create in an island bed. Sometimes it helps to step back and look at the 'big picture'. You might have a stack full of clever little plant combinations but it is the general scene that most people remember when they see your garden, not all the minutiae. So make sure any island plantings relate to the grand plan.

## Keep it simple

Whether it is shrubs, climbers or even tall perennials you choose for your backdrop, remember that the best living backgrounds are just that: backgrounds; so keep your screening simple. Like a theatre set your choice should be bold and dramatic but it shouldn't grab the attention from the main players in front.

*Bougainvillea* 'Scarlet O'Hara' dresses up an uninteresting wall. The planting in front of lychnis and epidendrum orchid celebrates rather than turns its back on the blazen backdrop.

It is so easy to try and cram the background full of interest and colour with a chocolate box of different species. The plants we choose should instead give a hint of the overall theme, but they shouldn't steal the show. Maybe a toon tree streaking in flamingo pink can be excused for a few weeks in spring before it settles into a more sedate green but a bank of yellow privet or flaming photinias will just hijack any bright ideas you might have for the planting in front.

Even a garden bed sculpted like a coastline will start simply at the back and become more intricate and detailed toward the front. Therefore in an informal design try and plant your backdrop with variously grouped plants rather than single specimens.

## Hedges

The hedge is the classic background for a more uniform and formal effect. Sleek, neat and subtle (unless planted in photinia), a wrap-around hedge is as sexy and timeless as a little black dress; the only trouble is it takes rather more work. Hedges work so well because their brutal simplicity unites all the planting in front as neatly as a ribbon wrapped round a present. Furthermore, being generally wide and flat, a hedge's strong sense of horizontal form counter-balances any strong verticals you might include in your planting like flower spikes and topiary spires.

If you have an attractive fence or wall but want to screen neighbours, pleached trees are a good idea. Plant a row of large shrubs or small trees and train them up and along horizontal wires to create a hedge on stilts. Species like callistemon, tilia and *Leptospermum nitidum* 'Copper Sheen' are good for this.

For background hedges, as with all screening, plants in quiet colours, such as the neutral grey of corokia or a classic dark green like camellia, work best. Be aware of bold foliage too. It can become a distraction in a border of soft and subtle species. Griselinia, for example, though it would make an excellent hedge for a native or tropical border, becomes overpowering behind a soft ethereal bed of perennials where it cuts a dash as subtle as a jumbo jet careering through a cloud. Plants with fine foliage generally make better background hedges because their small leaves recede into the distance, which makes your border seem that bit deeper. Hedges don't have to be straight — it may sound obvious but often when presented with a linear boundary we unthinkingly lay our plants out in a line. Scallops, zigzags and random curves can create intimate bays of planting which in a large border are useful for breaking up the monotony. Often these convoluted hedges leave gaps behind that can be filled with a feature tree, or as a hidden place for compost or a wheelbarrow store.

> ★ **PLANT PICKS: BACKGROUND HEDGES**
>
> *Abelia grandiflora*, camellia*, *Choisya ternata*, *Coprosma* 'Beatsons Brown'/'Beatsons Gold'/*repens*/*virescens*, *Corokia* x *virgata*, escallonia*, *Feijoa sellowiana*, *Griselina littoralis**, *Laurus nobilis**, *Muehlenbeckia astonii*, *Olearia albida*/*solandri*, *Osmanthus heterophyllus**, pittosporum, *Podocarpus totara**, *Rosmarinus officinalis*, *Spiraea* x *vanhouttei*, tecomaria, *Thuja plicata*, *Viburnum tinus* 'Eve Price'*, *Waterhousea floribunda**
>
> * suitable for shady conditions

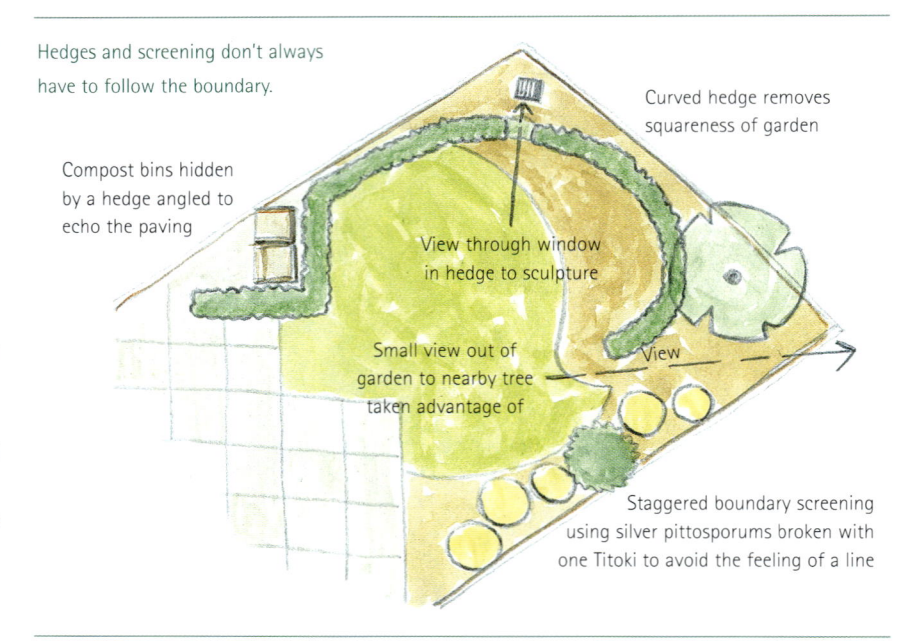

Hedges and screening don't always have to follow the boundary.

Curved hedge removes squareness of garden

Compost bins hidden by a hedge angled to echo the paving

View through window in hedge to sculpture

Small view out of garden to nearby tree taken advantage of

View

Staggered boundary screening using silver pittosporums broken with one Titoki to avoid the feeling of a line

Neither does a hedge have to look like a hedge. Plant one species irregularly across the back of a border rather than in a line and it can be lightly clipped into a cloud-like billowing screen.

**Opposite**

The brutal simplicity of a *Corokia* x *virgata* hedge binds up the complex planting in front as effectively as ribbon around a box of chocolates. The small leaves and gentle colour are the perfect backdrop for plants like *Craspedia globosa* (centre).

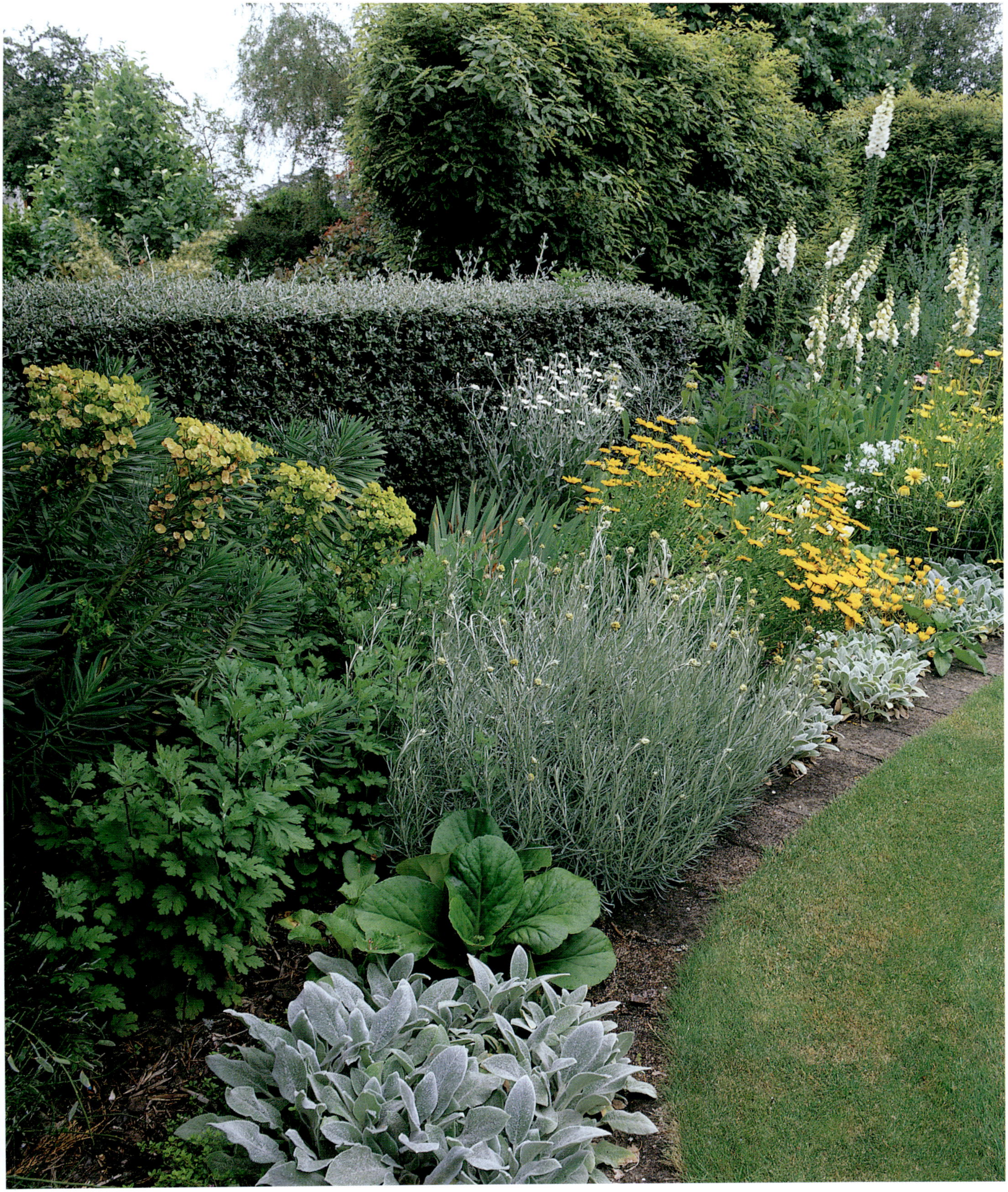

### Walls and fences

If you are lucky enough to own an attractive fence or wall then make the most of it. A good honest fence is nothing to be ashamed of and in more intimate spaces, painting such boundaries can add some permanent colour to our gardens and will show off our plants and foliage. Pale colours like creams and smoky greens and greys tend to recede and make the garden feel larger but they can easily get discoloured with algae and lichen. Deep colours like plum and midnight blue can look stunning, showing off lush foliage and flowers, but they tend to pull the boundaries in visually.

While powerful background colours allow you to design borders with foliage instead of flower power, you need to be confident that you love the colour because, unlike the flowers, it will be in your face for 12 months of the year! Coloured walls (and pots) can sometimes be a cop out from designing borders where the flowers pull the colour punches. With nature the effects are often more subtle and if you don't like them they are easily changed and reshuffled.

When a boundary is a feature in itself as with many modern urban gardens there is no need for heavy planting in front. Strongly structured and well-spaced plants work best. If sensitively lit they will cast dramatic shadows and act like pieces of sculpture. Below there will be an opportunity to play with finer tapestries of plants without the need for screening and height. With attractive walls neither are we limited to an evergreen palette because even when deciduous plants go bare the background will carry the garden.

## The front of the border
### Hard edges

A good edge not only defines a garden border — framing it and tying everything together — but it also has a practical aspect, stopping bark and soil from washing out onto paths and preventing the lawn from 'leaking' into the undergrowth. The biggest danger with formal edging is that it becomes too visible and we end up looking at the concrete mowing strip round the flowers rather than at the flowers themselves.

A well-constructed edge is often

*Pale walls recede and make narrow spaces feel larger. This coral pink shade is handled confidently with vireya rhododendron, spiky* Dracaena marginata *'Tricolor' and neoregelias.*

a necessity but it can also become a distraction. Gone are the days when we could just cut a 'V' round the edge of the lawn and whizz round with the edging shears to stop the wandering tentacles of kikuyu from having their wicked way with the roses. To me a good honest lawn edge is nothing to be ashamed of — well maintained, it is easy to keep sharp and tidy, but we seem to feel the need for something more sophisticated these days. The paved 'mowing strip' has become the low-maintenance panacea to all our woes — even if we do still need to get out a lawn edger from time to time. Certainly a strip of paving at the edge of a border can be useful but not just to reduce lawn edging. A proper edge if wide enough can act as an access path too for gardening in wet weather and as a place for plants to flop and billow naturally without being ravaged by a hungry lawn mower. Used like this, even harsh materials will be masked and softened with generous planting and the boundary where the planting ends and open space begins looks less contrived.

### Edging materials

Always use materials that are sympathetic to your style and low-key enough so that you notice the landscape rather than the landscaping. Choose materials that blend with existing features, particularly the house. Grey pavers will complement steel garden ornaments, bleached decks and pebbles, while warm, sandy colours and wood work well with terracotta pots, red brick and sandstone. The best edging is made of quality materials like brick or wooden sleepers firmly cemented in place and, when used well, they form an integral part of the garden's framework rather than looking like an after-thought. Punga logs, laid on their side, drilled and held in place with metal rods, make a soft and funky retaining for native and Pacific rim-style beds and simple pebbles and driftwood are just the ticket for a cruisy beach look with succulents lapping at the shore.

These more natural materials are preferable if you have serpentine and irregular bed shapes where concrete and brick might argue with the relaxed feel.

The worst kind of edging flaunts itself at the expense of the plants behind. Stones laid end to end can look the part for an informal seaside or Pacific-themed planting but if painted white they will look like a set of old dentures. It's a look that you may have got away with if you happened to own a rural motel back in the sixties, but it will hardly make the cut in the heart of the city. Concrete is hard to get right — it can look tacky and cheap or, on the other hand, funky and chic. The difference is scale. Poured by the truckload and polished to make monolithic walls and slabs, concrete looks stunning, but the edging strip sort you can buy precast into an 'L' shape will just make your border look like the verge of a state highway.

## Raised edges

Where planting is raised, garden edges are especially visible. Raised beds make a lot of sense. On heavy soils they are an opportunity to improve the drainage — in narrow spaces they allow us to lift our planting to display it better. Low walls can tame our jungles of precious plants and form the bones of our design. They make unofficial seats from which to weed or to stick our noses into the flowers and, best of all, they make the platforms off which any plant with an adventurous spirit can cascade and show off. But like all edges there are pitfalls and the worst is when the soil level behind the wall settles and sinks so low below the rim that trailing plants can't pole-vault over the top.

## Plants as edges

No matter how many weeds are sprouting in our garden beds, when the lawn is cut and the edges trimmed every garden looks fresh and tidy. It's the same with the plants that we put around the edges of our planted areas. Get these right and we will give the impression that we have our act together — no matter how scruffy our planting has become. You only have to look at those vast herbaceous borders of English stately homes to see how Lady

*Good edges show off rather than compete with the planting. In smaller gardens like Ian Fryer's, with quality materials, confident planting and well-thought-out shapes, edges can become a feature in themselves.*

Marchmont disguises all her bad planting and shoddy maintenance. When the delphiniums have come crashing down in a gale and the tansy is having its wicked way with the achilleas it's the tightly knitted hem of box hedging that contains the chaos and covers up the mess.

A retaining hedge is like a sticking plaster on a bad border — it instantly suggests a sense of style and stops the suicidal plants like geraniums from throwing themselves into the path of the lawn mower. Box, of course, is done to death but there are many other tidy plants that can make good hedges to create a neat edge. Not all of them are shrubs; you can do a very good stitching together job with self-supporting perennials such as dwarf asters and solidago. These plants may die in winter but they will still give a respectable hedge-like fuzz through the cold months.

Before we all rush out to wrap hedges around our borders bear in mind that a hedge is only suitable if it reflects the atmosphere you are trying to create. A hedge, whichever plant you choose, imposes a certain sense of formality on a garden and dressing up an informal lawn with clipped box can look as silly as insisting that a surfer wears a tie. Remember too that although hedges support flopping plants they prevent you from showcasing all manner of interesting and charming groundcovers and trailers. These might have otherwise spilled out of your beds and softened your planted edges in a less formal and low-maintenance way.

## Semi-formal and formal edges

Gardeners seem to be divided into two camps on edging. There are those who find it as artificial and constrained as seeing a lion caged behind bars, and there are those who get addicted and happily weed, divide and trim literally kilometres of regimented alyssum, lamb's ear and marjoram in piped edging around their planting.

In the semi-formal approach a single species of plant is repeated as a continuous band around a garden bed to give a definite frame without the fuss or impact of a hedge. Around informal beds, this approach of edging exclusively with one plant type can look over-contrived and unnecessary, but in more formal schemes and near to the house it adds a sense of unity and style to a planting. Any reasonably well-behaved groundcover will do the trick but evergreen species will be more practical. In a potager the upright form of chives or tulbaghias (society

---

### Above left
Low hedges are especially useful for caging in boisterous planting, particularly where paths are narrow.

### Above right
Gravel is the perfect invisible edging — it allows plants to express themselves.

### Opposite
Paths and steps should be a stage set for plants as much as a way from A to B. When we make them generously proportioned we won't begrudge growth billowing out and softening the harsh lines.

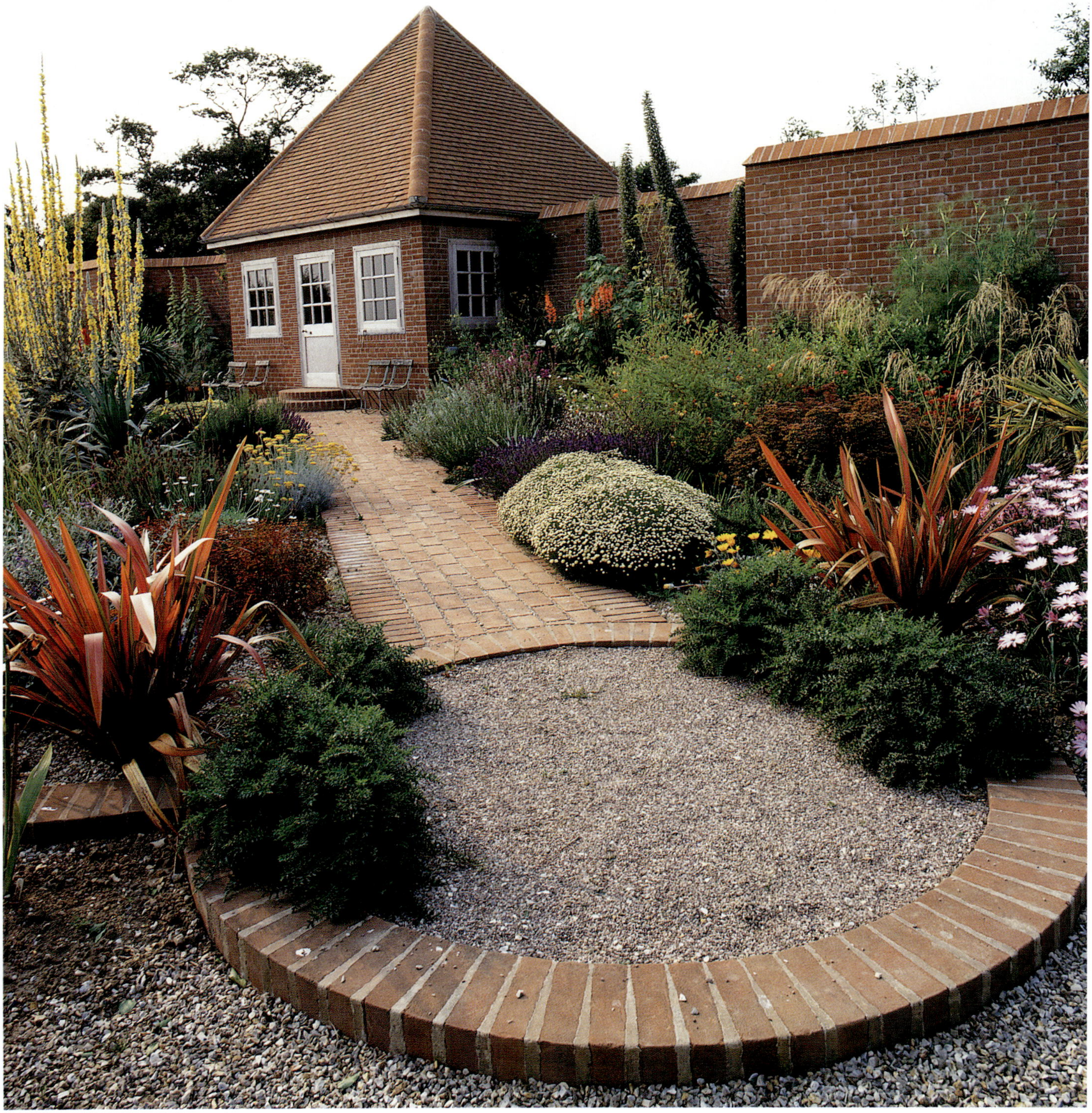

garlic) will not flop onto narrow paths and will deter bugs from the vegetables. In the flower garden mats of pinks and thrift are soft and comforting while traditionally the stronger foliage of bergenia and stachys (lamb's ear) have been valued. All these plants, even if you don't choose to plant them in lines but rather in informal splashes, will make great edging plants to the border.

The informal approach to edging is simply to let a mixture of plants lap at the shore between lawn, path and the planted earth. Here our shoreline approach comes to the fore — tall plants can fill to the edges and low carpeters can seep out into the depths of the border. The only real constraint is to make sure small, sun-loving plants near the front are getting enough light and air and are not being engulfed by over-enthusiastic neighbours.

## Diffusing the edges

Though gardeners used to get very worked up about the state of their edges, today we are much more relaxed and fluid about our garden boundaries. There is no unspoken law that says that edges need to exist at all — all of nature is one great, interwoven tapestry after all, where each habitat drifts imperceptibly into its neighbour.

In naturalistic settings, especially in larger country gardens, by resisting the temptation to dig a little ditch between the green sweep of the lawn and your borders, a seamless join will be far more friendly than any scaled-down version of the Berlin Wall. Use a weed eater or a herbicide and allow the grass to flow into and under the drooping leaves of anemones or to thin and peter out under the heavy shade of trees. With good foliage plants at the edge of borders and judicious use of gaps, your planting will ebb and flow nicely and the lawn will do the same.

Where planting meets hard surfaces the best way to blur the boundary is to let your plants do what they do best — flop and flow. Go for species that will consciously bulge out and melt like candlewax down low walls and across paving. Cushion plants like gazanias, arctotis and dwarf conifers or hebes planted close to the edge are ideal for this sort of softening. They weld together the hard landscaping and the planting, and create a unified design.

## Gravel gardens

One of the most exciting ways of landscaping that has emerged in recent years is when plants are allowed to spill out and not be contained in well-defined spaces. Instead, they are threaded through areas of harder landscaping so that the boundary edges between 'borders', paths and entertaining become blurred. In nature, of course, plants are never hemmed into flower beds so this style of planting is perfect for a fluid and naturalistic look reminiscent of deserts, riverbank or seashore.

Landscapers and gardeners like John Brooks, Beth Chatto and in New Zealand Ted Smyth have led the way in making gravel gardening immensely popular. Gravel sets plants off well; it is clean and fresh looking, is hard enough to walk on but malleable enough to let plants pop up and seed about. Most plants seed enthusiastically into gravel so avoid laying it on bare soil if you want a low-maintenance mulch. Instead, lay weed mat underneath. In gravel the weeds come up along with the aquilegias and poppies but at least, with all its air holes, the undesirables will pull out easily. The thicker you lay gravel, the less seeding you will enjoy or suffer depending on your outlook.

For the plants the great virtue of gravel is that it shades their roots and conserves water in summer. In winter too, because the top layer is so free draining it also plays an important role in keeping

---

### PLANT PICKS: LOW HEDGES

★ *Agonis flexuosa* 'Nana', argyranthemum, *Azalea* 'Kurume'*, *Berberis thunbergii* 'Atropurpurea', *Buxus sempervirens**, *Camellia* 'Baby Bear'*, *Coprosma* 'Cutie'/'Evening Glow'/'Fireburst'/'Karo Red'/'Cappucino'/'Mangitangi', *Cuphea hyssopifolia* 'White Whisper', *Erica carnea* 'Springwood White'*, *Escallonia* 'Red Dream', *Euonymus fortunei* 'Emerald Gem'*, *Euonymus japonicus* 'Macrophyllus'*, *Hebe topiaria*/'Beverley Hills'/*diosmifolia*/'Margaret', *Ilex crenata**, *Lavandula stoechas*, *Leptospermum scoparium* 'Nanum Kea'/'Nanum Kiwi', *Metrosideros carmineus*, *Nandina* 'Gulfstream', *Parahebe catarractae* 'Snowcap'*, sarcococca*, *Teucrium fruticans/chamaedrys*

★ **Non shrubs for edging:** alchemilla, allium (chives), armeria (thrift), aster, eg, *A. lateriflorus* 'Horizontalis', bergenia, dianthus, *Erigeron* 'L.A. Pink', felicia, *Hemerocallis* 'Stella d'Oro'/'Sherwood Gladiator', *Libertia ixioides**, nemesia, *Nepeta* 'Superba', petroselinum (parsley)*, solidago (dwarf), stachys (lambs ear), tulbaghia, grasses like carex, helictotrichon and festuca

*suitable for shady conditions*

**Above**

Lapping at the shores: planting in gravel can be wonderfully fluid. When bulbs or annuals, like these petunias, ebb and flow with the seasons, with such an attractive mulch below, the garden will still look complete.

**Right**

On a bend a dramatic 'set piece' is filled with heuchera and wrapped up neatly with *Carex hachijoensis* 'Evergold', which adds formality and style but is less work than a hedge.

## TIPS FOR GRAVEL GARDENS

In choosing and using plants in gravel areas it is worth considering a few points.

- **Choose good lookers.**
  Because planting can be sparse and diffused, this style of gardening relies particularly heavily on plants with good all-round looks.

- **Don't worry about plant heights.**
  Because we can walk between and around everything, enjoying the planting from all angles, planting heights can be varied endlessly.

- **Keep things light.**
  Natural gravel areas like beaches, braided rivers and mountains tend to be exposed and harsh environments that often dry out severely in summer. Though tropical plants look good in association with pebbles, it is the lighter drought-adapted plants that look most at home and will provide translucent veils of planting — often these plants have small waxy or glaucous leaves.

- **Take the gravel look and apply it to other media.**
  Crushed shell, scoria and bark chip can all be used to create a sort of fluid interface where plants merge imperceptibly with our living areas. Usually there will still be conventional areas of thicker planting, often at the rear to hide garden boundaries, but as the planting thins, tall, veil-like and architectural plants can form headlands and islands with inlets of mulch between.

- **Keep on top of maintenance.**
  For all its romance the drawback of this style of gardening is that gravel, even with weed mat beneath, often suffers from weed problems after a few years. If you include self-seeding plants as part of your selection, nature will quickly turn your oasis into a thicket so stay busy and restrict the use of self-seeders.

dry the necks of plants like succulents, alpines and Mediterranean shrubs, which easily rot off in cold, wet soils. For the gardener though, gravel just looks good, and as herbaceous plants and seasonal bulbs are cut down or die away the spaces left, whether temporary or permanent, always look attractive.

The diffuse look and intermingling of plants and living space can be incredibly dynamic and exciting in the gravel garden. As planting thins out, in the clearings we can have chairs and tables, paths and places for sculpture. Plants can swell and peter out in an uncluttered way. Where in a traditional border we would feel the need to plant up all the gaps to hide the bare ground, in the gravel garden when plants die and are cleared away we can leave a seasonal space knowing that the gravel looks good enough on its own.

## FOOD FOR THOUGHT

☆ Are you making the most of any borrowed views from your property?

☆ Which sections of your boundary need better screening? Should the screening be formal or loose, of one species or several?

☆ Is there a place you could create a gravel garden where the border/living space boundary is blurred?

☆ Have you considered using perennials as an alternative to low hedging?

☆ Hedges can be overdone — they can straightjacket a garden. How is your design in this department?

☆ Are your border edges too obtrusive? Do you notice them before you notice the plants?

☆ Are your edges a pleasing shape? Wiggles and straight lines never mix well.

☆ Have you allowed plants to flop and soften the edges of the garden?

Chapter 14

# Added Extras

*garden features and pots*

THE COFFEE STAINS were only skin deep. As the layers of paint rolled back, softened by the stripping chemical, the original glow of the oak wood started to show through. Over the years someone had added an intricate beading around the top and claw feet on the legs to give the table extra height but these were gently pulled away and a week later the restoration was complete. Gone was the bright green paint, as well as the superfluous adornments and the crusting of years. We were left with beautiful bones: a strong and simple kitchen table just as it had been intended — no frills, but classic good looks.

## Do you need extra interest?

A perfectly good garden can easily become spoilt with too many added extras. It seems that a place to sit and some good plants aren't enough these days. We have mags and spoilers for the car, face plates for the phone and the garden too has to have its adornments — lighting, water features, sculpture and pots, pots, pots. They are all very beautiful but in decorating are we not — quite literally — trying to gild the lilies?

My dad is great out on the open golf course but his game turns to custard on the mini golf. As gardeners we can be the same — good at arranging plants in a garden border but without a clue when it comes to placing, choosing and using all the added extras which seem to come with the modern garden.

Though magazines and makeovers would have us include fairylights and red walls, mirrors and neon mobiles, most often it's simply a pot, a seat, a piece of sculpture or a water feature that we choose. These features often cost far more than any of the plant material and usually become a major focal point so we need to choose and site them carefully.

The first question to ask when considering such additions is: do I need a point of extra interest in this part of the garden at all? When we are ruthless often

Added extras can help enliven a planting. This is a cheap and simple use of bamboo poles stepping out a rhythm and fortifying the blue of Chatham Island forget-me-nots in Gwyn Masters' Taranaki garden.

the answer will be 'no'. As we have seen, 'dull' patches of subdued or simple planting can be valuable in themselves as restful breathing spaces as part of the grand plan. Other unsatisfactory beds might better be enlivened with improved planting rather than another dominating and often expensive element. In our age of makeover gardening it's always tempting to throw in a feature like a pot or a statue because it can provide an instant fix, but often these superfluous distractions can shatter the unity and flow in a garden. With features, less is definitely more.

## Providing a sense of focus

While it is relatively easy to cram plants together and get away with it, a glut of 'features' can produce something restless and fragmented. Such gardens start to resemble a bric-a-brac shop rather than a relaxing haven. The trouble with a garden packed with pots or features is that, although it's exciting and stimulating, the charm is short lived. Like a real junk shop, you may enjoy a visit for an hour or so, but you wouldn't want to live there and our own gardens have to be livable.

Where a definite focal point is needed in a design, however, often at the natural termination of a narrow space or at the crux of a bend, it's perfectly desirable to provide something to lift and enhance the planting to a more sophisticated level. Large pots and sculptures used in a purposeful way are like the conductor of an orchestra — they give a sense of focus to a particular part of the garden and can give a heart to a group of plants which otherwise had no anchor point. Topiary and feature plants have the same function, of course, but they never have quite the clout of something more definite and high profile.

# Principles for choosing features

Whatever basic features you include, here are seven basic principles to follow in choosing them so that they enhance rather than detract from your plants.

### 1 Choose the feature to fit the setting

It would be less than inconsiderate to arrive home having bought a new pet doberman dog without first consulting your family. Yet how often do we return home with a pot or object that we bought on the spur of the moment without considering the effect it will have on our other garden elements and planting?

Any piece should relate to the overall style of your garden — a red glazed vase, for example, will look far too sophisticated and smart in a rambling country garden and conversely a piece of driftwood might look too casual and raw in a city courtyard of steel and polished stone. Sometimes it's good to have a few oddballs thrown in for the shock factor but only where you have already established a strong sense of identity in the garden as a whole and can confidently break the 'rules'. A common mistake is to buy the right pot but underestimate the size and find that it looks inadequate in its new home. Always do a dummy run at home first with another pot, a bit of wood or cardboard to remove the guesswork. Impulse buying of garden features purely because they appeal is a mistake — buy them instead because they will do the specific job you have in mind for a particular corner of the garden.

### 2 Choose a setting to fit the feature

The more complicated or ornate the pot or feature the simpler should be the setting. Small pots look lost in bold foliage and large pots tend to look incongruous — like a bull in a china shop — among fine planting and fiddly jumbles of leaves.

If you can, try to contrast the texture of pot and planting. For example, a shiny bronze urn would sit well among a carpet of dull chocolate-coloured carex because it's a harmonious colour but a very different texture.

Bright-coloured pots and sculpture are always difficult to integrate into the garden. It is best to echo the colours in the surrounding foliage. If the colour spreads out from the central feature the harshness of the colour will be diffused into the body of the border.

### 3 Less is more

Too many distractions can disturb the unity and flow in a garden. Aim for as few features as are needed rather than clutter.

---

Opposite above left

Native tussock and alpines enhance the rugged feel of these hypertufa sculptures by Stan Matovich.

Opposite above right

Rustic features collected locally make excellent focal points. This lightning conductor has a suitably rusty backdrop of *Carex flagellifera*.

Opposite below left

Classical statuary would look out of place in the jungle but Jeff Thomson's corrugated-iron cow is right at home munching among the nikau.

Opposite below right

Intricate sculpture and pots need simple settings. This airy piece is ideally placed in simple green foliage where we can see through to the sea.

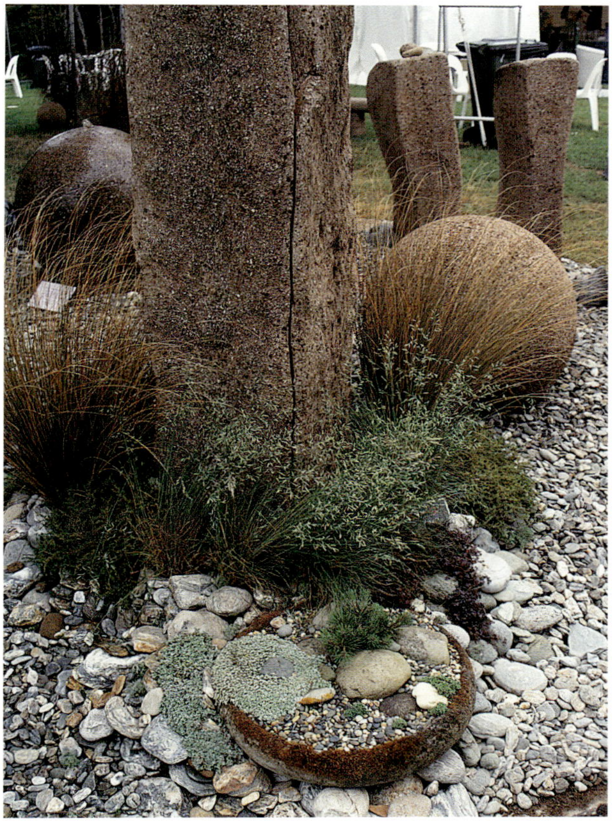
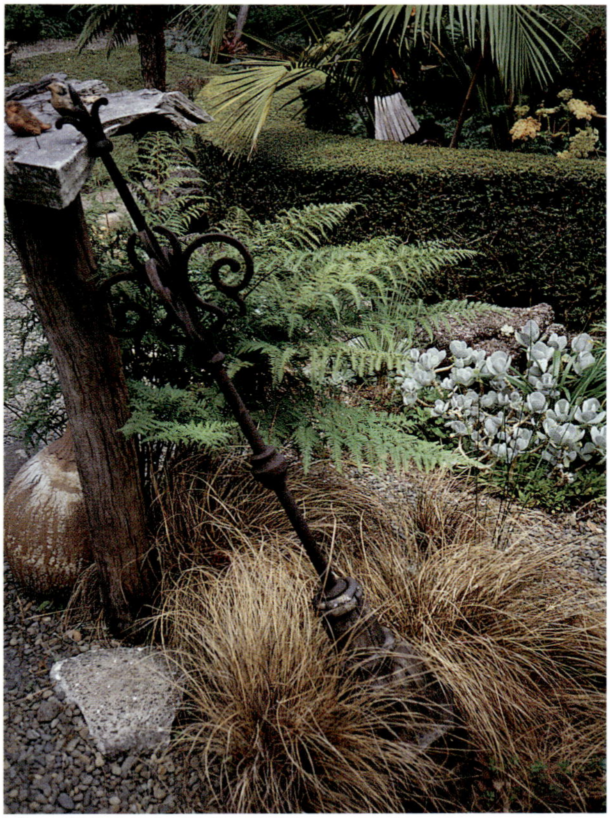
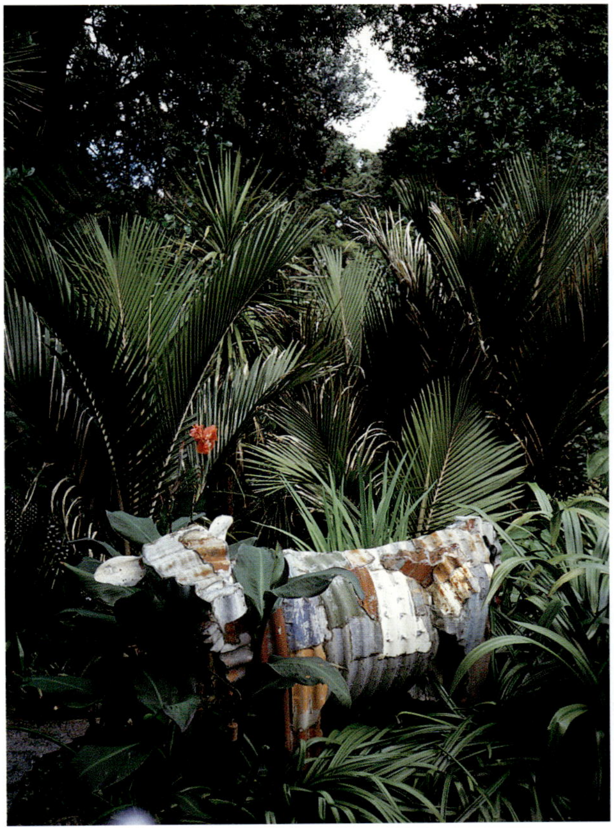
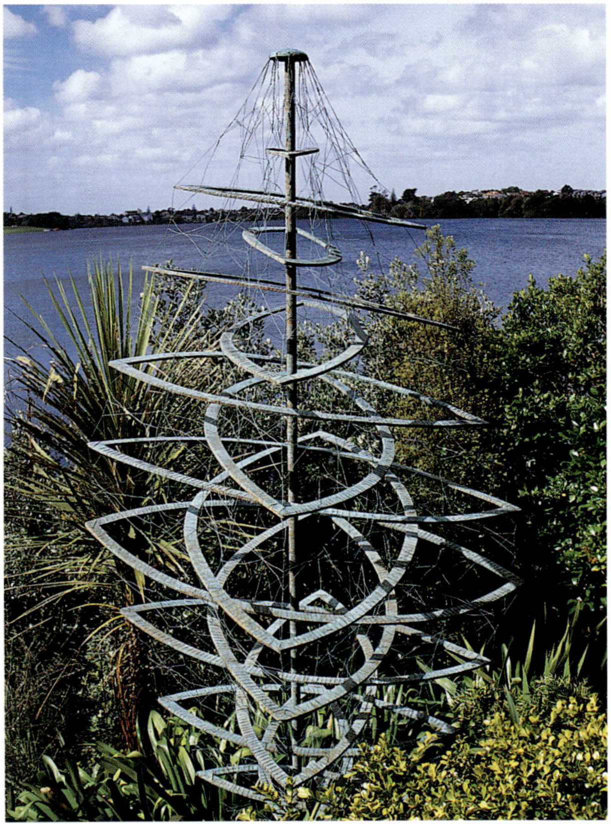

### 4 Choose materials sympathetic to the site

So often we get given pots in a kaleidoscope of colours and styles. If the different features in your garden don't relate either in style, materials or colour, they will look uncomfortable together and will blur your sense of style. As with your own family, plants, pots and sculpture should each have their own unique identities but should look at least vaguely related to one another.

### 5 Nestle features in

Sometimes because we have spent a lot of money on a feature we put it in the most obvious place in the garden where everyone is bound to trip over it and comment. Some people garden as if every dollar they spend has to be seen from the living-room window. When features are nestled into nooks and crannies, however, with perhaps just a tantalising glimpse, the garden becomes a treasure hunt and we are led out to discover what's around the next corner. Like a Jelly Tip ice cream, a good garden reveals its inner layers, only after a bit of blissful excavation.

### 6 Features need to be in scale with their setting

Sometimes the features we have in the garden have shrunk out of scale as their surroundings have grown and burgeoned. Our eyes are terrible at guessing the size of things from a distance so we get clues from our surroundings. For example, a terracotta oil jar may look huge at the far end of a lawn but when someone unexpectedly walks past we see that the pot doesn't even reach their waist.

Similarly, if planting around features is low and composed of small-leafed plants (and there are no nearby buildings or fences to give our eyes a sense of scale), a feature can look larger than it really is when viewed from afar. Conversely, if the plants around a feature are large and lush-leafed, the feature will look dwarfed by its surroundings. This optical effect is worth taking note of.

### 7 Big features are best

Get the wallet out and always buy the biggest pot or sculpture you can afford. Regardless of your garden's size boldness equates with confidence and confidence suggests style. In a large, open garden a small feature will look lost in the scale of the setting so features on a theatrical scale are especially important.

One way to place smaller objects to maximum advantage is to position them in confined areas where we can't view them from a distance. When we see objects close-to, the scale of the surroundings becomes less important as we are more focused on the object. Even the biggest of gardens have hidden corners where small pots will look at home.

Don't be tempted, though, in a small garden to only use pint-sized features. Knickknacks might look appropriate as details and surprises, but to increase the sense of space in a tight area go for an oversized piece of sculpture or pot. For some reason the confidence and boldness of such features pushes out the boundaries and lends a larger-than-life feel to the entire garden.

*Not all added extras need to be 'in your face'. Hidden in a corner, this fern-inspired sculpture is almost upstaged in summer by a bank of lively iresines. Sculpture is very much part of the Pacifica style.*

## Inflating your features

If you have pots or sculpture that you like the position of, but realise that they might be out of scale with the adjacent planting, there are ways of pumping up the impact. Here are six angles to try.

### 1 Raise your pots and sculpture

Planters often look best nestled in foliage but why hide something you paid good money for? It's easy to swamp small features in foliage so raise them up on bricks or wooden blocks and hide these with the foreground planting. Pots still look best sitting comfortably in the surrounding plants so try and get a balance, blurring the edges of a pot with planting but still creating impact. If you choose an attractive material that is sympathetic (not necessarily identical) to the main feature you might even go so far as to create a plinth or column that will elevate a feature further. Though visible the column should not take the limelight from the pot; for example, don't put a red glazed jar on a red pole!

### 2 Package your feature

Make more of small features by creating an eye-catching formal backdrop that becomes part of the focal point and increases its impact. In the shop window scenario, imagine a diamond displayed raw on a wooden block. Now imagine the same diamond on a bed of red satin in a smart case — same feature but the difference is good packaging. Pots and sculpture can be placed against trellis panels, feature walls or more subtly set in clipped topiary alcoves or within frames draped with climbers to bolster their sense of importance.

### 3 Illuminate with leaves

One of the more subtle ways to increase the impact of a man-made feature in your planting is to highlight it with suitable foliage. As we have already seen cream, white or grey foliage naturally draws the eye, so if you place these around a feature pot in the border you are sending a clear message where the focus of attention is to be. Dark features made of wood or bronze especially benefit from being thrown into relief by a light backdrop.

Any coloured leaves can be used en masse to grab the eye, but it's important to take your cues from the colour of the pot or piece of sculpture. Copper ages to an especially unusual patina stained with turquoise, so by linking this in with blue conifers, succulents or plants nearby like *Acaena caesiiglauca* you not only reinforce the impact of your container but help to acknowledge its presence in a planting.

### 4 Acknowledge a pot's presence

Have you ever been invited to a party and been left standing like a turkey in the middle of the room — feeling like everyone's eyes were on you for all the wrong reasons? Often we buy an extrovert pot, place it in a vacuum of subdued planting and wonder why it sticks out like a sore thumb. Brightly coloured pots and sculpture are notoriously difficult to sit comfortably in a border, but it will help

---

Four ways to increase the impact of pots.

1. Create a backdrop — a formal trellis, screen or clipped hedge. Good packaging is everything.
2. Raise your planter. A pedestal can be ornamental or hidden with greenery.
3. Put dramatic plants in your pots, planting in scale to the pot.
4. Group your pots — either the same-size pots repeated formally or a 'family' group as shown below.

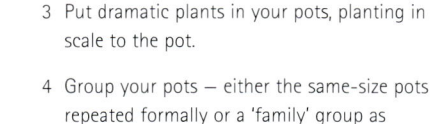

enormously, having set your heart on that canary yellow tub, if you drizzle a thread of gold through the surrounding planting. I call this acknowledging the presence of a pot. As mentioned earlier, the shared colours echo and spread out from the central feature and the result is a diffusing of the harshness into the body of the border.

### 5 A storm in the calm

Rather than drawing attention to a feature by raising the drama using coloured foliage and backdrops you can go to the other extreme and calm the planting down to such a subdued level that a feature stands out in the surrounding quietness. This approach works particularly well with features that are highly ornate in their detailing and require a calm setting to play against the busyness of the details.

Subdued backdrops also work well with quietly coloured features made of materials like wood, copper and lead, which find it hard to compete for attention with bright surroundings. For quiet backdrops use a single plant species repeated. Dull textures and small, simple green leaves work well. Clipped hedges and topiary are classic ways to wrap up subtle surprises in this way.

### 6 Safety in numbers

It's a fact that part of the reason zebras developed the herding instinct was to appear larger and more formidable in the face of predators. When we group puny pots together they look less lonely for a start and increase their impact in the garden setting. Related to this idea is that of duplicating a feature for added impact. One large pot might look good but five placed through a planting randomly or marching through with a formal rhythm will give an added sense of confidence and style. It's a trade secret of design that if you repeat your mistakes often enough and with conviction it will look like you know what you are doing.

In gardening, in the absence of knowledge, confidence is the next best standby. So don't leave that single blue vase perched in the border like a piece of lost baggage on the station platform; get several more and thread them through and everyone will applaud your courage and flair. Even something as simple and inexpensive as a family of bamboo poles painted a strong colour can become a piece of abstract sculpture woven through your plants if you carry the idea off with conviction.

Above

This seat and sundial feel very much part of this scene because their colours are carefully acknowledged in the planting around them, like the honey colour of libertias and *Sedum adolphi*.

Opposite above

Classical statues are notoriously hard to integrate into modern gardens. But with a bit of moss and the help of a tree trunk even a classical marble nude finds a comfortable place to undress at Ayrlies.

Opposite below

Bright mosaic work and bold patterns suit the swagger of succulents but care needs to be taken that as they swell they don't upset the proportions and make the pot seem small.

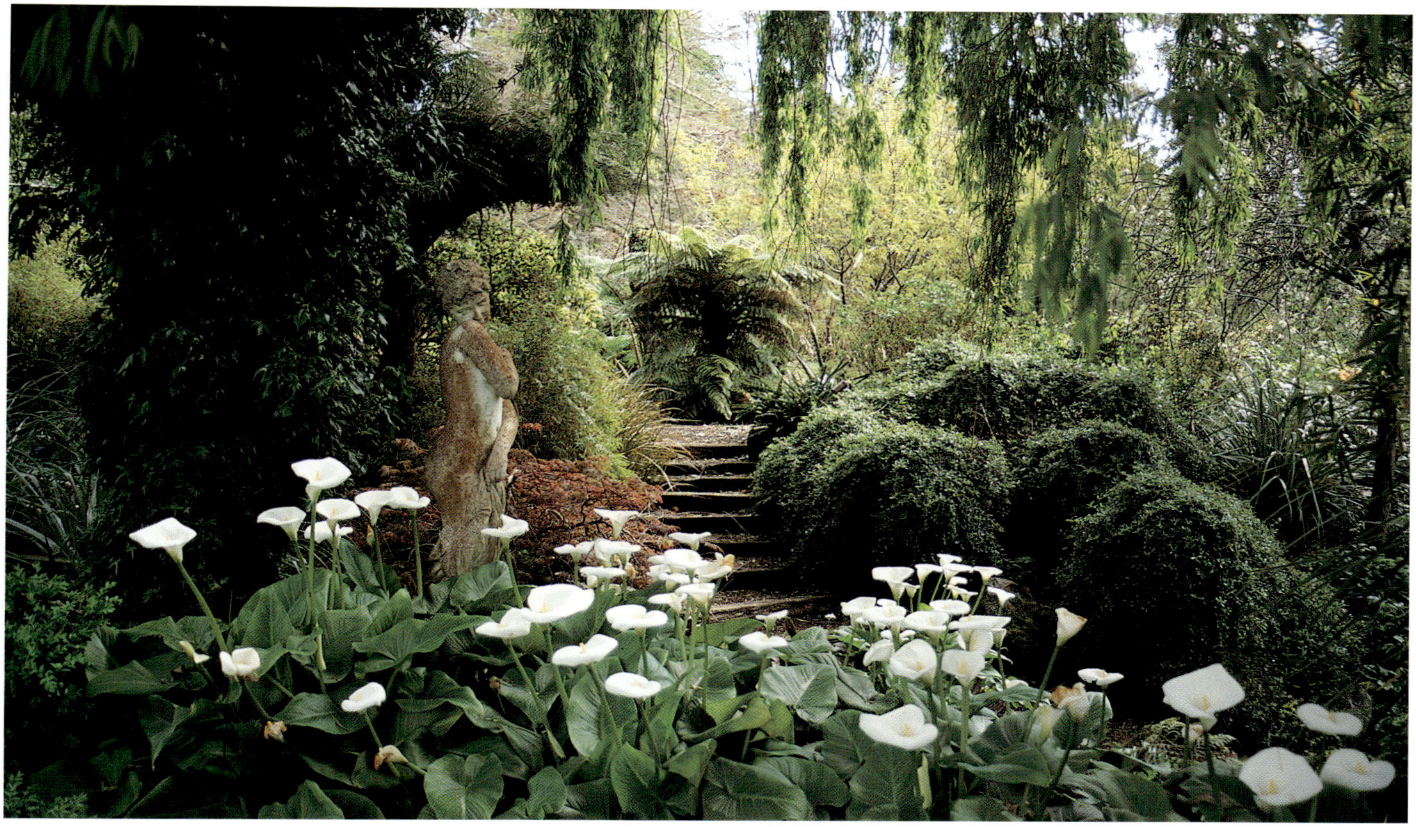

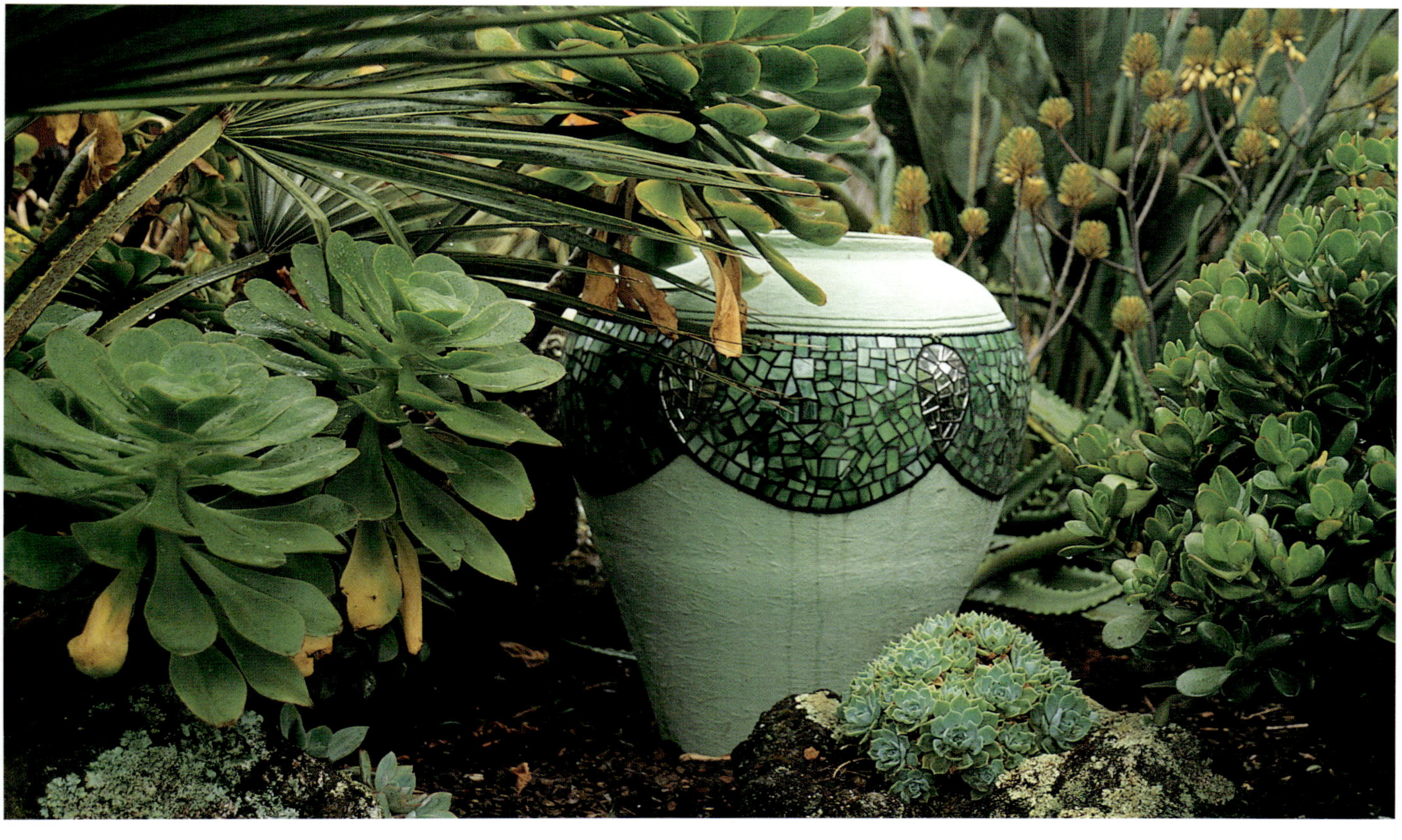

On a terrace or deck a row of identical pots will have far more impact than one or two. Again in a less formal way, a family group of containers of varying height will become a major focal point rather than if they had been spread out like a rag tag scattering without any apparent purpose.

## Pots

Pots are a special kind of garden feature. They are the one added extra most of us own and using them purposefully takes particular skill. We fall down mainly with pots when we have too many, too much of a mixture and we group our pots poorly or not at all.

### Pot-crammers' syndrome

The simplest way you can improve the look of your garden is to throw away most of your pots; it is the piece of advice I give out most often to clients. Gardeners seem to collect pots as fast as a bookshelf gathers dust. We dot them around like confetti round a church gate under the mistaken assumption that a pot will cheer up any dull corner. Pots rarely cheer anything up; more often than not they clutter things up. Forgotten plants hang around clinging gloomily to life, crying out to be put out of their misery. The brighter the colour these pots are the worse is the offence. In the depths of winter when the garden should be allowed the decency of taking things easy a bright blue oil jar is about as appropriate as a belly dancer at a funeral.

Fortunately, though, pot-crammers' syndrome is curable — all you need is a sledgehammer and a skip and the first place to lay the hammer is on your pint-sized pots.

Small containers have little impact in the garden yet often they are to be found swarming round our decks like aphids on a rose bud. They are not just fussy, they are impractical. Plants don't dance in ballet-shoe-sized containers — they wilt and die as soon as you turn your back so lay the boot in. A good guide about what to discard is to bin anything you can lift easily.

If you can't bear to throw containers away herd all your superfluous pots to a space behind the shed. Let them be joined by any other knickknacks — gnomes, photographic plant labels and poems on sticks that have crept into your borders and there, out of harm's way, create a shrine to tastelessness and clutter.

In the end pots are work. Unless you live on solid clay most plants will grow better out in the open ground. Though beautiful and useful near to the house on patios and decks to soften hard surfaces, in a flower bed there is little need to have your plants in pots unless you want to create a sense of formal rhythm or a focal point, or show off something special.

---

The same plant repeated in several pots brings a unifying sense of calm to a terrace or deck — especially if your pots are a mixture of sizes.

## What to put in a pot

Many books cover at length container gardening so we won't go down that path. Planting principles are the same whether you are planting a 50-foot square border or a window box. A container, however, is a special little presentation of plants. It is raised up and dressed up so your planting has to look especially good and for a decent length of time.

Pots are treacherous places for plants so it's best to choose the real toughies that will forgive you if you go on holiday and abandon them. Here are a few more design issues to consider which might make your container gardening more pleasurable.

## Drama or subtlety?

Plants in a pot are rather like the hairstyles we choose to complement our face. Cheap and nasty pots need a bit of glamour upstairs and classy pots need something simple that won't steal the show. It's an unofficial rule that the amount of money we spend on a container is inversely proportional to the number of plants we put into the top of it.

With an ornate and flashy pot you don't need to gild the lily — just play it simple with the hairpiece on top and use a single species preferably without eye-grabbing flowers. Better still, forget the plants all together. If a pot is attractive enough and sculptural enough to stand alone then resist the need to plant it up at all.

## Mixed planting or not?

Cramming several different plants into a small pot is about as attractive a habit as those who stack their plates with everything on offer at a smorgasbord. Yes, it is nice to have a bushy plant, a poky plant and a trailer jostling together but save it for a half barrel or something with the diameter of a dustbin lid where there will be room to create a proper composition. Bedding plants and bulbs, topiary standards with a froth of flowers beneath — all such combinations work well in larger containers.

Always try and limit sophisticated planting to formal areas near the house where they are easy to water and place them in simple settings. Conversely, if a container is sited in a garden bed among mixed planting, always plant it with something classically simple and bold.

## Use the same plant in lots of pots

This trick is especially effective where you have a mishmash of different containers and you want to create a relationship between them. By avoiding the temptation to have a different specimen in every pot you will enhance the unity and restfulness of your garden. At Ayrlies a bright blue swimming pool was made to look less incongruous by placing groups of hypertufa bowls on the surrounding paving, all filled with icy *Echeveria elegans*.

## Use a big plant in a small pot

Not normally the rule, you can only get away with this if the plant looks comfortable in its toe-crunching home. Epiphytes like vireya rhododendrons, epidendron orchids and bromeliads all thrive in cramped accommodation and look strangely at home. Tough natives too, like an astelia or cabbage tree, can look good in a cosy setting where they add a slight Dr Seuss quality.

## Never use a small plant in a big pot

Awful! Pots need to look exuberant — like they are overflowing. There is no place for hesitant plants in containers.

## Avoid too much dangly planting

Trailing plants in a pot and planting around the base are useful for softening a feature but you don't want to hide your pot — that is, unless it is cheap and nasty when it will be highly desirable to cover it up. With fancy pots make sure the greenery is not masking the beauty and impact of your feature.

*The more you spend on a pot, the less you put in it. These sempervivums will swell but they won't dangle and swamp this elegant vase. The planting of heuchera and black mondo below ensure this feature is anchored into its setting.*

A haircut to suit the face: tall, thin containers suit extreme plants, either tall themselves or flat and weepy.

### Use extreme plants in extreme pots

People always tend to put tall plants in tall pots. This is a good rule of thumb, creating some good upward thrust, but you can also get away with putting a totally prostrate plant in a tall pot. It works because the droopy plant and upright form of the pot present a nice contrast — and for the practical reason that a tall pot gives plenty of scope for some serious dangling. Tall pots are an extreme shape so they suit extreme plants. What they despise is average-shaped plants moving in on their space — these average 'joes' will just extinguish all the drama.

Short, low pots and wide dishes are different again. Tall plants look very odd in these so go for something dribbly and flat.

### Shuffle your pots

Containers are a great place for luxuries and treats that can be wheeled on stage for their finest hour then swapped with something else. Bring house plants out for a summer holiday. Shunt spring bulbs off the stage when they have finished. Put them behind the shed and wheel on your summer lilies. Never put up with sad-looking plants tapping at the French doors. Move them out of sight until they get their act together. There will, of course, be your sedentary elements but as for the rest — have fun. Mobility is one of the inherent beauties of pots. With suitably themed planting you can produce show-stopping seasonal splashes of interest at significant times of the year.

### FOOD FOR THOUGHT

☆ Have a pot count up. What are your added extras saying? Are they placed in a meaningful way — repeated or grouped as focal points, or are they scattered?

☆ Have a look at the materials and colours of your garden features — is there an obvious harmony and relationship? Do they nestle in or stick out?

☆ How about your pot planting — is it exuberant and appropriate, not just for the pot beneath but for the setting too?

☆ Are you blending bright pots into the landscape by picking up on the colour with the planting around?

Chapter 15

# Tight Fit

*making the best of small spaces*

Line up, but don't shut up: they may not have much room to play but these creamy caladiums and scented nicotianas are not letting it dampen their spirits.

THE AIRPORT WELCOMES with a labyrinth of chrome posts and blue tape — we snake around the maze trying not to ram the ankles in front with our trolley and ask the eternal question — why is the next queue moving so much faster? New Zealanders hate to queue yet we find ourselves doing it more and more. At the bank they dress up their meagre staffing levels with a tasteful zigzag of polished wooden railings and a few pot plants. There we can read a leaflet about taking out a second mortgage or watch a telly on the wall as we shuffle forward. Traffic lights, supermarket checkouts or firing squad — it's all the same: line up, shut up and shuffle forward.

## Pint-sized borders

In today's smaller gardens plants are increasingly having to wait their turn and line up as flower beds get more emaciated and lose ground in the demand for outdoor living. Everywhere decks, terraces and low-maintenance gravel areas are eating away at our green spaces, but that doesn't mean we have to be unimaginative when it comes to planting what remains.

In fact the less room we have to play with, the greater the need to be cunning in the way we treat these pockets of planting. Narrow beds that edge a driveway or a fence, or wrap around a courtyard area, are often the mainstay of the garden. But being universally long and narrow it is hard to arrange our plants so they don't look like thugs lined up for a police mug shot. Here are some ideas that will help.

## Plant across the space

In a thin bed it seems the most natural thing in the world to plant your plants in lines. When plants are planted like this our eyes are swept along and as well as a feeling of movement the border seems even longer and narrower. But if we fight the urge, go against the flow and let our plants cut across the natural line we can make a narrow border feel wider and more spacious, whether we do it in formal bands of planting or natural ribbons.

For the informal look, it is especially important to fight the overriding sense of narrowness, the rigidity and the strong horizontal lines of walls and fences. So vary your plant heights and widths and plant in blocks and ribbons that cut across the border rather than following it along. In formal schemes repeat plant groups symmetrically across any central path.

## Keep it simple

Reduced space demands a reduced palette of plants. Each plant is more visible and cannot blend in with the crowd so we will need top performers that will work hard as a team.

Nearly always in a narrow border the first planting technique to employ is repetition. For a formal look a blatantly minimalist treatment is often the best approach. The planting can get as sophisticated and complex as you like in places where beds fatten but along the base of fences a single strip of one species can give a classic simplicity that will create an overall sense of unity and purpose. An impeccably smart line of clipped bay trees down one side of the garden or along a side passage draws the eye along quickly and easily.

## Choose slimline plants

Do away with more voluminous shrubs — those gut-busting embarrassments which develop middle-age spread — in favour of more streamlined specimens. Say your goodbyes to the likes of hibiscus, pittosporum, hebe and griselinia unless you are prepared to perform rigorous trimming and training. Instead, bring in climbers, slimline plants and looser toe

Two narrow beds. In the right-hand drawing the planting is lengthwise, accentuating the long, thin dimensions. In the left-hand drawing the planting is across the bed, making it feel wider and shorter.

A ribbon of farfugium cuts diagonally across this narrow bed, breaking the predictability of the space and contrasting with finer foliage of buxus and liriope.

ticklers, which will flop but not trip you up. Shrubs in tight spaces are often problematic. They have the nasty habit of growing out as much as they grow up but there are a few which will watch their waistline including the likes of bamboos, nandina, pseudopanax and cordylines. Many shrubs which look fabulous at a nursery are really unexploded missiles which, when you get them home, will launch themselves up and out of your garden in no time. So choose the slower-growing spires, paltry palms and tidy perennials, such as echinacea, with finite height.

The last thing you want is too many upswept specimens standing stiffly to attention like a regimental lineup. If fences need hiding, use evergreen climbers instead and keep your upright plants for creating rhythmic effects and to add emphasis at key places.

## Use hangers out

Taros are especially useful in a narrow situation because they hang out in a beautifully relaxed way while keeping their feet firmly under the table and out of harm's way.

If nothing is allowed to splay beyond the confines of a planter or bed your garden will begin to look rather uptight and frigid. Moreover, larger plants hanging out in your face will just be annoying. What's needed instead is a little foppish casualness at knee level. Where there isn't constant foot traffic, low plants that will hang out, spread and droop in a moderate way will soften a hard edge or dribble down a low wall. Plants like fuchsias, ferns, hemerocallis, libertias and clivia enjoy themselves while remembering their table manners.

## Create rhythm

Having laid a simple thread of plants along your space, be it climbers, toe ticklers or both, next consider adding a sense of rhythm to break this long monologue into bite-sized chunks. There's nothing like a little regular punctuation to make a long, thin border feel shorter and more stylish.

Try not to always reach first for the obvious — the pin sharp architecture of topiary, a cabbage tree or a perky pseudopanax. It may be better to create a more blurred suggestion of rhythm along a fence. While upright shrubs help to hide or break up long stretches of fence or wall, distinct panels of climbers like native *Tecomanthe speciosa* or star jasmine are just as effective at breaking up the monotony and they allow you to cover over a multitude of sins along the way. Don't be afraid of leaving lengths of fence bare with a few key climbers spaced out with gaps between.

Alternating one plant with another is the most boring way of creating a formal rhythm. There are many ways to repeat a key plant or plants along a border to give a bolder and more interesting look. Generally the longer your bed, the bolder your blocks of repeat planting need to be.

## Use height well

In narrow beds the only way is up. Against fences and walls it is especially important to try and have interest at all heights and for this, climbers will be your biggest ally as they will head up and away rapidly and take up little room.

Where plants like spires with a strong sense of upward movement are chosen, try to balance that with something trailing down. In a formal look spires and columns of topiary and standardised shrubs will be invaluable for providing a feeling of exuberance and height without the volume. Containers, water features and sculptures too, can all play a vital role mounted at key places onto fences and walls.

*The puka may get a little claustrophobic but other natives, like* Pseudopanax lessonii *and* P. ferox *and arching* Chionochloa flavicans, *will stay slim and make an energetic combination.*

Different ways to repeat plants along a narrow space. The more plants are arranged in blocks or groups, the less 'busy' is the effect.

## The side passage

Most of us have a narrow piece of land down the side of the house that we don't quite know how to deal with. If it is quite wide, say more than 4 metres, there may be scope to create the feeling of a small garden room, but if it is any narrower the space will always have something of the feel of a passageway. If this is the case then the challenge is to make it look like a meaningful part of your garden picture rather than an embarrassment.

Some houses today are so hemmed in that the entire garden is a boxed set of side passages. Often positioned along the ugliest side of the house, many have strips of soil as long and as impossibly thin as shoe laces — often with such scenic highlights as dustbins, washing lines or air conditioning units, and here you will really have your work cut out.

Planting the anorexic perimeter of a side passage means taking a different approach than that taken with a slim flower bed out in the open garden. The difference is the way that we view them. In the open garden the planting is often seen from straight on and from a distance, while down the side of a house, apart from the odd direct view sideways from a house window, the planting is seen from one end or the other.

Invariably passages have tricky microclimates too. The rain shadow cast by house eaves, fences and walls will make some of the area dry as dust and often cast it in deep shade.

### Does it need planting?

The first question to ask in these most unpromising of places, even if you love gardening, is whether you need planting here at all. Will those minuscule strips ever look like anything or will they be a constant niggle, draining time and resources that could be better spent in the main body of the garden? Don't be afraid of removing beds all together and allowing a narrow passage to be just that.

### Bold and simple

Often there will be scope for some beautification so take a look at the width of your space and consider how it might be realistically used — do you want people to linger or to move on quickly? Often narrow places are just that: places for passing through rather than for stopping so the planting can and should be bold and unfussy. It will make an impression even if we don't stop to look at every leaf and flower.

Reliable unfussy foliage, not dazzling variegations or floral effects, will work best. Your plants should have a business-like air about them as if they are saying politely, 'Let's get on with it' rather than showier plants that would give more of a 'Stop to look at me' sort of message.

Simplicity in a narrow space is key. The last thing you want is a side passage that looks like a dumping ground for the motley collection of rejects evicted from the main garden. Like green glue, simple planting of a single species will unite all the bits and pieces down the back of a house — effectively binding together a disparate mixture of different fences, drainpipes, dustbins and changes in paving into a meaningful whole. What you need is not fancy tricks but reliable, good doers.

In narrow spaces tall plants are essential for drawing the eye upwards and away from the narrowness so you will have to be especially careful to choose slimline plants.

With two borders either side of a path to play with, zigzagging a feature plant can really push out the boundaries as our eyes bounce from side to side and don't rush down the middle. A zigzagging thread, say of a gold upright euonymus, can set up a nice sense of formal rhythm.

### Softening hard angles

Narrow passages are often dominated by hard features. The overpowering verticals of walls and fences crash head-on into the horizontal plane of a path, creating

*Imaginative use of Spanish shawl (Heterocentron) to make a vertical 'lawn' down a retaining wall and the gentle swing of the path help relieve the boredom in this passage. Breaking the path into sections also helps broaden the dimensions.*

*Zigzagging the planting diagonally across this narrow path draws the eye from side to side, making the space feel wider while making the two sides feel unified.*

a harsh angle. A good cushion of leaf at the junction will inevitably soften this awkward collision and make the space feel more appealing.

While prostrate plants like ajugas would grow well, groundcovers like this tend to mould themselves to the shape of the space rather than softening any awkward angles. Using them in this instance would be rather like trying to paint over a crack with a thin emulsion paint. What we need are fillers — plants that are large enough to look generous but compact enough that they don't obstruct the path. Although flax and astelias grow well in such conditions and are relatively upright, they are notorious for throwing strappy leaves across paths — a real trouser soaker on a wet day and a trip-me-up the rest of the time.

Try instead the stalwarts such as a dwarf arthropodium like the variety 'Te Puna'. The upright leaves of liriopes and libertias work well too, or more graceful hen and chickens ferns, hellebores or hakonechloa grass, which will lean out over a path but will not get in the way. Don't forget clivias either; they are indispensable under dry, shady eaves.

If you are really cunning you will position the climbers so they coincide with any house windows. Even though the foreshortened view out may not be a million dollars at least you will have provided an amphitheatre of leaf on the boundary. Suitable climbers for this would be those with reliable foliage like fatshedera, *Hedera canariensis*, akebia, *Clematis montana* and the luscious *Clematis armandii*.

### Altering path design

One way to create more room for creative planting with a narrow space is to move a path against the house and lose the bed nearest it so that you create a wider border on the outer side. This is the place, after all, that often gets more natural rain and is seen more easily from house windows.

Similarly, if you zigzag or meander a passage path from one extreme side to the other, you will remove the strait-jacketed look and in the process create wider and more interesting planting bays. If planted lushly these can add an element of surprise and discovery as you walk along and dustbins and air-conditioning units might be effectively screened in the more generous recesses.

### Informality in a narrow passage

Treating a side passage in an informal way is more of a challenge as the geometry of house and boundary are so compellingly formal. By repeating a key plant in irregular and bold blocks you will at least rattle the cage of formality. A grey plant like *Liriope muscari* 'Silver Ribbon', a gold *Acorus gramineus* 'Ogon' or the lightening effect of creamy variegations can be used to suck the eye onwards. The zigzag style of repeat planting mentioned earlier can be just as effective but stagger your signature plants more randomly down the path. Any planting that cuts across rather than following the dominant lines of fences and path will help to soften the space.

---

### PLANT PICKS: SIDE PASSAGES

★ **Slim-line plants:** (see climbers, spires and upswept plant lists)

★ **Shrubs and larger plants:** aloe, *Bambusa gracilis*\* (fairy bamboo), camellia\* (narrow types), eg, *C. japonica* 'Night Rider'/'Alpen Glow'/'Blondy'/'Cinnamon Cindy'/'Fairy Wand'/'Fairy Blush', *Carica pubescens* (pawpaw), *Colocasia esculenta*\*, *Cordyline nigra*\*, *Dichroa versicolor*\*, fatshedera\*, mahonia\*, *Nandina domestica* 'Richmond'\*, osmanthus\*, *Plectranthus fruticosus*\*, *Pseudopanax* 'Sabre'\*, *Rhopalostylis sapida*\* (nikau), *Toona sinensis*, vireya rhododendron\* (tall types)

★ If trained to a wall — ceanothus, chaenomeles\*, citrus, garrya\*, itea\*, pyracantha\*, sophora

*\* suitable for shady conditions*

> **PLANT PICKS: NARROW SPACES**
>
> ★ **Smaller plants:** *Agapanthus* 'Streamline', *Arthropodium* 'Te Puna'*, bromeliads*, *Calamagrostis* 'Karl Foerster', cannas, *Carex hachijoensis* 'Evergold'*, clivia*, epidendrum, ferns* (especially asplenium and polystichum), fuchsia*, *Hakonechloa macra* 'Aureola', hedychium, *Helleborus argutifolius/foetidus*, *Hemerocallis* 'Stella d'Oro', *Iris foetidissima* variegata*, *I. evansia*, libertia*, *Liriope muscari*, *Orthrosanthus multiflorus**, sarcococca*, sisyrinchium, *Strobilanthes anisophyllus**
>
> *\* suitable for shady conditions*

## Wider passages

When a narrow garden space is 3–6 metres wide there is more scope to create a distinct garden at some point rather than a mere passageway. A small scene with its own atmosphere to stop and enjoy will break up the length. Plants, after all, are ever the optimists and if given the chance most will make a purse out of a sow's ear, transforming a cold and lifeless tunnel into a leafy enclave.

In these wider places, long paths need to be broken. Stepping stones will slow down the feel of a long path but even more effective is a wide swelling of gravel or paving. You might have to forgo any borders at all at this point just to create a reasonably sized area to stop and linger and to push out the boundaries. A feature such as topiary, a pot in the centre or even a small water feature will create a focal point from either end and suggest a definite garden space. Here you can break any regular rhythmic planting you have been using to suggest a place to pause.

Announce any lingering point clearly with a new plant or plants in addition to those used along the rest of the space. Full stops of clipped topiary or a special climber thrown over a fence can be particularly arresting.

## Outside windows:
*looking out on small spaces*

Where important windows of the house look out onto narrow passageways or courtyards you are presented with another design challenge. More than any other part of the garden, here the view is uncompromisingly boxed in and you will need that shop window flair. Gardening here really is like painting a picture, which will be viewed rather statically from within so it needs careful composition.

If you choose formality you might go for topiary or raised planters arranged symmetrically with perhaps a trompe l'oiel, a piece of sculpture or trellis panel as a focal point. If a wall or fence is very close to a window such highly composed arrangements can look rather contrived and predictable, and understatement often works better. A simple line of one repeated plant, or a sheet of climbers, are tried and tested solutions but try and be adventurous with your plant choice. Climbers of varying textures woven together can make a subtle tapestry effect by themselves, especially if you introduce the dimension of scent to waft in at the windows.

You may, however, want to up the sense of drama by mounting wall planters featuring an architectural plant like an astelia or a trailing succulent. Even baskets of seasonal bedding can look good in such places to bring freshness and life. Bromeliads, orchids and other epiphytes can be either glued or tied to a wall or an old branch and arranged to

---

*Left*

Opposite a prominent window this stylish widening turns an alleyway into an event. The topiary placed diagonally gives the impression of symmetry from both sideways and lengthwise.

---

*Opposite*

Suspended animation: anything that can possibly hang or trail is wired to driftwood and palm trunks — bromeliads, orchids, airplants and (at the far end) an elkhorn fern (*Platycerium*).

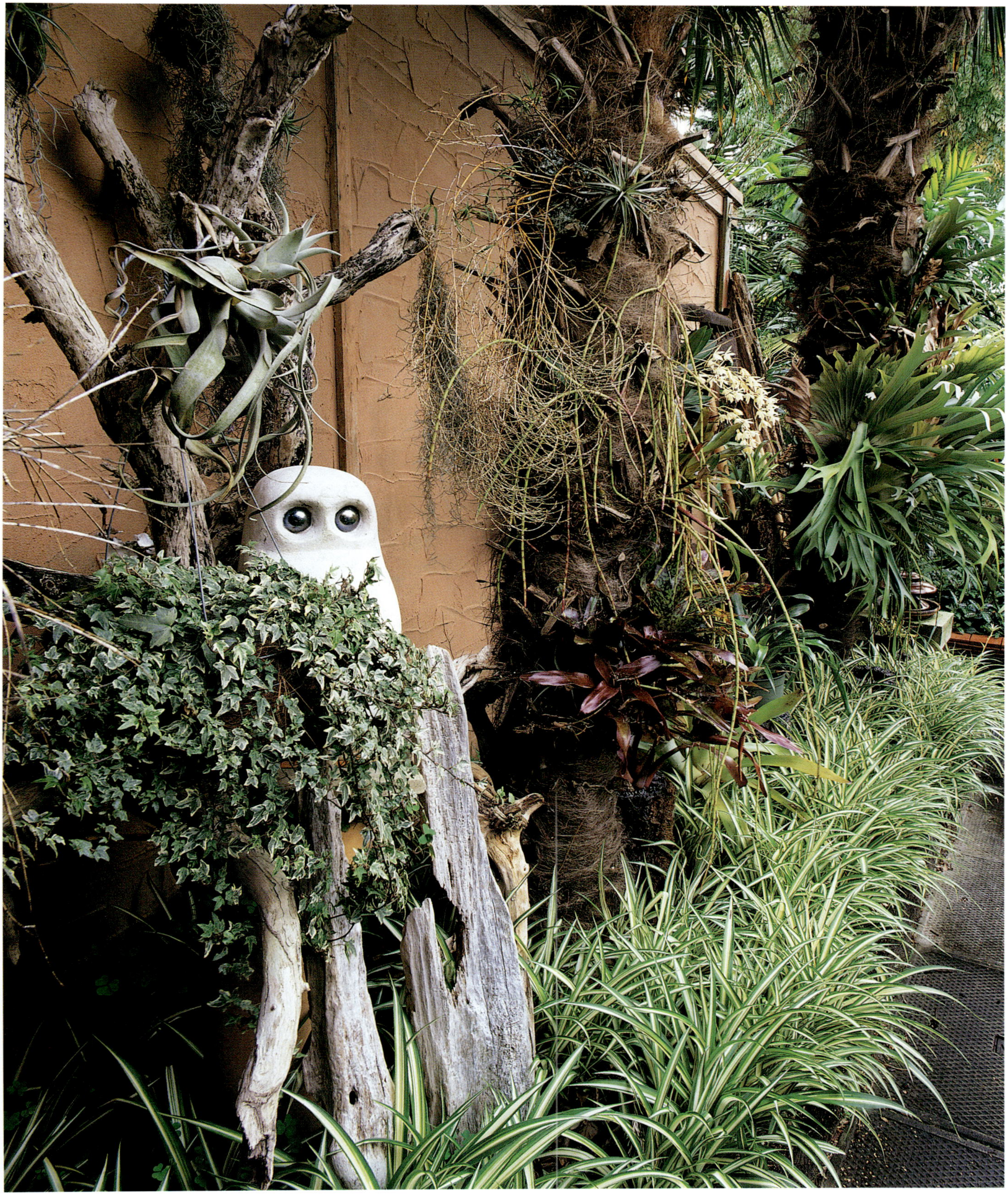

appear at the window. Tall plants like epidendron orchids or cane begonias in subtropical areas can be planted along an outdoor path and will get high enough to make an impact from inside.

By using wires set in patterns — either splayed in a fan or grid pattern — scramblers like trachelospermum or ivy can be trained up to provide intricate decoration for a more dramatic treatment. Such features will need careful and regular clipping.

If you are lucky enough to have attractive outside walls there is no need to cover them. Just break them delicately with light, architectural plants — anything from bamboo canes and dracaenas for a contemporary look to nandinas or maples for a gentler effect. These can be lit from below to cast shadows at night and bring a sense of movement and space to indoor rooms. The use of a single plant with a simple backdrop can have a beautiful Zen-like simplicity and will be a welcome break from the more exuberant parts of the garden.

### Trees in tight spots

If there is an ugly view perhaps out into a neighbouring property you will need more than sculptures and wall hangings. A good solution is to use standardised trees or topiary clipped with its back to the boundary. If maintained regularly, these can be especially effective because they burgeon just at the right height to screen out neighbours but allow a certain amount of leg room beneath to get past. A looser deciduous tree like a Japanese maple or crab apple set against a wall of evergreens works well too.

A more ambitious alternative is to erect a set of horizontal wires above the fence along which to train a climber like a vine or even a row of trees for a pleached effect. Once the fiddle of erecting a stout framework is complete, it's surprisingly easy to pleach a tree and create a sort of hedge on stilts. Each year the stronger growth is tied in along the wires and all other shoots are spurred back along the sides for a manicured and compact look.

Simply planting a row of standards like callistemon close together will give a similar effect. Just clip the tops to merge them together. Trees near windows need to be chosen with attractive foliage in mind. Lime, liquidambar, fig, plane, maple and whitebeam will all look dramatic from inside and for evergreen screens try *Prunus lusitanica*, *Ficus hillieri*, or even peppertree (*Schinus*) and titoki before you opt for the ubiquitous waterhousea or eugenia.

If your trees are part of a line along the side of a house, make the spacing

Alchemilla and nicotianas provide a simple strip of planting combined with the rhythm of lime trees just ready to be pleached to a trellis screen.

slightly irregular if it means you get your trees to balance symmetrically outside prominent windows. The irregularities are never obvious when seen from either end of a narrow space anyway.

## Other pocket-sized beds

Often the most exciting part of a garden is where plants leap out of the conventional flower bed all together and set up shop in other places — that crevice by the drainpipe or that crack in an old wall. Just see how huge weeds love to dazzle and surprise in a neglected bit of guttering! To the minimalist, small bitsy crevices will be like acne on their sleek and simple designs — an annoying and unnecessary distraction from the purity of form. But often they can add a layer of detail that enriches and adds charm to a planting scheme and a large expanse of boring paving. The secret is to plant simply and purposefully and to make sure your smaller planting spaces are an intentional part of the design in the first place and not just awkward gaps where the paving meets the deck at an odd angle. If this is the case just pave them over — they will be a nuisance and a distraction.

You wouldn't ask several guests to squeeze into the same seat so it's best not to shove a host of different plants into a crevice of soil hoping they will all get on like a house on fire. I try and plant any space smaller than armchair size with just one type of plant to avoid the cluttered look. I say 'try' because to the plant lover gardening is done with a mental shoe horn and there will always be room for 'just one more' plant!

A small flower bed is not the same as a container garden so don't apply a container gardening mentality to it. For some mysterious reason while you can plant up a container with a bevy of plants and (sometimes) get a wonderfully exuberant show, those same plants

**Right above**
Here a similar set-up to the photo opposite but with conifers like *Thuja orientalis* 'Pyramidalis' and a unifying thread of liriope at the edge.

**Right below**
Small planting pockets make a big difference in paved areas but need simple treatment. This block of aromatic balm is the perfect complement to some intricate mosaic paving.

Plants can sometimes seem tightly herded into garden beds. By carrying a plant across from a flower bed into a lawn or paved area it effectively blurs the boundaries of the garden and adds a sense of freedom to your planting. In this smart and semi-formal driveway there is just room to let some yuccas make a break for freedom. *Carex hachijoensis* 'Evergold' makes a tidy edge and the stunning tree is *Ficus roxburghii*.

---

if a feature plant or tree in the garden is repeated out on a lawn or paved area. This thread of repetition jumping across from the exuberance of the garden beds to the simplicity of open space helps to tie the two areas together and makes for a strong unifying feature. In our coastline analogy you are creating the stacks out to sea that link with the mainland.

### Bold and simple

Lawn plants need to be architectural enough to hold their own. Because you will view them from nearly every angle, it is nice to choose plants that look effective when back lit or silhouetted such as smoke bushes (cotinus) or sword-like doryanthes. Try to repeat plants if there is space to give your design a more intentional effect. On formal-shaped lawns consider the theatrical use of island beds — perhaps circles of restios rising from a frothy rim of alchemilla or a line of leucospermum mounds punctuating the edge of a path. Confidence again gets results and bold, simple ideas always work best.

### Lawn trees

A tree is the classic lawn plant. So often we limb them up into a lollipop shape when a multi-branched specimen would have looked far more interesting,

squashed into a permanent planter or small bed just look fussy and distracting. The reason is perhaps because of the setting. Plants in a container are often ephemeral in nature and are a display brought up closer to eye level and slightly separated from the garden planting as a whole, but garden beds, no matter how small, are still part of the fixtures and fittings. As such, they should relate to what's happening in the rest of the garden — not just in plant content but in the scale and simplicity of planting.

## Specimen planting in lawns

Some view any plant in a lawn as a potential menace to the mower but lawns aren't used enough to display specimen plants. It's rather incongruous having all our plants huddled round the edges of the lawn and total bareness in the middle — nature never segregates the two and some carefully chosen plants in the lawn can break up the bareness.

What we don't want is a random scattering. Often a garden looks interesting especially if you go for the feature bark of something like a guava or a *Luma apiculata*. With trees like birches, palms and *Acer griseum* the classic design advice is to nestle them together in groups to emphasise the dramatic bark. Three is said to be the magic number but you may well have your own ideas. Out in the open is a sensible place for a tree — here they are good to sit under and won't shade out other planting in the main borders.

Often, though, a tree can look a bit lonely poking out of bare grass. A small trunk and a large crown look particularly incongruous so where this is the case, create a visual foundation for the tree. A wide circle of pebbles or crazy paving under a tree can make mowing round it a little easier and will remove any bare patches of grass that might have developed in the shade. Simple planting works well too. The size of the bed should match the size of the drip line of the crown or perhaps be a little smaller. Keep the planting low so that you don't obscure the trunk and use only one or two plants to give a subtle feel, which will be appropriate in this simple setting of lawn and canopy. Planting a ring of daffodils under every lawn tree has become an overworked cliche, so give them space. If you are using bulbs under your lawn trees, creating a garden beneath will prevent you mowing the leaves off too early and will allow you to hide the dying mess with successive planting.

## Steps and paving:
### adding plants

There is nothing like plants for softening and enlivening large areas of paving and steps. Many of us enjoy the romantic self-seeded look in the gaps between paving to break up the harshness but often we need to build in small planting pockets to allow us to do something more substantial.

Carpeters like thyme, thrift and chamomile can create oozing drizzles of colour and greenery — a sort of rockery without the busyness of rocks. If you lay paving from scratch it is worth the trouble of making plenty of room to accommodate such plants because they usually enjoy a cool, deep root run and excellent drainage too. Open paved areas are harsh environments for plants. Impossibly hot in summer and often exposed to strong winds, the soil beneath, though cool, can be very alkaline due to the proximity to concrete foundations so choose plants carefully. Many Mediterranean species are ideal like euphorbias and cistus as they love heat and a wind in their sails. Sunny terraces mimic the exposed microclimate of mountainous regions — especially if you live in a cold district so try alpine groundcovers, compact hebes and native grasses that love an exposed micro-climate.

Low carpeters look best placed carefully so that they don't easily get trodden on. No matter what romantic notions we might have, thyme hates to be stamped on. In places where there is foot traffic it is better to use taller plants that will be seen. The spires and wands of plants like dierama and verbascum too can be used to great effect in paving where they have the baking heat they love and where their strong sense of architecture can be enjoyed without the

---

Stepping-stone steps are a great opportunity to allow plants to move in: here Vivian Papich allows mondo grass to seep forward, placing vertical ranks of sansevieria behind.

Steps can be a stage for plants and a safe place to allow self-seeders. On these theatrical platforms by Edwin Lutyens, ferns, erigeron and ox-eye daisy hang loose.

clutter of other plants. When using architectural plants choose the types that won't need staking and contrast them with the softer mats and blobs.

A large area of paving or gravel, with several scattered pockets of planting, can be treated rather like a large garden border. The same principles of composition, form, texture and drama apply but everything is more spread out so each plant needs to be good looking enough to hold its own as well as relating to its associates. In this respect it's good to link through a theme plant to avoid a complete scattering of liqourice allsorts.

### *The topography of a terrace*

Steps and walls are a great opportunity to display plants in an imaginative way because they have built-in topography and a well-defined structure to link together the planting. Steps need to be designed large enough to incorporate planting without compromising ease of use. Plants look stunning cascading down a slope so use a theme plant to create a ribbon of continuity down a wall or steps.

Retaining walls can be very visually obtrusive but by blanketing them in exciting trailing plants and repeat planting key elements both above and below you will cut across the strong horizontal lines of the wall and make a dynamic composition. So often we plant along the top of a wall in a predictable way so instead it's good to cut across the contours with some tumbling rivers of foliage, be it trailers, spires, spikes or blobs.

## FOOD FOR THOUGHT

☆ Have you turned your back on landscaping your side passages?

☆ Are there plants in tight spaces, which constantly get in the way, trip you up or drip water on you whenever it is wet?

☆ Take a look out of every window of the house. Are you making the most of each framed view — raising plants up, using climbers, containers, pleached trees or effective lighting?

☆ Have you used repetition and rhythm down your narrow spaces?

☆ Have you pushed out the boundaries in your narrow spaces with zigzag planting, stepping stones or paving that meanders or bulges?

☆ In long, thin garden beds how have you broken up the length — with repeated shrubs, bold blocks of foliage or planting that cuts across the space rather than following the line along?

☆ If there is room, consider breaking a path with a wider garden room to make the space feel bigger.

☆ Do you have walls, steps and paved areas large enough to accommodate some pockets of creative planting?

Chapter 16

# The Tortoise and the Hare

*the maturing garden*

Enjoy your youth but invest in the future too. These fast-fill pine and poplar provide instant shelter but will need removing promptly before they grow into monsters. The lavender hedge too will go off the boil quickly but here the daylilies and slower shrubs will prevent a mid-life crisis.

PLANTS GROW LIKE the raindrops down a window. There are the foolhardy plungers that career down the glass in frantic haste as soon as they hit the glass. There are the slow but sure droplets which descend with considered aplomb, and then those completely stubborn beads of water that don't move an inch. Imperceptibly swelling and gathering strength, they suddenly take off when you least expect it and plummet to a sticky end on the sill.

Camellias plod along, abutilons roar into action and hellebores — well, hellebores like to bide their time. Aloof for the first year, they weigh you up and decide if they like you. If you are lucky they'll nod approval with a flower or two and, once seed is set, they move in lock, stock and barrel and you suddenly find yourself overwhelmed.

Every plant dances to the beat of its own drum and chases the years at a different speed. Beyond the seasonal cycle there is one aspect of planting which is rarely considered: how the garden matures over the years. Gardeners take a different approach to educationalists. While teachers reward high achievers and those who get ahead, in the garden a plant that over-achieves is set upon with a chainsaw! The process of curbing over-enthusiastic plants is a bittersweet experience. While there is certainly a sadistic pleasure to be had from setting upon a defenceless shrub with a saw and loppers, it's also sad (not to mention back-breaking) to have to cut out some perfectly healthy plant because it is smothering its neighbours.

### Planning for growth

Having carefully considered our site and soil and chosen a team of plants of satisfying shape, texture and seasonal interest we sometimes fall at the last hurdle. We forget or misjudge future growth rates and spread, and plant our gardens in a way that will only end in tears a few years down the track. In New Zealand's equitable climate we need to be especially vigilant about growth rates and habits because plants tend to either sulk and die, but more often they like us so much that we can find ourselves suffocating in their embrace.

Every plant we invite to live with us is either a zoomer or a zimmerframe and as we get to know our garden things turn out very much like the Aesops fable about the tortoise and the hare. There is no clear-cut line between which plants are the villains and which are the heroes — in fact we need both characters to make the story exciting, but as in the tale, often it is the plants that take the slower route that reap the rewards.

Television gardening cannot show the process and the beauty of ageing. The process and the fun of gardening takes time and it will be a year or three before things really start to become mouth-watering, so hang in there and enjoy.

## Fast growth equals high maintenance

We live in a society that wants instant results. Children today have little concept of the principle of delayed gratification and when we buy a home it is for five years rather than 50. So in the garden instant results and quick effect has become the underlying requirement.

The great paradox, however, is that while we are looking for fast-growing plants and instant effects we also demand gardens that are low maintenance and it is almost impossible to have both. Fast-growing plants are always the high-maintenance option.

### High-octane monsters

The reason that quick-fix fillers are a lot of work is that while they may have excellent jet propulsion, they usually come without a braking system and will continue to shoot up and outwards until they have outstayed their welcome. Fast growers, to fuel their athleticism, are also greedy for nutrients and water so you will have to stay busy keeping them fed.

The classic examples are those cheap and cheerful background plants we use to quickly hide a fence or to screen out a neighbour — the likes of pittosporum, griselinia and waterhousea. Like wolves in sheep's clothing, they often skulk into the shrub department of a garden centre when in truth all will make medium-sized trees if left to their own devices. We take them home and have a very amicable first three years but the honeymoon period is short and sweet. Soon our 'quick fillers'

Palms are the poplars of the future. Even this turbo-charged planting will get left in the starting blocks by a queen palm (*Syagrus*) with a head for heights.

*While some perennials need regular reducing and division, others like these slow-plodding paeonies will thrive with minimal attention and will look as good a decade later.*

get to the teenage years and beanpole upwards. As they balloon out at the top they lose all their leaves at the base and – to add insult to injury – they steal your light, dry out the soil and leave you once again staring at the fence you hoped they would hide.

Palms are the classic modern example of plants that look lovely when young, grow well and are quick off the starting blocks but which will become far too large for most urban gardens in the future. Certainly there are small and slow palms but most slow growers are time-consuming to produce so nurseries don't focus on them; that's why they can be difficult to obtain and expensive when you do.

In a way the palms are the macrocarpas or poplars of the 21st century and in 50 years the sound of chainsaws will be the drone heard through suburbia as the current honeymoon glow dissolves. There is no middle ground with a palm; while we can top a pencil conifer or decapitate a cabbage tree and it will regrow, with a palm we either leave it alone or remove it completely.

## Compromise between boom and bust

Many speedsters tend to be comparatively short-lived compared to the slow plodders. Like fireworks they can explode on the scene but leave you with a lot of clearing up in the morning.

Gum trees are a typical example. In our climate they grow unnaturally quickly but pay for their youthful enthusiasm with a greatly reduced shelf-life. In their native Australia they take longer to reach maturity but have a greatly increased life innings.

If we fill our borders only with fuel-injected plants then fights will inevitably break out and we will be forever stepping in to sort things out – slashing and pruning. On the other hand, if we use well-behaved, slow plodders exclusively then things will look a little constipated and measly for several years with gaps between one plant and the next.

The best approach is a good compromise. By planting a mixture of hares and tortoises it is possible to enjoy some quick fixes while knowing that other parts of your planting are there for the long haul and, like a good wine, will mature and only get better as the years go by. As your slower-growing plants become your permanent classics the high-octane plants will have done their dash and can be cleared away.

Managing the speedsters alongside plodders will take a bit of care, however. If we view the faster-growing elements as ultimately expendable then we can plant them alongside slower shrubs, knowing that just as they begin to knit together your quick-fix plant can be thinned out to let the more-choice specimens swell. Attacking plants that appear to be thriving for the sake of the slow plodders in between is one of the hardest decisions to make in gardening but the long-term future of your planting depends on it. If you leave thinning out until too late, the tortoises will have been all but choked to death and may never get to a ripe old age.

## Soft fill: perennials

Perennials are much the same as trees and shrubs in that the fast growers tend to get themselves into trouble much more easily. Perennials at least have a set height limit. The trouble comes as they spread outwards.

We have already looked at those which run wild from day one, but even the slower growers eventually need lifting and dividing to prevent them from engulfing neighbours. More vigorous varieties are often easier to grow and are highly desirable, but their enthusiasm comes at a price so keep a close eye on them. Many like cannas and daylilies, salvias and dahlias form the mainstay of the summer border, but they need good feeding to give the best results as well as dividing every five years to keep them flowering well and to reduce them in size.

It's often the case that when a garden lacks drama and crispness it's because the perennials have become tired and have leaked into everything, forming a flabby mass. Yet if we are willing to manage the perennial 'boy racers' of the border we can harness and enjoy their enthusiasm and generosity. If you are fit, lifting and splitting a canna or dahlia can be a fantastic job — it's like breathing fresh air into the border and if we chip away and tackle a few plants each year the garden will retain its sense of youthful vigour. Remember to include too those perennials — the likes of eryngiums, rodgersias, hellebores, astilbes, paeonies and aconitums — that need far less care, and love to be left alone.

## Fast and slow mixes

In planning your tortoise and hare mix, plan your planting on two levels. First work out your slower, long-term plants, spacing them to allow room to grow and expand. Then interplant with quick-fill plants which will give you an instant sense of maturity.

Short-lived, sun-loving shrubs like argyranthemum, felicia and lavender are especially useful between plantings of camellias and viburnum, for example. They will enjoy the initial openness of the site and as the slower shrubs develop they will naturally die away as they are shaded out and run out of steam. What you don't want as filler plants are thugs that will impede your long-term plants. For lower planting choose well-behaved perennials like gazanias and brachyscome, which will carpet (but not smother) the ground before the main planting expands and swells.

For screening a neighbour, fast shrubs with light foliage like lavatera, buddleia and alyogyne will afford a degree of instant privacy but will leave room and allow light to get to longer-term shrubs like hollies and feijoa that you may have planted in between. Large perennials like eupatorium and miscanthus grasses can also be useful for adding instant body to a new planting while more permanent shrubs fill out. Such quick-fill perennials have a set height limit and allow plenty of light in to slower-growing plants in winter when they lie down — they can be sprayed or dug out later.

Annuals and biennials are especially good at filling in gaps at the early stages of a planting and then graciously bowing off stage when the long-term stars find their feet.

With any border that is started from scratch, if you can put up with the bareness, give your long-term plants a year or two to themselves to allow them to find their feet before you flood the bed with the rest of the rabble.

## Dealing with the ageing garden
*Sun and shade*

We grow too familiar with our gardens. Sometimes distancing ourselves and looking at them afresh can highlight many areas for improvement. I find the first few days after a holiday is the perfect time to look at everything objectively and plan major changes. As time passes we see our gardens so frequently that it is hard to notice how much they have changed with the years. The most common change that we sometimes fail to notice is how gardens that start out sunny often lose their openness as trees and shrubs mature and fill out. Under trees, plants are limping along in the gloom, giving a mediocre performance. Often it will be easy to replace such planting to inject new life under a tree but sometimes some judicious pruning and limbing up may be all that's needed to allow the sun back in.

Occasionally it will be worth taking the bull by the horns and removing larger garden elements altogether if they are getting in the way of the look you are after. Decisions like this need to be made when you are feeling ruthless and angry — perhaps the day you get the credit card bill. Plants that are adapted to a sunny

---

Opposite above

Treasure your monsters: the octopus tentacles of this pohutukawa are shown off by an underplanting of monstera on a suitably grand scale.

Opposite below

Dying with dignity: by planting a young upstart euphorbia in the belly of this grand old whipcord hebe (*Hebe cupressoides*), Christopher Lloyd turns an exit into an encore performance.

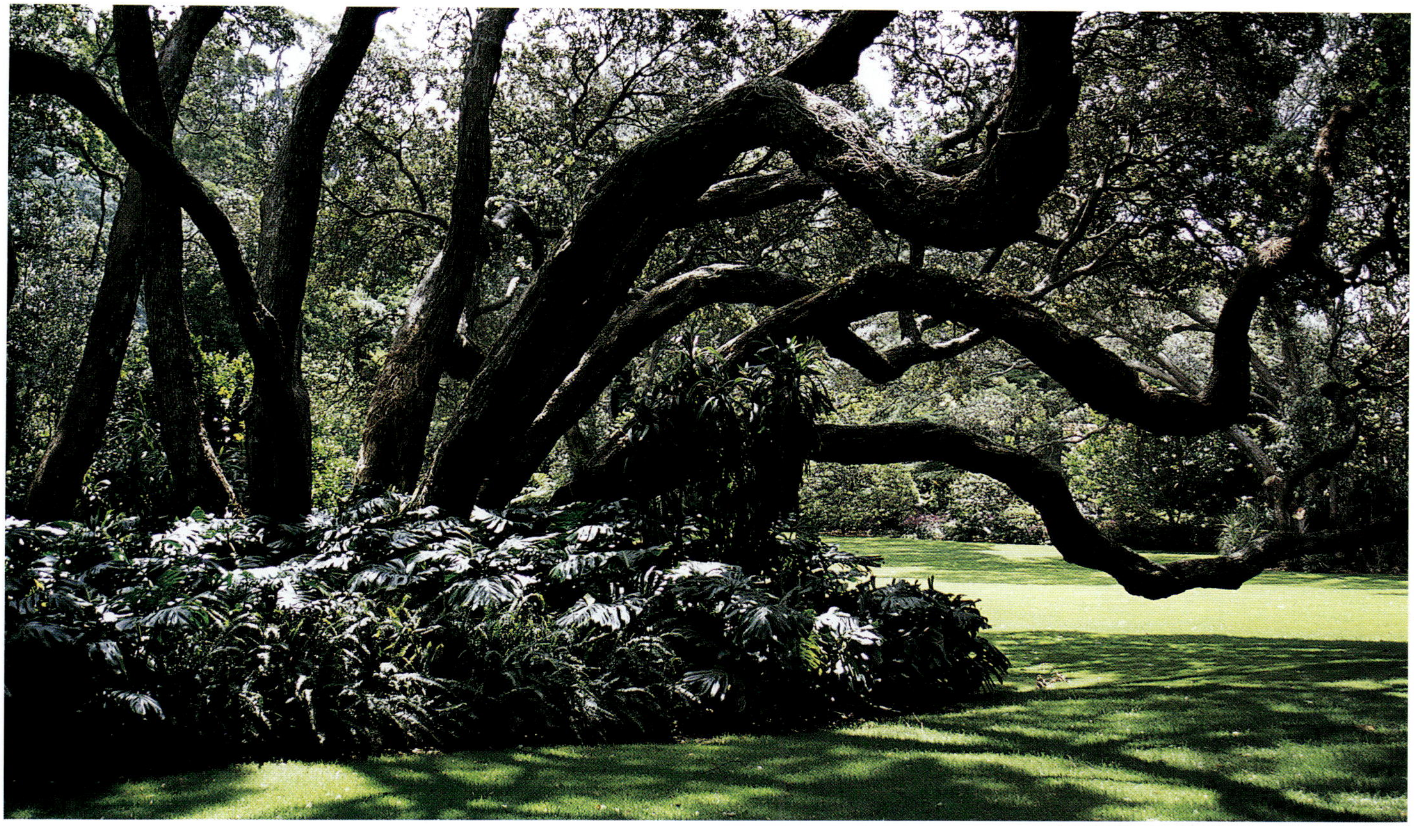

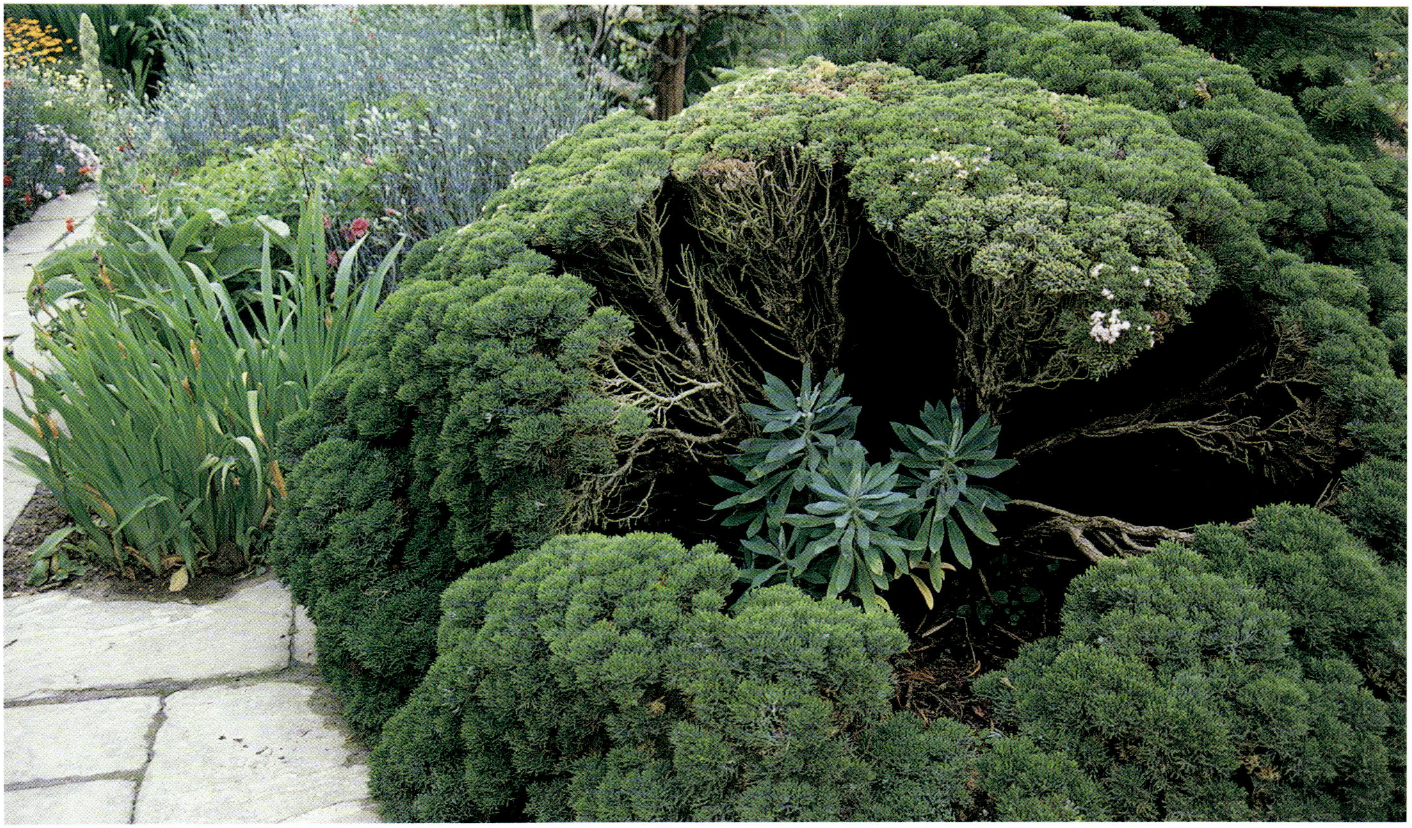

aspect often struggle in shade; they go drawn and leggy and fail to flower well. Shade plants in contrast seem more adaptable and although they will grow in shade they often do just as well (sometimes better) if you cut down a tree or prune a shrub and brighten their outlook. A good water through the dry months will often help such woodlanders cope with life in the great wide open after you have had a major clean out.

## Proportion: the size staircase

As well as sun and shade the other most important thing which affects the ageing garden is the relative proportions: how things of different size relate to one another. I think of it as a sort of size staircase, so that ideally an object of one size steps down or up to the next without a big break in between. In the garden we need to avoid places where, for example, a very large feature — usually a tree, wall, lawn or paved area — meets a very small feature: what's needed is something of medium size in the middle. A classic example is a deck. A small strip of deck looks out of place next to a very large house but would sit happily next to a smaller, single-storey dwelling. As the garden matures and your (perhaps) carefully contrived shop window composition grows up, everything grows at different speeds and proportions get very distorted. We inevitably end up with something that resembles a baggy old jumper with lumps in all the wrong places — a receding waistline and arms down to the ground. Now a baggy jumper is perfectly nice and charming but there comes a stage in any baggy jumper's life when enough is enough and it gets resigned to the cat basket.

In a garden the most frequent problem occurs when a tree rockets away and turns into an elephantine monster that no longer relates visually to the planting scratching around at its feet. In this case there is no easy answer. Beyond pruning the tree to reduce its size the best thing to do is to consider how you might introduce a linking element in that size staircase — a plant that will grow big enough to be a visual intermediate between the vastness of the tree and the diminutive plants below. In a woodland garden I found the simple addition of a group of cabbage trees around a large oak was enough to soften the incongruity between it and the fine planting beneath.

Simplifying and enlarging the planting under larger trees is another helpful idea to help blend the proportions better. In this case you are boosting the proportions of the underplanting so they come closer to that of the tree. Using dominant foliage such as flax or acanthus is especially effective at adding weight to the underplanting — giving the feeling that the tree has firm foundations.

It is not just trees that can look out of place; a dominant hedge or any bulky shrub situated next to intricate or low-lying planting will look uncomfortable because of the harsh dichotomy between the scale of the two elements. Add in some plants of medium height between the two, however, and a better balance can be reached.

## Shrinking pots in the ageing garden

Another scenario where the maturing garden can trip itself up visually is where you have introduced man-made focal points or set pieces in the planting. At Ayrlies Garden in Auckland we placed a wonderful, but rather small, oil jar in front of a group of new tree ferns but just three years later the dynamics of the scene had changed beyond recognition. Seen against the gargantuan trunk and leaves of the maturing ferns, the pot looked ridiculously inadequate as an eye catcher. The size of a pot or bench gives a very strong and inflexible indication of scale and size and so it is especially vulnerable to being dwarfed by its surroundings.

As the plants around swell and grow a pot or water feature that looked initially so well proportioned and comfortable in

Think of proportion as a size staircase. The drawing on the left shows what often happens as gardens mature. Trees leave the planting far behind and from a distance we notice the trees but not the plants below. Adding a shrub or a beefy mass planting of foliage like astelia or flax, as shown in the drawing on the right, can draw our eye down from the tree to the planting below, acting as a middle stair in the size staircase.

its setting eventually ends up looking like a piece of dolls' house furniture in King Kong's jungle. As with large trees next to small plants, the proportions are all wrong and a bit of adjusting will help balance things.

In Chapter 14 we looked at ways of visually boosting pots and man-made extras but often the simplest solution is to relocate a pot or piece of sculpture to a more sympathetic spot.

Proportion is a hard concept to grasp but most people know when something looks out of kilter, even if they can't explain it. Sometimes a very large plant next to something small can be stimulating, but on the whole it is best to create a natural progression, whether it is in the relationship between plant elements or between plants and their surroundings. A single yucca might be fine in an intimate setting for instance — if it is in a planting seen across a large lawn, you will need yuccas in groups of five or ten to create the exaggerated impact suitable for the scale of the setting.

## Regular care, little and often

Beyond the poetic decay of autumn each year, there is the more permanent slide into old age for all plants. But the twilight years needn't be tinged with sadness — the secret is in keeping your garden youthful in part and refusing to allow it to run out of steam. Treat your team of plants like the clothes in your wardrobe. We don't throw all our clothes away every 10 years and buy a complete new set; neither do we wait until sweaters have holes in the elbows before we give them the boot. Rather we are constantly buying new items that grab our fancy and for each new shirt we buy (in theory) we chuck out an old one. Thus the wardrobe is a dynamically changing mix of the old and the new. A garden full of only old plants is in danger of collapsing overnight. It's far better to remove some plants before they get ratty and decrepit to make way for new blood.

As well as new arrivals and swift exits, attend to the plants in between, making sure you squeeze an Oscar-winning performance from them. Garden maintenance is like time spent with kids — it is not quality time that is important but quantity time. Feeding, mulching, dividing and trimming are best done a little and often.

A conifer or shrub that is pruned annually from an early age will make a bushy and sturdy specimen. If you leave trimming until the last minute, however, when the plant is pushing out over a path, hack it back and you may well end up with an ugly bald patch.

Some people see maintenance as some sort of perpetual battle against nature. They leave the garden for months, even years, on end and then wade in at the eleventh hour like Bruce Willis in the

*Above*
Modesty isn't a virtue when you're a small pot in an ever-expanding world. This oil jar at Ayrlies soon became swamped by the tree fern behind.

*Below*
Miss Wilmott's ghost (*Eryngium giganteum*) loves fresh soil to seed into and will be with you forever if the garden is regularly cultivated.

final scenes of a *Die Hard* movie trying to put out fires that never should have started in the first place. It is no wonder people think gardening is hard work.

## Growing old gracefully

The life of some plants is short and sweet and they should be enjoyed as such. You may only have a ceanothus, a caryopteris or a lavender for four or five years. Like fireworks, their light is bright but brief yet it still makes them worth the effort — their demise will leave you with an exciting new space to try out a new idea and ring the changes.

Some plants shrug off this mortal coil with an ugly splutter and need removing promptly, like a leucadendron that turns brown seemingly overnight. Others grow old gracefully and we should enjoy every part of the process. Some plants in our team go on seemingly forever, getting better and better until we could never bear to lose them — like a gnarled old wisteria or a rusty-barked guava.

To enjoy this process is part of gardening. You may have to lay aside pre-conceived notions of what looks beautiful and acceptable. Often beauty is associated only with tidiness and the vigour of youth but as bushes recline and go bare at the centre, perhaps revealing sculptural innards, look for the beauty and enjoy the process. Hedges will sag a little at the seams and that lagerstroemia you bought as a bush will defiantly turn into a spreading tree with flaking bark. The juniper you wanted straight as a die will lean drunkenly towards the light and the stump of a long-felled redwood will send up a forest of side shoots.

If you can bear to let your garden walk with its shirt hanging out you might find much to enjoy.

---

### PLANT PICKS: SLOW GROWERS

★ **Trees and shrubs:** *Acer palmatum* cultivars, *Beaucarnea recurvata* (ponytail palm), *Ceratopetalum gummiferum* 'Rubies 'n' Lace', cercis, chionanthus, cornus*, *Diospyros kaki*, dracaena, fothergilla, franklinia, hamamelis*, ilex* (holly), loropetalum*, *Podocarpus totara*, *Rhopalostylis sapida** (nikau palm), stewartia, styrax

*\* suitable for shady conditions*

---

### FOOD FOR THOUGHT

#### Tortoise and hare

☆ Are your borders full of instant fillers with no slow plodders?

☆ Could some high-maintenance, fast-growing plants be removed now and be replaced with some more choice species?

#### Light and shade

☆ Reassess the corners of your garden. Identify which areas get sun all day, half the day or not at all and whether this has changed over the years.

☆ In the shady places ask yourself: is your planting textbook shade planting or is it sun-loving plants making the most of a bum deal?

#### Proportions

☆ Looking at your trees and large shrubs, are there middle 'stairs' of height and size between these and the smaller plants in the garden or do they stand aloof like tall poppies?

☆ Look at pots and focal points. Do they look ill-fitting in context to the size of plants and foliage all around?

☆ How might you change this?

☆ Across large areas of paving or lawn, is your planting dramatic enough seen from a distance?

#### Old timers

☆ What old plants do you enjoy in the garden?

☆ Is there a good mixture of youthful and aged plants in your garden?

Chapter 17

# Putting It All Together

Gardening books usually tell us to take inspiration from our architecture! Sometimes it is best to turn a blind eye. A clean-slate approach to planning a border can seem daunting at first but at this bach the world is your oyster.

MY MATE GARY patiently explains rugby to me. I know less than nothing. 'In a team there are the forwards and the backs.' (Sounds easy so far.) 'In the backs you need the wings and the fullback to work together — these are the fast players — the weavers and dodgers with the fancy footwork. In the forwards it's the flankers who are the fast guys: it's their job to dive on the ball and scamper around like terrier dogs.'

Gary moves on but my mind is still with the terriers — they are scampering now through a meadow towards some nice trees...

'There's loosies and locks,' continues Gary excitedly, 'props built like tanks, and a half-sized halfback who shouts a lot!'

It all sounds so complicated it's a wonder anyone knows what anyone else is doing out on the pitch — and I thought it was just about getting the ball over the line.

## Design principles working together

Just like a rugby match, planning a garden is about choosing the best team you can — letting each plant do what it does best and providing as much support as possible. On the day we can only hope the players will work together and turn on that winning magic. With the best planning in the world, when we send our plants out onto the 'pitch', personalities, the elements, the vagaries of the soil and the dog that escapes from next door will mean that we can never predict exactly how the game will turn out.

In this last chapter we are going to look at how the many different design principles come together in practice.

As in the dynamics of rugby it is hard to say for sure where every player fits and what qualities each should have. Flexibility on the day for plants and players is part of the strategy, after all, but hopefully here is a rough plan of action.

Some of us are starting with a beautiful, bare canvas — maybe you've just moved to a new property or want to expand your existing garden. The alternative (and more likely) scenario is that you want to alter your existing planting. If you are like me you often find that what started as a spring clean ends in an all-out war — hacking and slashing with makeover zeal. The fact that most plants can be moved around, reduced, retrained and resown makes this part of the game so interesting. The pleasure (as in rugby) is as much in the tackling and grappling as in the creative rebuilding but it's the promise of something fresh, exciting and very individual at the end that makes all the hard work worth while.

## Overhauling an existing bed

### Pulling it all apart

In improving an existing bed the process inevitably begins with some carefully considered destruction, shuffling and removal. There will probably be much that you already like about your existing garden. The things you enjoy and merely want to enhance will provide you with a definite starting point.

Already there might be a sense of maturity — a good tree or an imposing shrub around which you want to create a new and dynamic team of plants.

In revamping an existing planting here are some steps through the process so that as you wield the spade you don't lose the plot.

### Step 1: Wait and look

If you've just moved to a property with an established garden the best thing you can do is to hold back and live with the garden for a year before ripping into existing planting — that is, of course, unless the existing planting is very basic. In previously well-loved gardens there will be treasures for you to discover; bulbs will pop up in unexpected places and that monstrous hibiscus you hated at first will, in time, become invaluable when you discover how it shields the deck from a westerly wind. With time you will notice how the sun moves round the garden, the frost pockets and where the damp and dry areas are situated.

Waiting and looking often save us reinventing the wheel at a later date and will save money too.

### Step 2: Get a notebook

A garden has to be constantly moving on or it will stagnate. Before secateurs and trowel, a notebook is the most essential tool you can have in the garden. Back at Sissinghurst Pam and Sybille, the brilliant head gardeners, always kept a moth-eared journal in the potting shed grandly entitled 'Great thoughts'. These days a pocket diary with a pencil might be more practical to let you record ideas and observations instantly before you can forget. I get through two a year. At different seasons I write down combinations of plants to try together. Inspiration can come from sources as diverse as something seen on TV or magazines or glanced on a road verge.

You may not think that you have a great deal of flair or imagination. It doesn't matter. If you make the effort to use your eyes and translate what you see around you and adapt it to your own garden then you will create something special.

As well as plant ideas make a note of maintenance jobs to do and areas of the garden or particular plants that are not pulling their weight.

Spending plenty of time staring and daydreaming is all part of the creative planning process. Stop and take a moment and the 'great thoughts' will come.

Plan your structural and feature plants first. With a sunny, well-drained site and a blue/lemon colour theme, *Phormium cookianum* 'Tricolour' and helictotrichon grasses add the structural, evergreen framework here with *Salvia nemorosa* 'Blue Hills' and gold sedum dribbled through to strengthen the theme.

*Step 3: Consider garden size and shape*

Do you really need garden beds in certain places at all? Are the existing planting spaces a good general size and shape? Could a row of clipped trees or pots along the fence or just a clean, painted wall create a calmer, crisper setting than what presently exists? Just because you have always had plants in that particular place doesn't mean it has to continue that way.

Ask whether the various pockets of planting around an area work together or do they give a bitty look. Could some fiddly beds be enlarged and some ineffective and labour-intensive beds be grassed or paved over to streamline the design and direct attention to where you can group plants in a more dramatic way?

*Step 4: Find the faults*

Try and identify why the present scheme isn't working. You may initially think that everything is wrong. But as you look closer you will identify a few key faults. Here is a checklist of some of the common faults and how to correct them.

**Problem:** *The plants aren't happy.*
Often problems can simply stem from the poor health of your plants. If they are just looking a little sulky it is probably simple factors that need changing like light levels, soil moisture and nutrition. Often shrubs may be nearing the end of their life – some can be cut back, fed and rejuvenated but many will need the boot.

**Solution:** Some good old TLC mixed with a dose of brutality. Incorporate buckets of grit and compost to improve aeration, drainage and nutrition. Be extravagant because, let's face it, how often are you going to repeat the job? A soggy hollow might need draining, and planting will need to be revised to allow for the present microclimate that may have changed since the border was first planted. Most perennials will benefit from being lifted and divided.

**Problem:** *There is no sense of style.*
The plants look like a motley group of strangers at a railway platform rather than a happy family.

**Solution:** Form a clear idea of what you hope to achieve in this part of the garden. Do you want simplicity or drama? What sort of feel do you want the planting to evoke? What sort of colours do you want to use? Often an existing tree or shrub that you want to keep will suggest a planting style or a colour scheme. This master 'wish list' will guide all the other decisions you make. If you didn't have set ideas before, your style statement will suddenly help you identify what is wrong with the present planting.

**Problem:** *There is too much going on.*
In your enthusiasm over time you (or the previous owners) might have added just too many plants fighting for attention or too many added extras like pots, statues or bits of topiary. Unity is one of the basics you need to get right.

**Solution:** If there are lots of self-seeding bulbs, biennials and annuals these are often the first to go so you can get back to some good bones. Before you start, identify what is causing the busyness. Is it merely the colours or too many different shapes? Often plants need repeating and gathering into distinct groups. Chapter 7 covers simplifying a bed in detail.

**Problem:** *There isn't enough going on.*
The opposite scenario is a boring border with a limited range of plants. It may look, as a composition, simple and tasteful or it might just look bare with gaps between but if you feel bored with it, it is time to inject some life.

**Solution:** Add something bold and definite. Provide drama with new structural plants and add detail planting too for seasonal effects. If planting is already generous, punch a few interesting holes, bays and gaps to make way for new blood. If the general shape and composition is good consider adding some interesting details – a light climber over a shrub, a few bulbs for a blast of seasonal cheer or a dusting of self-seeders to add some spontaneity. Whatever you add must complement what you keep.

**Problem:** *There is something wrong with the backdrop or edges.*
Either too much ugly fence or wall is showing and dominating the scene or you might be looking through to next-door's orange house. Worst of all, the neighbours are looking through at you from their elevated deck! Edging might be too wiggly, too bright or non-existent.

**Solution:** Change the edges, paint the fence, build a wall and plant some simple screening with repeated plants or climbers.

**Problem:** *There is no structure and form.*
Here someone has been busy with all the pretty bulbs, annuals and perennials and forgotten the architectural or structural elements.

**Solution:** Add a backbone: one or two types of structural plants. Go for at least one with good year-round leaves, one

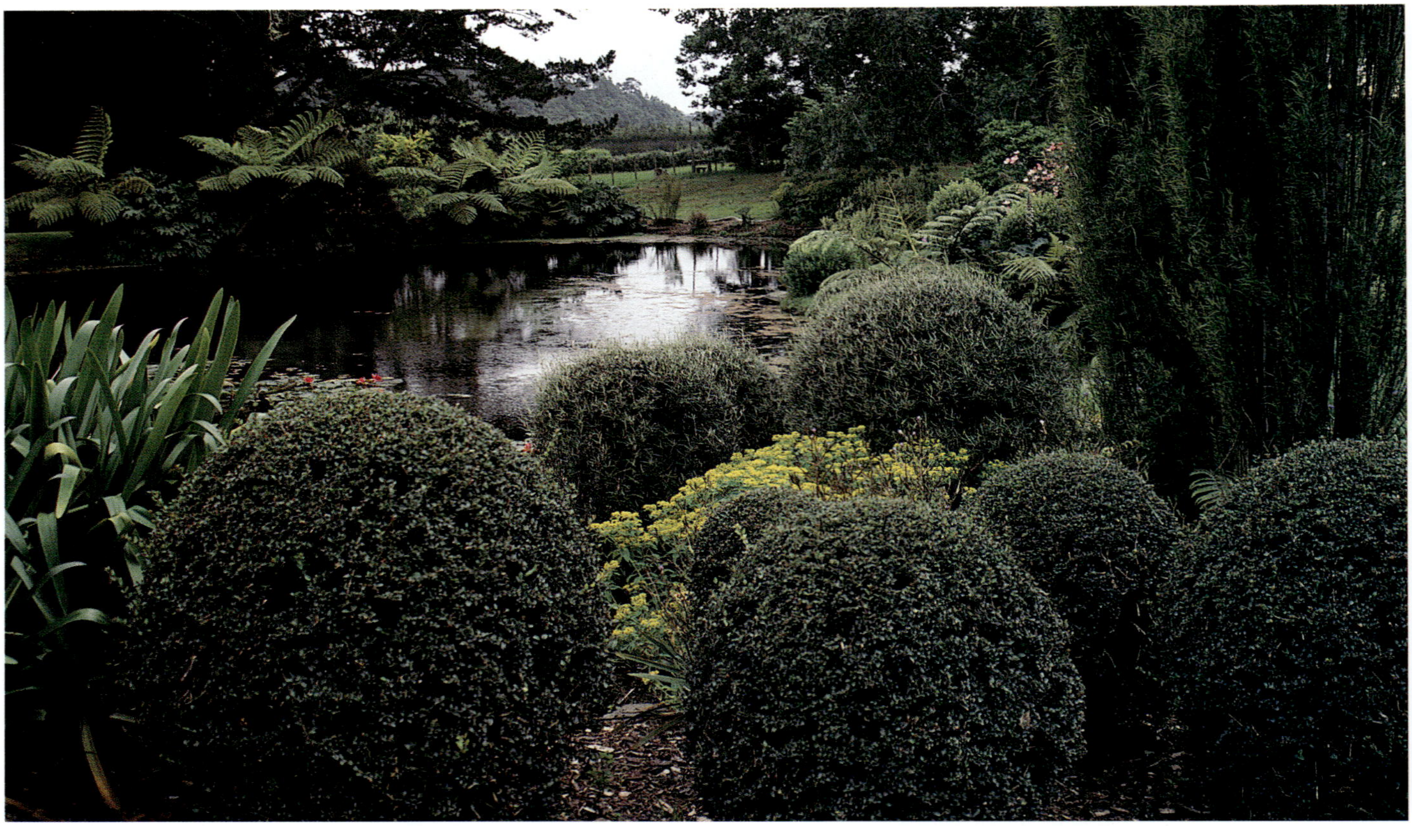

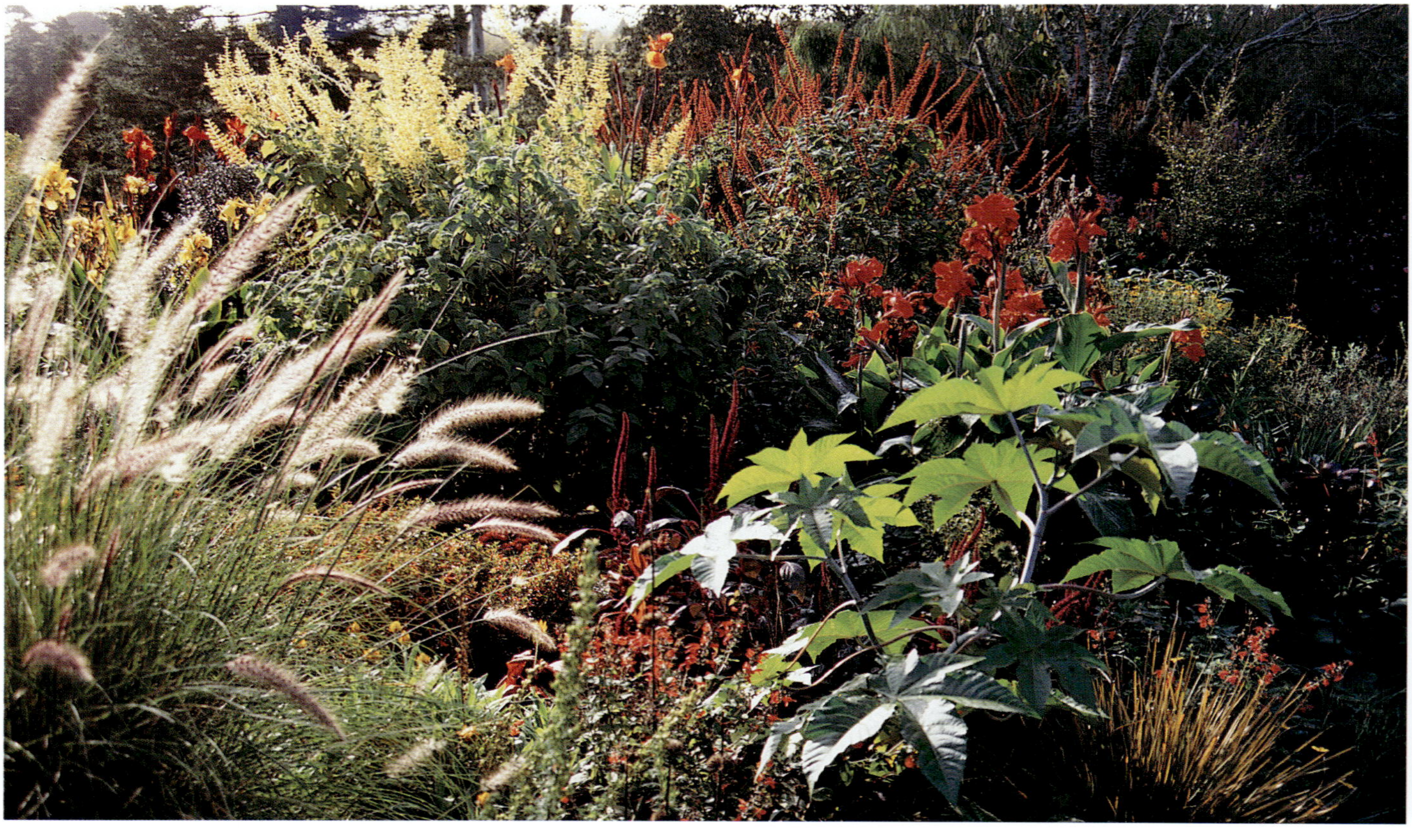

with strong form and maybe a third with contrasting form.

Notice which times of year there is nothing going on. Sometimes a low ebb is just a seasonal glitch, which can be smoothed over with a plant that will bring drama at that particular time (neighbours' gardens are good for inspirational ideas at key months).

In a boring border if there is even one redeeming feature, one plant you really like that looks happy and healthy, then that might be a good place to begin to build a stronger planting. You might repeat that plant and thread it through the new border as a firm starting block. Large shrubs and established trees will take several years to replace so even if you aren't mad on them, carefully consider all their qualities and consider keeping them. A tree may be the wrong colour and drop leaves in autumn but it may also screen a neighbour or have a beautiful branch structure, which might mean it is worth keeping after all.

Problem: *The proportions of plants are wrong.*
Sometimes a vigorous plant is doing so well that it has taken over the show or there is a plant that is doing well but you would like to see more of it. Be careful of acting on impulse when this is the case as some plants are only attractive for a short time — they are luxuries and you don't want to make them main players in the design. Often a prima donna may be stealing the show from other plants. Where you want harmony, consider sacrificing dominating plants such as gladiolus with bright red flowers or strongly variegated foliage for the sake of the common good.

Solution: Get the spade out. It is amazing how being brave and taking out one jarring element can make what's left look a hundred percent better. Removing gold coleonemas is the classic example. Propagate the plants you want to increase.

Problem: *A bed has no topography.*
If the planting is just a big wad of swelling undergrowth like a beached whale with no intriguing inlets, headlands, spires and caves it's time to do some sculpting. On the other hand your plants may be scattered rather than arranged in family groups to give a definite composition.

Solution: Slash, burn and prune. Knock some holes in monotonous banks of lavender and prune up those old camellias to show a bit of leg and make intriguing shadowy caves.

Problem: *A bed is too formal or not formal enough.*

Solution: Overly rigid repetition can easily be remedied by removing one element and loosening up the planting in between. To increase formality identify a feature plant to repeat through the planting. Consider using a wall or fence behind or pots, topiary and sculpture to formalise a bed.

Problem: *The border doesn't relate with the rest of the garden.*

Solution: Here repetition is essential. With your overall theme clearly in your mind choose a new plant or pick an existing plant in the garden to be a signature plant that you can weave across from border to border, creating a thread of unity. Reliable evergreens make good link plants. If you choose a link plant based on flower colour the effect will only work for a season. This might make a good secondary signature plant but you'll still need other repeated elements. Architectural plants and topiary make good linking elements, as do species with strong foliage.

Problem: *I've got the wrong kind of plants.*
Do a check up of your desired theme and the key shape ingredients you have already and their distribution along the border. Are there enough structural plants to anchor things down such as architectural plants and some solid blobs of leaf and form? Sometimes there might be just too much variation in foliage and form — a glut of prima donnas without a supporting cast or an over-emphasis on flower power at the expense of good foliage.

Solution: If it is all too hard and angular add some softness. If it's all too flat add some spikes and spires. If it falls apart in May add some daphnes or proteas — it's all pretty obvious really.

*Step 5: Hack and slash*
Now the fun begins. Remove what you see as the weak, the sick, the overpowering and the downright ugly. Reduce the space wasters and destroy

---

Opposite above
Get the main structure in the garden sorted and everything else will fall into place. This well-shaped scene is at Woodbridge near Auckland.

Opposite below
Backlit magic from *Salvia confertifolia* and *Salvia madrensis*. Even what may seem like a chaotic jungle has its moments, so live with your existing planting before rushing in with a spade.

those boring little plants that sit there doing precious little all year. Make plenty of delicious space to be creative – dig in compost and feed the gaps. With the planting left behind you may need to group them a little more meaningfully straight away or fill the gaps with more of the same.

## Step 6: Take a break

Before planting any new plants, having refined your original planting and sorted the wheat from the chaff, the next important step is to sit back and WATCH! Live with your garden for a while. New planting ideas will pop into your head in the context of your already vastly improved border. The new look needs time to grow on you or the opposite might happen – those plants you thought that you wanted to retain will suddenly become very annoying. It may be time for that skip again and some more editing!

## Step 7: Plug the gaps with framework planting

Begin by looking at the existing topography: where are there hollows that need filling or headlands that you want to create?

Choose the trees, shrubs and larger perennials that you want to put in these places. Obviously the site situation and soil will determine on a practical level which new plants you choose, but on a creative level you need to consider all those important factors like contrasting plant shapes and foliage, and then aspects like colour and flower season. This is the time to add those dramatic structural plants (see Chapter 6). They might be repeated in groups or might form occasional highlights. Place any focal points like pots or seats at this stage also.

## Step 8: Keep it simple

With bare ground, resist the urge to plant a plethora of new plants. Try to plant in multiples. If all your new plants are single specimens alarm bells should be ringing. Keep the back of the border and behind the scenes places particularly simple to cut down on maintenance and allow easy access for weeding. If you are a plant lover and tend towards a busy look, consciously create at least one large slab or ribbon of mass planting somewhere in every bed to offset your inevitable slide into busyness.

## Step 9: Put the icing on the cake

With the main elements in place your border should look almost complete but hopefully you have left enough gaps to add in the luxuries that will add seasonal highlights, perhaps soften the edges or just create an element of richness and surprise. If you have got the structural body of the border right (your cake) you can afford the luxury of having something special to top it off.

## Step 10: Change your mind

Invariably a friend will come over for a drink and put the spanner in the works. They will point out something you missed, quote a gardening guru or simply beat you into submission with bullying tactics, convinced that their taste is invariably better than yours. Worse still you will visit a garden centre and get tempted. Changing your mind and altering an initial plan are all part of the process.

---

**Left**

A subtropical mix relying totally on contrasting foliage for the drama. Natives like astelia and scleranthus mix with an impressive *Kalanchoe beharensis* in the centre.

**Opposite**

As trees grow up a sunny border can become a woodland glade and the planting beneath needs to evolve. This bevy of shade lovers includes a thread of heuchera and gold hakonechloa grass with a silvery comfrey (*Symphytum* x *uplandicum* 'Variegatum').

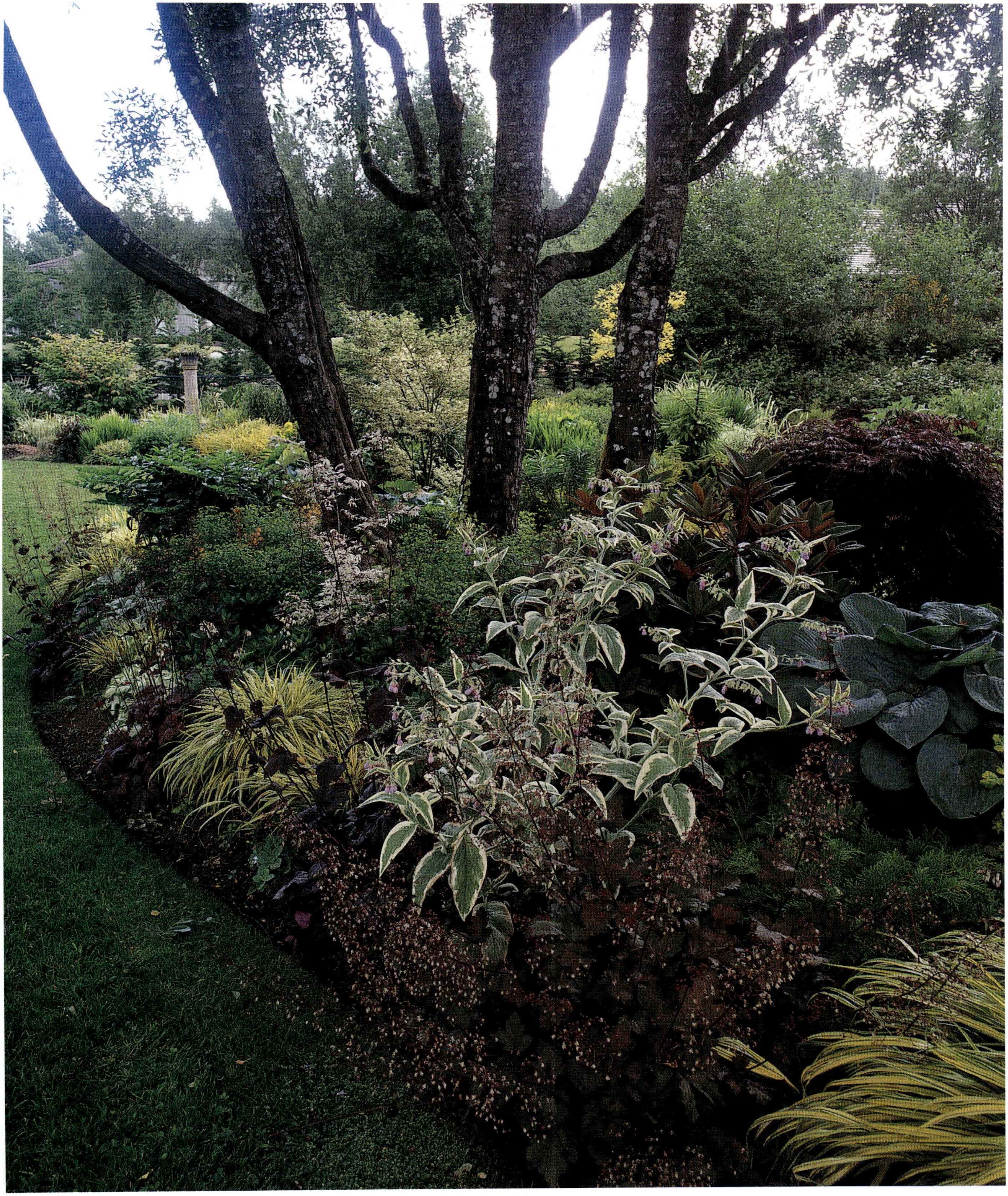

## Creating a new garden bed

The clean sheet approach can be daunting – if things go wrong we can't blame any problems we inherited, except perhaps an atrocious soil or a harsh aspect, which are the first considerations when planning any type of planting. If you have just moved to a new house, often there will be only a whisper of topsoil spread over inhospitable subsoil. If this is the case then it's essential to spend the time and money investing in plenty of additional topsoil and organic compost to build up the beds to create a free-draining and more hospitable start for your plants.

Some people love to have a detailed plan and others prefer to do things on the ground. I find that a combination of the two is best; I love constructing a cunning plan and then inevitably find (much to my own disgust) that when I get out there I change my mind and get even better ideas when I can see the proper scale of things. Physically laying out at least your most important structural plants is an essential part of the process. Be realistic as you anticipate the width and height that everything will grow — this is the time to ensure your slow but eventually substantial tortoises are placed first.

Most of the 10 stages set out in pages 178–182 are relevant when planning a new border, but here are some extra thoughts and a suggested order for the project.

### Step 1: Make a wish list
I find writing a wish list of suitable plants is essential. Make it as long and creative as you like for maximum choice. The only absolute requirements for all plants on your list is that they be sympathetic with your theme, and that they will, in all probability, enjoy the particular soil and situation.

### Step 2: Shorten the wish list to make a planting list
Now get real! Reduce your list severely. When it comes to the final choice we have to be ruthless in culling to prevent busyness.

### Step 3: Plan things on paper
Even if it is just a scribble on the back of a cornflakes packet, getting your ideas on paper will immediately help you see if you are on the right track and will help you develop your idea. A plan needn't be to scale but that will be useful in a large area. Some people like to do a plan before thinking about specific plants. They like to plan the shapes, humps and hollows first then find plants that will fit the requirements. I work the other way by making a list of possible plants and using that as inspiration for my plan.

A plan is especially useful for planting the main structural bones in a design. A plan like this has a good variety of contrasting shapes set to create islands, headlands and a cave under the tree.

1. Tree to hide neighbour's deck.
2. Some fat blobs (eg. upright rosemary) grouped to pad out the border.
3. Smaller shrubs (eg. choisya).
4. A cluster of fuzzy shapes (eg. citissus) strengthens the corner.
5. A weeping shrub (eg. juniper) sticks out to form a headland.
6. Five architectural stars (eg. cordyline) to add drama.
7. Large drift of evergreen perennials (eg. acorus or carex). Other drifts of perennials and bulbs, and a scattering of annuals, will be added later.
8. Spires to help anchor down the more amorphous shapes.

## Step 4: Mark out the site and the structural planting

For planning your numbers and to get an idea of the feel of your planting, for larger beds it is important to mark out at least the more structural elements like larger shrubs, trees, topiary and architectural elements. Use buckets, bricks or bamboo poles — possibly colour-coded — so you can tell what represents what. At this stage you may well revise your plan.

## Step 5: Planting

If you moved into a new house you wouldn't lay out your book collection before you had lifted in the furniture and especially the bookcase. Likewise, in planning and planting a border there is a logical way to lay out the plants and plant them when they arrive. Although there is a rough pecking order it doesn't imply that any stage is more important than another. (Books are just as important as the bookcase, after all.)

Obviously the larger, longer-lived and more permanent plants like trees need the most careful placement and will be considered first. The smaller and most ephemeral ingredients can be sprinkled around at the end. Within each of the groups of plants listed below I find that it's best to give the evergreen plants consideration first so that in winter they will give a pleasing composition.

### Larger structural backbone plants

Lay out and plant these first. They will mainly be trees, shrubs, perhaps large grasses massed in groups and drifts. Most often you will want a simple mixture of shapes and foliage — evergreen and deciduous. These structural plants will become your backdrop and might screen out neighbours, so plan them like the headlands at the coast.

### Dramatic feature plants (permanent)

These will grab the attention for much of the year. In smaller borders often the architectural plants like topiary, flax or large succulents like aloes provide both the drama and the main sense of structure. In larger beds, however, often in being so dominant they will be less numerous and will be grouped around softer but larger structural elements. Plan them like rocky stacks at the beach: in family groups or stepping out a rhythm, either formally or informally.

### Dramatic feature plants (non-permanent)

Cannas and grasses with their good form, dahlias with their flowers, and plants like cardoons and acanthus, which provide both, make for striking stand-out stars. Though they come and go, they have high impact when they are firing on all cylinders so they need careful spacing to relate well. Use them as one-off wonders or grouped and keep them distanced from too many other high-drama plants. Simple backdrops of structural plants will work well.

Large, evergreen perennials like these — *Phormium* 'Yellow Wave', *Ligularia reniformis* and hemerocallis — should be planted before the more ephemeral members of your team.

### Medium shapely plants

The many perennials and small shrubs with good form and foliage can be grouped and drifted around the taller elements. Position your shrubs before perennials.

### Small shapely plants

Create drifts and pools of textural groundcovers and small, well-behaved perennials. By now the gaps should be closing but, if you want, leave up to a third of your bed for the luxuries.

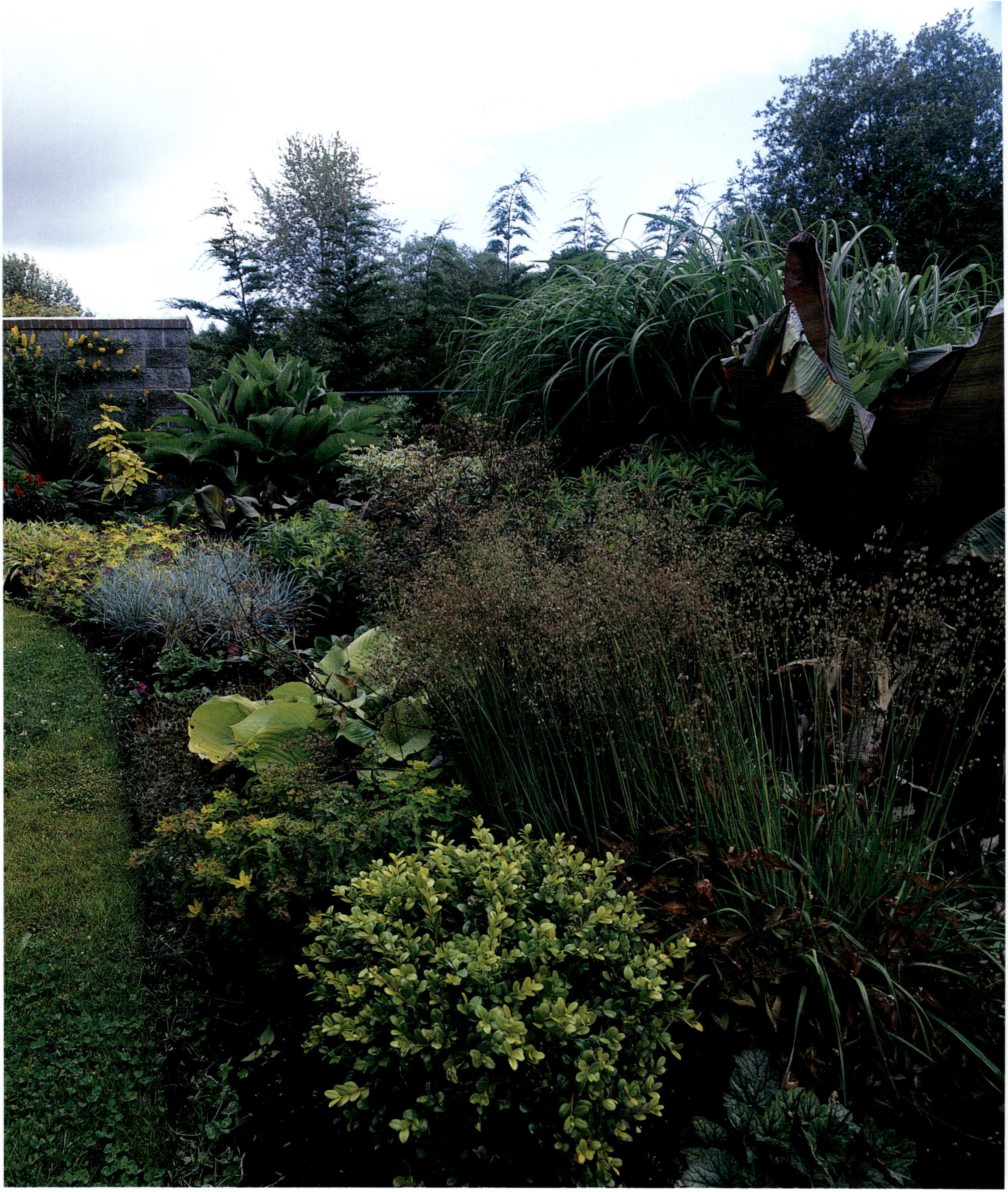

### Long-lived luxuries

Only when all your structural and textural stalwarts are in place can you consider your luxuries. Begin with the permanent ones such as bulbs and perennials. Some luxuries like geraniums are good fillers to soften out the border but other luxuries will primarily provide flower power, either at a useful time of the year (helenium and echinacea) or for long stretches of the season such as cupheas.

### Nomads

Many small seeding perennials, annuals and biennials provide that wonderful detailing and lubricate the more structural elements. A few notable exceptions like architectural *Nicotiana sylvestris* and biennial verbascums are so imposing that they might need to be planned earlier in the process. But for most of these fly-by-nights the fun and beauty will be in allowing them to work out their own place in the picture.

## Step 6: Polish

The final look of a border is greatly affected by the finish — the way you maintain, clip, weed and polish your garden. The finish depends largely on your particular taste and personality. Some of us are naturally neat and precise: we hang things up and put things away, and our gardens reflect this. A weed is only a plant growing in the wrong place and a tidy gardener will have a much longer list and a much shorter tolerance to unplanned visitors than a more casual gardener.

**Opposite**
Threads of bronze banana and *Persicaria* 'Red Dragon' along with gold hosta and buxus knit this modern border together. The veil of deschampsia grass adds some essential lightness.

Smart and tidy gardens where the shrubs are pruned tightly, paths are swept regularly and weeds don't even get a foothold look crisp and perky. Plant shapes are better defined and the garden looks loved and cared for. This approach is especially suitable near the house and along the edges of beds that are seen easily. The manicured approach is also essential in minimalistic gardens, which rely on clean spaces and a lack of clutter.

In contrast, a relaxed treatment can be more beneficial to wildlife and it can save us an awful lot of hard (some would say unnecessary) work. Autumn leaves left to lie will be dragged down naturally into the soil by worms and studies have proved that the old and fastidious techniques of pruning roses are now obsolete — a clip over with the shears will do. The laid-back approach can produce a more naturalistic look that is especially suitable in the far reaches of the garden and at the back of borders that aren't seen so easily.

Your feet may be firmly in one camp or the other on neatness. There is, however, a place to combine both

Woodland gardens lend themselves to a more relaxed maintenance regime. Here *Acer palmatum* cultivars, foxglove and gunnera do the weepy-blobby-spiky thing brilliantly.

approaches in the same garden and sometimes when the manicured look meets a ragged approach there is a refreshing spark. An example is a loose and 'messy' wildflower meadow that is complemented by a manicured and close-mown path cutting through the middle.

## Step 7: Reassess everything as it grows

I once bought *Euphorbia* 'Fens Ruby', thinking it would tickle itself into a corner. Instead it enveloped two metres of border in a tidal wave of growth. We need to keep our eyes open — cosset the slow plodders and beat the thugs senseless. Life isn't perfect. Sometimes the plant we bought is not the colour we hoped for or the effect of a particular shrub is too dominant or too subtle. Even with the best plants in the world, nature will surprise us — the mistakes and the unexpected surprises become our favourite bits and nature and time add their final brushstrokes to the picture.

Gardening is not, after all, about a finished design that when implemented means the garden is finished — it is a journey with no end point.

## The most important things

If you have got nothing else out of this book I hope at least that you feel inspired to look at the way plants interact in your garden a little closer and determine to enjoy the exciting process of design. Much of the time these days we are passive consumers but making a garden is one of the best ways to revel in the pleasure of a personal creation rather than consumption. Of the many principles of design here perhaps the three most important are to:

- Contrast foliage shapes and forms.
- Repeat key plants through your borders.
- Try and stick to a style, theme or colour scheme.

. . . but even these are not the most important thing.

### Heart and soul

What will set your garden apart is when you stamp your own personality on the place. Beyond sound principles of design if a garden doesn't have this most intimate spark it will lack heart and soul.

Some gardens just feel loved. You can sense the difference between one that has been designed by a designer and then 'maintained' and one that has been nurtured and gardened by a gardener. A dramatic design full of gimmicks and flashy planting is like watching a *Star Wars* movie. It's an expensive blockbuster. Though it may grab our attention with special effects, the dazzle is skin deep — if it lacks atmosphere and character then it won't grab our emotions at a deeper level.

The funny thing about soul is that you can't buy it off the shelf — it doesn't come with an instant makeover or by reading a book such as this. Neither is a soulful garden necessarily stylish, fashionable or even tasteful. What is required to create it is that we pour ourselves into the place. Whether you are a deep thinker, maybe a spiritual person or a joker with a light and fresh approach, whether you are methodical or a scatter brain, your personality is the greatest gift you can inject into your planting.

Good gardening and great gardens start and end with two things: love and passion. The less we try to copy other people and be ourselves, the richer will be the garden that we make. That's not to say we can't be inspired and affected by what others are doing but that we take our own slant on what we see rather than mindlessly regurgitating the latest fad and fashion.

### Enjoy

Even when our attempts to design and cultivate are atrocious nature graciously steps in time and time again to clean up the mess and to delight and surprise us with a bursting bud, an unfurled leaf or a dusting of frost and dew.

So be sure to stop the weeding, digging and planning from time to time and just for a minute, instead of all the 'doing', allow yourself to just 'be' in the garden. It is rather like a hot bath; you may not always have the time to get in and soak but we need to do it once in a while to keep us sane. We should never become so obsessed with improving and fine-tuning our particular patch that we become our own worst critic, never able to enjoy what we have achieved so far.

Gardens are for the enjoying and the process of gardening is primarily a hedonistic pursuit — like a rugby match there will be some pain and struggle but inevitably the sweet taste of victory. Edwin Lutyens was certainly right — gardening is a game and in the end nobody is going to shoot us if we get it wrong. We just need to get out there, head down the step, grab the spade and enjoy our time on the pitch.

---

Team spirit: *Ajania pacifica, Magnolia* 'Little Gem' and agave — very different characters working well together. If you're having a ball it will show in your planting.

# Index

Page numbers in bold indicate illustrations. Plant names in the text have not been indexed.

*Acacia baileyana purpurea*, **88**
*Acaena caesiiglauca*, **104**
*Acer palmatum*, 30, **187**
*Achillea millefolium* 'Red Beacon', 31
   *A. m.* 'Salmon Beauty', **93**
*Acorus gramineus* 'Ogon', **18**
*Aeonium arboreum* 'Atropurpureum', **124**
   *A. a.* 'Schwarzkopf', **10, 101**
*Agapanthus* 'Streamline', **9**
*Agave attenuata*, **58, 66**
   *A. parryi*, **104**
aging garden — see maturing garden
*Ajania pacifica*, **188**
*Alcanteria imperialis* 'Silver Form', **5**
alchemilla, **164**
aloe, 77
*Aloe aborescens*, **85**
   *A. ferox*, **85**
   *A. thraskii*, **28**
*Alstroemeria* 'Red Baron', **101**
anchor planting, 42, 72
angel's fishing rod, **133**
annuals, 88, 127–8, 172, 187
*Anthemis tinctoria* 'E.C. Buxton', **105**
architectural plants, 33–6, 42, 179–80, 181, 185
   positioning, 36
*Artemesia* 'Silver Queen', **7**
arum lilies, **30, 87**
autumn, 89
Ayrlies Garden, **42, 70, 87, 101,** 112, 174, **175**

backdrops, 135–40, 179
balance in planting, 41–6, 90
banana, **186**
biennials, 88, 127–8, 172, 187
billbergias, **112**
blobs, plant shapes, 17–19, 117, 181
blocky planting, 43–4, 75–6, 78
blue plants, 104
bold planting, 74, 160, 166
borders, 128, 131, 140–4, 179, 181
   small gardens, 157–9
*Bougainvillea* 'Scarlet O'Hara', **137**
bromeliads, **11, 54,** 163
brown plants, 100
*Brugmansia* 'Noel's Blush', **93**

bulbs, 123, 131, 132
busyness, 68, 69–72, 179

*Campanula* 'Elizabeth', **130**
   *C. latifolia*, **102**
canna, **106**
*Canna* 'Assault', **7**
   *C.* 'Parkes', **101**
cardoons, 37
*Carex* 'Frosted Curls', **115, 120**
   *C. elata* 'Aurea', **87**
   *C. flagellifera*, **123, 149**
   *C. hachijoensis* 'Evergold', **58, 144, 166**
   *C. siderosticha* 'Variegata', **115**
   *C. testacea*, **27**
carpeters, 25–7, 167
*Centranthus ruber*, **59**
Chatham Island forget-me-not, **147**
*Chionochloa flavicans*, **159**
*Clematis* 'Perle d'Azur', **133**
climbers, 23, 64, 136–7, 128, 164
colour, 62, 65, 70–1, 74, 81, 91–106, 127
   classic partnerships, 106
   foliage, 96, 118
   seasonal, 88, 89
   trees, 64–5
contrasts, 16–17, 61–2
   colour, 95–6
   leaf shape and texture, 109–18
*Convolvulus cneorum*, **51**
*Coprosma* 'Beatsons Brown', **42**
   *C.* 'Hawera', **27**
   *C.* x *kirkii*, **72**
*Cordyline* 'Red Fountain', **35**
   *C. australis* 'Albertii', **35**
*Corokia* x *virgata*, **139**
*Cortaderia selloana* 'Gold Band', **22**
*Corydalis flexuosa*, **83**
cottage style, 55–6, 127
cotton lavenders (santolinas), **76**
*Craspedia globosa*, **139**
*Crassula ovata*, **15**
*Crinum moorei*, **22**
*Crocosmia* 'Lucifer', **31**
*Cupressus sempervirens*, **39**
*Cycas revoluta*, **113**
*Cynara cardunculus*, **37**
*Cynoglossum amabile*, **56**

*Dasylirion*, **15**
depth, 11, 12–13
desert style, 52–3, 114
design principals in practice, 177–88
details, 11
*Dierama pulcherrimum alba*, **133**
diffuse planting, 74–5, 78
   edging, 144
dinner-plate shaped foliage, 110–2
divaricating plants, 18, **18**, 27, 28, 52, 116–7, 119
dotty planting, 45–6
*Dracaena marginata* 'Tricolor', **140**
dramatic planting, 57–66, 185
drifts of plants, 76, 78

*Echeveria* 'Chocolate', **66**
   *E. elegans*, **77, 104**
*Echium pininana*, **67, 129**
   *E. plantagineum*, **59**
edging, 128, 131, 140–4, 179, 181
elkhorn fern, **163**
*Eryngium giganteum*, **175**
espalier, 29
*Euphorbia charachias*, **51**
   *E. cyparissias* 'Fens Ruby', **124**
   *E. glauca*, **124, 129**
   *E. lambii*, **109**
   *E. polychroma*, **126**
evergreen plants, 108–9, 181

faults, correcting, 179–82
features, 147–56, 174–5 — *see also* water features
farfugiums, **158**
fences, 140, 181
ferny leaf shapes, 113–4
fescue grass, **64**
*Ficus roxburghii*, **166**
flower beds, 11–14
   removing, 14
focus, 10–1
foliage, 107–20, 181
   coloured, 96, 118
   highlighting a man-made feature, 151, 152
formal planting, 50–1, 78–81, 181
   edging, 142–4
foxgloves, **56, 187**
framing the garden, 135, 162–4

furcraea, **108**
*Furcraea marginata*, **8**
fuzzy leaf shapes, 116–7

gazanias, **80**
*Geranium macrorrhizum*, **13**
grasses, 115–6, 133–4
gravel, as edging, **142**
gravel gardens, 144–6, **145**
green plants, 97
grey plants, 99
groundcovers, 25–7, 64, 76
   partnerships, 123
growth, planning for, 170–2

habits, plant, 125–34 — *see also* climbers
*Hakonechloa macra* 'Aureola', **30, 183**
hand-shaped leaves, 114
hebe, **64**
*Hebe cupressoides*, **172**
hedges, 138–9, 141–2
helictotrichon grasses, **178**
hemerocallis, **103, 124, 185**
*Heterocentron elegans*, **160**
heuchera, **145, 155, 183**
hibiscus, **63, 124**
honesty, **98**
horizontal plant forms, 29–31
hosta, **83, 186**

informal planting, 50–1, 80–1, 161
*Inula magnifica*, **131**
iresines, **150**
*Iris foetidissima variegata*, **107**
   *I. tectorum*, **123**
island beds, 14, 137

jack-in-the-box plants, 131–3
Japanese style, **49, 50**, 60
Jekyll, Gertrude, 29, 30, 81

*Kalanchoe beharensis*, **182**
   *K. daigremontiana*, **91**
knot garden, **63**
kowhai, **18**

lawns, groundcover, 26
leaves, 109–18
   hand shapes, 114

indistinct, 118
leafy shapes, 117
sounds, 119, 133
spring growth, 119–20
texture, 118–9
translucence, 120
*Leucanthemum vulgare*, **126**
libertias, **152**
light whisperer plants, 133–4
*Ligularia reniformis*, **185**
liriope, **79**
living spaces, balance with garden, 13–14
lobelia, **123**
loose weaver plant shapes, 31–2
*Lunaria annua* 'Alba Variegata', **98**
luxury plants, 86, 181, 187
lychnis, **126, 137**
*Lychnis chalcedonica*, **59, 131**
*Lysimachia atropurpurea*, **99**

*Magnolia* 'Little Gem', **188**
maintenance, 90, 169–76
maples, **30**
mat plants, 25–7, 167
maturing garden, 62, 169–76
   proportion, 174, 175, 181
   sun and shade, 172–4
Mediterranean style, 51–2
Mexican hat, **91**
minimalism, 68
miscanthus grasses, **88, 129**
mondo grass, **69, 167**
   black, **11, 155**
monstera, **173**

narrow gardens, 160–1, 162–4
neoregelias, **140**
new garden bed, creating, 184–8
nicotiana, **157, 164**
*Nicotiana sylvestris*, **106**
nikau palms, **73**

*Olearia cheesmanii*, **136**
*Ophiopogon*, **11, 155, 167**
oreganum, golden, **11**
ox-eye daisies, **126, 168**

*Pachystegia insignis*, **64**
paeonies, **171**

partnerships, plant, 122-4 — *see also* contrasts
colour, 106
paths, in side gardens, 161
paulownia, **112**
paving, 140, 165, 167-8
penstemons, **103**
perennials, 19, 88, 89, 123, 127, 131, 132-3, 172, 187
*Persicaria* 'Red Dragon', **186**
personality plants, 121-34
*Phalaris arundinacea* 'Picta', **13**
*Phlomis russeliana*, **102**
phlox, **103**
*Phormium* 'Platt's Black', **130**
    *P.* 'Yellow Wave', **185**
    *P. cookianum* 'Tricolour', **178**
*Physostegia virginiana* 'Lavender', **130**
*Pisonia brunoniana* 'Variegata', **58**
*Pittosporum tenuifolium* 'Tom Thumb', **100**
pizza topping planting, 27
plant shapes, 15-32
    combining, 17
    horizontal forms, 29-31
*Platycerium*, **163**
pleaching, 29, 39, 138, 164
pohutukawa, **173**
pollarding, 39, 40
potagers, 142, 144
pots, 148, 150, 151, 152, 153, 154-6, 174-5, 181
*Primula helodoxa*, **87**
*Pseudopanax ferox*, **159**
    *P. lessonii*, **159**
puka, **111, 159**
punctuation plants, 81-2
purple plants, 105

red plants, 101
repetitive planting, 61, 73-82, 181
*Rhopalostylis sapida*, **73**
rhythm, 73, 77-82, 159
ribbon planting, 30

*Rosa* 'Cathayensis', **130**
*Rudbeckia fulgida*, **89**

*Salvia confertifolia*, **180**
    *S. elegans*, **106**
    *S. madrensis*, **180**
    *S. nemorosa* 'Blue Hills', **7, 178**
santolina, **76**
*Santolina* 'Lemon Fizz', **103**
*Scadoxis multiflorus* subsp. *katherinae*, **107**
scattered planting, 77, 78
screening, 136
sculpture, **149, 150, 151**, 181
seasonal interest, 83-90
*Sedum adolphi*, **152**
seeding plants, 125-8
sempervivums, **155**
*Senecio cineraria*, **47**
    *S. serpens*, 27, **80**
set pieces, 65-6
shapes — *see* flower beds; leaves; plant shapes
shrubs, rounded, 17-19
Siberian iris, **86**
side gardens, 160-4
simplicity, 11, 67-72, 74, 158, 160, 166, 182
Sissinghurst, 26, **26**, 67, **67**, 92, 178
sisyrinchium, **99**
small spaces, 157-68
soil preparation, 12
*Sophora prostrata*, **18**
sounds, leaves, 119, 133
space, 69
Spanish shawl, **160**
specimen planting in lawns, 166-7
spikes
    leaf shapes, 114-5
    plant shapes, 28-9
spires, plant shapes, 23-5
spreading plants, 125
standards, 39-40, 164
steps, 167-8
strappy leaf shapes, 112-3

structural plants — *see* architectural plants
styles of planting, 10, 16-17, 47-56, 179
subtropical style, 54-5
swamp cypress trees, **70**
*Syagrus*, **170**
*Symphytum* x *uplandicum* 'Variegatum', **183**
*Synadenium grantii* 'Rubra', **117**

*Taxodium distichum*, **70**
thalictrum, **16, 103**
themes, 10, 16-17, 47-56
*Thuja orientalis* 'Pyramidalis', **165**
*Tillandsia usneoides*, **134**
tobacco plant, **106, 157, 164**
toetoe, variegated, **22**
*Toona sinensis*, **15**
topiary, 37-8, 162, 164, 181
trailing plants, 20, 22
training plants, 64 — *see also* espalier; pleaching; pollarding
trees, specimen, 166-7

upswept plant shapes, 19-20

variegated plants, 65, 71, **108, 109, 114**
*Verbena bonariensis*, **35**
vigorous spreading plants, 125
vireya rhododendron, **140**
*Vriesea splendens*, **11**

walls, 140, 181
water features, **57**
weeping plants, 20, 22
white plants, 98
woodland plants, 88

yellow plants, 102
*Yucca elephantipes*, **79**

*Zantedeschia*, **30**
    *Z. childsiana*, **87**

# Photographic and garden acknowledgements

All photos by the author, except those by Gil Hanly (GH) including front and back cover.

Abbott, Marilyn (West Green House): p. 47
Arnet, Sandra: p. 61
Beveridge, Sam & Downs, Tony (Shigeki Gardens): p. 49 (GH)
Blundell, Bee & John (Ngaranui): pp. 109, 118, 187
Brady, Peter: pp. 60, 72, 140, 142, 149, 163 (GH)
Carew, Sharyn: p. 166 (GH)
Christchurch Botanic Gardens: p. 64
Cleary, Graham: p. 154 (GH)
Cochrane, Linda: pp. 183 (GH), 186 (GH)
Coney, Miles & Anne: p. 63
Cooper, Cilla: p. 28 (GH)
Coyle, Jocelyn & Peter (Totara Waters): back cover; pp. 7, 10, 77 (GH), 153
Disley, Brett: p. 170 (GH)
Filoli-Woodside, San Francisco: p. 44 (GH)
Fisher, Joy & Gordon: p. 53 (GH)
Fryer, Ian: p. 141 (GH)
Garrett, Barbara: p. 162
Gillies, Geraldine: pp. 15 (GH), 33 (GH)
Government House, Auckland: p. 175
Greene, Isabelle: p. 80 (GH)
Henderson, Sophie & Collier: p. 51
Higgie, Clive & Nicki (Fernwood): p. 129 (GH)
Hudson, Norma & Bob: p. 82 (GH)
Kilsby, Kevin: pp. 35 (GH), 57 (GH), 150 (GH)
Kreutzberger, Sibylle & Schwerdt, Pamela (Gloucester): p. 46
Lagzdins, Elga: p. 68 (GH)
Laity, Judy (Cottonwood): pp. 71, 124
Lawrence, Pat & Selwyn: p. 126 (GH)
Lewis, Pam & Peter (Sticky Wicket): p. 46 (GH)
Lloyd, Christopher (Great Dixter): pp. 38, 74, 89, 131, 132, 168, 173
Lockhart, Lynette: p. 145 (GH)
Lowther, Karen: pp. 99, 122
Lynn, Elaine & John: p. 165 (GH)
Macfarlane, Richard & Susan (Winterhome): p. 67
Marshall, Geoffrey & Hayward, John: p. 157 (GH)
Masfen, Joanna & Peter: p. 56 (GH)
Masters, Gwyn (Aramaunga): p. 147
Matovich, Stan: p. 149
McConnell, Bev (Ayrlies): pp. 11, 16, 22, 27, 42, 59, 70, 85, 87, 88, 101 (GH), 104, 106, 107, 108, 113, 115, 117, 123, 130, 133, 137, 153, 175, 178, 180, 185
McMaster, Ben (Stowe): p. 39
Meyers, Barbara: p. 91 (GH)
Milne, Tony: p. 116
Morris, Marion: p. 164 (GH)
Otto, John: p: 8
Papich, Vivian & Daniel (Belle Vue Gardens): pp. 7, 9 (GH), 18 (GH), 66 (GH), 96 (GH), 111 (GH), 145 (GH), 152 (GH), 167 (GH)
Peek, Christine & Tony (Woodbridge): pp. 69 (GH), 86 (GH), 93 (GH), 180
Pope, Nori & Sandra (Hadspen House): p. 112 (GH)
Rive, Robin & Brian: p. 50 (GH)
Robeson, Graham & Gray, Alan (The Old Vicarage, East Rushton): pp. 143 (GH), 169 (GH)
Rogers, Barbara: p. 79 (GH)
Russell, Julie & Mike: p. 37
Sezincote p. 13
Sissinghurst pp. 26, 67, 85, 92, 142, 173
Smith, Geoffrey (Restoration) (The Masters Garden, Warwick): p. 24 (GH)
Thomson, Jeff: p. 149
Trengrove, John & Pauline (Cashel): pp. 98, 155
van der Pol, Rudi: p. 149
van Karthoven, Mark: pp. 134, 165 (GH)
Warren, Sir Miles (Ohinetahi): pp. 75 (GH), 171 (GH)
White, Xanthe: p. 73
Wills, John & Fiona (Trellinoe): p. 136
Wilson, Daphne: p. 94 (GH)
Worley, Ro & John: p. 139 (GH)

Photos on pages 21 and 45 are also by Gil Hanly.